The Oral Tradition of the
Baganda of Uganda

The Oral Tradition of the Baganda of Uganda

A Study and Anthology of Legends, Myths, Epigrams and Folktales

IMMACULATE N. KIZZA

McFarland & Company, Inc., Publishers

Jefferson, North Carolina, and London

Library of Congress Cataloguing-in-Publication Data

Kizza, Immaculate N.
    The oral tradition of the Baganda of Uganda : a study and
anthology of legends, myths, epigrams and folktales /
Immaculate N. Kizza.
        p.   cm.
    Includes bibliographical references and index.

    ISBN 978-0-7864-4015-3
    softcover : 50# alkaline paper ∞

    1. Folk literature, Ganda — History and criticism.
2. Ganda (African people) — Folklore.   3. Ganda (African
people) — Intellectual life.   4. Oral tradition — Uganda.
I. Title.
GR356.52.G36K59   2010
398.2089′963957 — dc22   2010002128

British Library cataloguing data are available

Cover images ©2009 Shutterstock

Manufactured in the United States of America

*McFarland & Company, Inc., Publishers
  Box 611, Jefferson, North Carolina 28640
  www.mcfarlandpub.com*

To my husband, Joseph Kizza,
and my daughters, Josephine and Florence,
a trio that brings out the best in humanity.

Acknowledgments

I am very grateful to the colleagues in the Department of English at the University of Tennessee at Chattanooga who received my idea and materials for this book enthusiastically and have cheered me all the way. My appreciation also goes to Anatole Kiriggwajjo at the Institute of Languages, Makerere University, Uganda, for his participation in collecting and translating some of the materials in this book. Josephine and Florence, I thank you for always being in my corner.

My greatest gratitude goes to my husband, Dr. Joseph Kizza, who proposed this book idea to me, sponsored my trips to Uganda to collect the materials, accompanied me to all the places visited, recording, taking pictures and guiding the narrators, helped me to translate, organize, draft, type, illustrate, proofread and edit the manuscript, and provided ideas, encouragement and moral support all the way!

To all the people of *Kyangwe* and *Kalubaya*, and all those who in one way or another contributed towards this project but whose names do not appear, I thank you.

Contents

Preface

After overcoming a series of hurdles in global literary circles, including the denial of its very existence, African literature has matured as a full-fledged discipline among global literatures. As African literature scholarship surges, literary scholars are increasingly pointing out that no serious scholar, student or even one casually interested in this discipline can afford to ignore the African oral tradition which is the genesis of the modern written African literature. Consequently, we are seeing increased interest and more refined scholarship being done on the African oral tradition; but primary materials for this scholarship have to be collected urgently because of two basic reasons: the death of the keepers of the African oral tradition — the elders — and the disappearance of African languages and cultures that anchor that tradition, due basically to technological trends, globalization and urbanization.

There are a significant number of collections of African oral tradition materials, mostly of folktales and proverbs, but very few comprehensive multi-subgenre collections like Wolf Leslau's *Garage Folklore: Ethiopian Folktales, Proverbs, Beliefs, and Riddles* and Emmanuel Matateyou's *An Anthology of Myths, Legends, and Folklore from Cameroon: Story Telling in Africa*. It is also important to point out that very few of those collections originate from East Africa in general and Uganda in particular. Okot p'Bitek's *Hare and Hornbill* is probably the most notable collection, and of folktales only, by a Ugandan who speaks the language of his people, the Acholi. Since there are significant differences among African peoples and their cultural traditions, histories and experiences as conveyed in their various oral narratives, a serious African scholar needs a variety of these collections from various regions, countries, and ethnic groups to participate fully in the ongoing, vibrant literary discourse on the African oral tradi-

1

tion. *The Oral Tradition of the Baganda of Uganda* is, therefore, a valuable contribution to this scholarship in three specific ways. First, it is a comprehensive multi-genre, specific ethnic group's oral literature collection and analysis, framed in the wider contexts of the multipurpose African oral tradition genre, modern African literature, and global literary studies. Second, it is a great study of the culture of the Baganda of Uganda because there are ample cultural explanations throughout the text intended to bring the reader closer to the cultural experiences of these people. Third, this text gives the reader a glimpse into the history of the Baganda in the context of Uganda in specific sections like "The Baganda: A Historical Perspective" in Chapter 2, and through historical explanations and references spread throughout the text.

The Baganda people have a very rich oral tradition of proverbs, riddles, myths, legends, idioms, songs and prose narratives, all of which are an invaluable window into their cultural traditions, history and experiences, but most of those in print are in *Luganda,* the most valuable of which are outlined by James Ssemakula in his "A Review of Selected Luganda Books" available at www.buganda.com/bitabopl.htm. The reader of *The Oral Tradition of the Baganda of Uganda* is, therefore, invited to immerse oneself into, and actively participate in, the discourse on the Baganda people's cultural traditions and history by carefully reading and, thereafter, referencing the comprehensive oral literature pieces and explanations given in this collection. In addition, the reader is also introduced to the enchanting tonal Luganda, the Baganda people's language anchoring Baganda oral literature. Luganda words and phrases appearing in the text are italicized and defined in the glossary, and other pertinent explanations, mostly cultural and historical, are enclosed in brackets.

The author traveled widely throughout the Kingdom of Buganda, visiting mostly elderly people and taping and video recording their narratives. Collecting oral narratives from native storytellers is not as hard at the dawn of the 21st century as it was before the current technological tools were available. Various scholars collecting such narratives before the technology we have today recount the difficult experiences they encountered then. With pen and paper in hand, the collectors would take notes as they were being told these narratives; sometimes the narrators had to repeat their narratives several times before the session would be over, but no matter how accurate the notes taker is, one cannot capture the essence of an oral narrative simply by taking notes at the spot. Keep in mind also that oral narratives are fluid: a person cannot repeat the narrative exactly as one told it the first time, the second time and so on. Every time a narrator tells a story, although generally it remains the same story, new content may be added, and some of that story's content may be altered or deleted. The narrator's attitude, mannerisms, tempo and so on cannot be static either. Both the narrator and the narration must always appeal to the audience physically present at the time the story is being told, and also fit in the existing context; that is the beauty of the oral narratives.

When I was collecting the narratives in this volume, I had two specific advantages over most collectors, especially earlier ones. First, I was armed with two simple but very practical devices: a tape recorder and a video camera, which enabled me to capture two renditions at once without distracting the narrators, by asking them to repeat, or myself, by writing continuously instead of listening and noting facial expressions, hand gestures and other such extras. Second, I am fluent in speaking, reading and writing Luganda, and firmly grounded in the culture and language of my narrators; I grew up hearing those very stories so that even if the situation was artificial, I had an idea of how each narrative would sound in a real storytelling setting, preferably an evening by the fire or simply sitting around grandma, with a live, and curious, audience prompting the narrator. An effort was actually made to surround the narrators with such audiences whenever I was recording the narratives, even if the setting was not totally ideal.

That said, it is important to keep in mind that no one language can be fully and accurately translated into another without losing some essence and nuances of it. Translating a live, oral Luganda narrative into a static, written English version leaves a lot to be desired; intriguing aesthetic features such as the accents, the tempo, the idioms, the phrasing, the gestures, the noises, the overall audible flavor of the language and its tonal nuances are almost all lost. Also often lost in such translations is the coherency and total accuracy of phrases, clauses and sentences because those grammatical aspects are not easy to transport among different languages. One author, Okot p'Bitek, who translated his native Acholi narratives into English, portrayed the process accurately by describing it as a murdering of the language being translated and a blunting of the warrior's weapon. The more different the two languages are from each other, especially culturally and structurally, the harder it is to accurately transport one into the other, and Luganda is as different from English as any two languages can possibly be. Compared to the complexity of Luganda from which the entries in this volume are being translated, these narratives are obviously very plain and simplistic, but as accurate as any such translations can be.

The book is arranged in five chapters. Chapter 1 is an introduction to the African oral tradition in general and to the Baganda oral tradition in particular, with emphasis on some of the issues that dominate the scholarly discourse surrounding the genre; the subgenres are also introduced. Chapter 2 focuses on the Baganda people by investigating who they are from two distinct perspectives, one historical and the other mythological. The Baganda people's most important legends and myths are also included and discussed, together with the physical locations associated with both. Chapter 3 examines epigrams, highlighting popular riddles and proverbs; these are cited in Luganda, each followed with a translation and short explanation, including rhetorical analysis where applicable. The prose narratives in Chapter 4, mostly folktales, are subdivided into various sections highlighting the functions and values of these stories in the cultural psyche of the Baganda; each story is concluded with a commentary focusing mostly on the themes within that story to aid the reader in close reading and discussion as well as to prompt that reader to notice the familiar human threads implicit in such stories even if most of those stories may not have sounded familiar to that reader. Chapter 5 is the concluding commentary on the value, status, significance and scholarly trends in the African oral tradition within the wider contexts of African and global literary studies. A glossary of Luganda words and phrases highlighted in the text in italics, as well as the "Appendix of Sample Luganda Songs" are added to enrich the reader's historical and cultural experiences, knowledge and interaction with the Baganda of Uganda.

The African oral tradition, more specifically its resultant oral literature, is at heart a people's literature, and Nadine Gordimer points out yet another significant difference between African oral literature and that of developed countries: Developed countries' oral literature is more of a subject of study in literary circles than a practical tool among ordinary people; literary scholars are more fascinated by, and consequently know more of this literature than the ordinary people in those countries. The African oral tradition, on the other hand, has always been, and still is, a day to day communication and practical tool for ordinary people to share, archive, authenticate and validate their existence and experiences. It is still largely respected as such. Because it is a multipurpose genre, the African oral tradition attracts a wide, diverse audience in literary circles where it can be studied from a variety of perspectives such as a cultural tool, as a rich and most authentic historical source, and a significant literary aspect that gave birth to and is still anchoring the genre of modern African literature. Even those readers who are not seeking literary excitement and fulfillment can still appreciate the African oral tradition, because it is quite entertaining; it engages one's imagination, and probably most important, the themes implicit in its literature highlight what makes us all human.

Immaculate Kizza
Department of English
University of Tennessee–Chattanooga

1

The African and Baganda
Oral Traditions: An Introduction

Issues in the African Oral Tradition

The significance of the African oral tradition cannot be overstated. Although there is a documented history of writing traditions among Africans, most of these people still privilege their oral tradition over the written ones as a valuable and very practical multipurpose tool that enriches and gives meaning to their day-to-day communication. In addition to its entertainment value, the African oral tradition is also an encyclopedia of the various peoples' histories, cultural experiences, traditions and values; a record of their feelings, attitudes, and responses to their experiences and environment; and also a tool for preserving and disseminating that knowledge both internally and globally. During the colonial period, the African oral tradition played a very crucial role of sustaining the essence of what it means to be an African within a hostile system that spared no effort to eradicate these people's presence so as to legitimately occupy both their physical and cultural spaces.

In literary circles, the African oral pieces that have been collected, transcribed, translated and at times explicated complement Phillis Wheatley's 1773 publication, *Poems on Various Subjects, Religious and Moral Tradition*. Wheatley's publication is memorable, among other aspects, because of two benchmark functions it accomplished, which are discussed by Henry Louis Gates, in his foreword to the Schomburg Collection of 19th century Black Women Writers. Wheatley's publication established both the African American women and African American people's literary traditions, as well as confirmed these people's humanity. Wheatley was subjected to an oral examination by eighteen renowned Bostonians to prove that she was the author of the poems she intended to publish. By successfully convincing these "notable citizens" that she had actually authored those poems, Wheatley contributed tremendously to a debate among the Europeans who had wanted to know, "since the beginning of the sixteenth century," as Gates points out, whether the African was of the same species as they were (Jacobs, vii–x). The ability to create literary pieces as displayed by Wheatley earned the African a spot in the human sphere.

Unfortunately this same debate resurfaced a century later when the same Europeans revisited the same continent. This time, as Achebe points out, "*presence* was the critical question, the crucial word. Its denial was the keynote of colonialist ideology" (Petersen); if they could argue convincingly that the physical and cultural spaces they wanted to occupy belonged to no one before their arrival, they could legitimatize their occupation. Since one cannot deny the presence of a people with a culture, a history, and so on, one embarks on marginalizing those attributes, and after successfully marginalizing them, one can concentrate on manufacturing and aggressively publicizing extensive lists of what those people didn't have, including, of course, history, culture, and religion. But the African oral tradition is tangible evidence that Africa had all those attributes long before they ever heard of Europeans, and the present study of the oral tradition of the Baganda, and many others like it, contribute to the debunking of that myth. In addition to African oral pieces confirming the humanity of Africans, they also, like Wheatley's publication, established the African literary tradition as known today.

In the wake of colonialism, African writers such as Chinua Achebe, Ngugi wa Thiong'o, Flora Nwapa, D.T. Niane and Jomo Kenyatta, to name but a few, embarked on a mission to debunk the colonial *presence* myth and reclaim their people's cultural spaces using these people's legends, proverbs, songs, mythology, epics, folktales — the list goes on. African writers since then have rewritten, and continue to rewrite, their history to set the record straight, showcasing their treasures and telling the world their version of the story of colonialism by appropriating the very languages and literary traditions in which they had been misrepresented and using their oral tradition as a springboard. It has been noted by those engaged in the study of African literatures that one cannot comfortably capture the essence of those literary pieces without having some knowledge of the African oral tradition which these writers use as a springboard in creating their works. For scholars interested in literary analysis, the African oral tradition is a rhetorically rewarding chest of treasures with tantalizing rhetorical devices such as similes, metaphors, personification, apostrophe, and sounds which contribute significantly to the study and enjoyment of not only African literature, but also of world literature.

Although valuable, the African oral tradition has not been getting as much attention in literary circles as written ones do, most of which are in European languages. As scholars like Finnegan point out, there is still a tendency to regard the African oral tradition as not warranting that much serious study because it is still being branded as so simple and primitive, and not so relevant in the global arena. A good number of Africans, hooked up on popular culture made up of western conventions and totally lost in the globalization fad, also contribute to the above sentiments. But as concerned Africanists like Kaschula and Bukenya point out, globalization should help the Africans to retain their oral tradition, which cannot go out of style so long as the Africans engage it in debating and seeking solutions to contemporary issues. The African oral tradition has proved to be an asset in contemporary dialogue, highlighting contemporary issues such as the marginalization of women, the functionality of political systems, and the search for solutions to health problems like HIV/AIDS. Foreign preachers find the African oral tradition useful as a tool they can use to connect with the "natives" and to make the Bible stories relevant to these people's experiences.

It is important to remind the readers that what actually keeps this tradition alive and contemporarily relevant is the society's involvement through the storytellers and audience. The stories being told are not fixed, unchangeable pieces as happens in the case of the written tradition; each storyteller is free to totally own the story one is telling and to try and make it relevant to one's audience through improvisation, omission, and addition of information as necessary. To the serious Africanist, the African oral tradition is anything but primitive, simple, and outdated, and as scholars who have given this genre its due attention can testify, it is a rewarding literary experience.

Another concern that scholars of the African oral tradition have is the speed at which stories that anchor this oral tradition and the languages that sustain them are disappearing with the passing of each generation of

Africans. Amadou Hampate Ba captured this sentiment accurately when he compared the death of each African elder to the burning of a library; Africanists lose a lot whenever an African elder dies. On the language issue, interested observers like Dennis O'Brien and Steve Connor, among others, point out that globally many ethnic languages are heading towards extinction in the near future; the statistics are alarming. "Many linguists predict that at least half of the world's 6,000 or so languages will be dead or dying by the year 2050," reports Rosemarie Ostler. African scholars have noticed that most of those rapidly disappearing languages are in Africa, where, in addition to technological trends and globalization, urbanization is also a contributing factor to the "death" of native languages. Since most African nations are made up of various ethnic groups, when these people make their homes in urban centers, they are forced to speak their nations' official languages for practical purposes, at the expense of their native ones. Consequently, generations of Africans living, being born and growing up in urban centers can hardly speak their own languages. This realization, that African languages are disappearing, has prompted African scholars to urge those who can to timely capture and preserve as many of the oral tradition treasures as they can while they still have a chance to do so. Efforts to collect and preserve African oral pieces are well underway all over the continent, as can be seen in the surge of publications on the topic, and scholars are often updating these pieces, stressing their fluidity and dynamism and their ability to remain contemporarily relevant.

In addition to the disappearance of our story keepers and languages, Isidore Okpewho, president of the International Society for Oral Literature in Africa (ISOLA, 2002–2004), outlined additional reasons why capturing these items timely was a must. In his 2003 call for papers for the Fifth ISOLA conference titled "The Preservation and Survival of African Oral Literature," Okpewho highlighted the changing environment due to technology and globalization. African youths, like youths globally, are more drawn to technological devices for entertainment than to their grandparents. And even those youths interested in listening to such stories may not have the time or be in the proximity of such storytellers since they (the youths) spend most of their formative years in schools, in many cases boarding schools or just away from home. Isidore Okpewho also pointed out the altering ethnic landscape, with people continually migrating globally and into urban centers as pointed out above, and even intermarrying.

In such an environment, it is hard to preserve ethnic oral traditions, let alone keep them relevant in those migrants' lives. Fortunately, the same globalization and technological advances that have contributed to the marginalization of those oral pieces have also been great assets to the scholars engaged in collecting and preserving such pieces. As pointed out in the preface of this book, this author's task of collecting materials was not as laborious as it used to be because of the available technological resources. In their works, African playwrights such as Wole Soyinka and many other globally lesser known ones have given life to many African oral tradition stories that would otherwise have disappeared. The filmmaking industry, both indigenous and foreign, has also been a great asset for the African oral tradition enthusiasts. The vibrant indigenous film industry is increasingly incorporating the oral tradition in story lines and scenes being portrayed in their films. Hollywood and other foreign filmmakers have also started to "borrow" African oral literature pieces for use in their films. These activities have rejuvenated the African oral tradition and made it more visible, relevant and popular to all generations globally, thereby ensuring its survival in the highly technological global village.

In the age of globalization, each group of people should bring something to the table, otherwise the concept of globalization loses meaning and purpose. The Africans are endowed with a rich, fascinating, dynamic, adaptable oral tradition which, if given the attention it deserves, including being studied for its literary merit, should widen the scope and enrich the study and appreciation of global literatures.

Subgenres in the African Oral Tradition

The benchmark of the African oral tradition is storytelling, and these stories come in various forms, the most popular being epigrams, songs, myths, legends and folktales.

One can safely say that **proverbs** are the most visible African epigrams and most intriguing literary pieces in the African oral tradition because they are brief and to the point, seductive in tone, and rhetorically enchanting. Because they are short, fortified with wisdom, and easy to remember verbatim, proverbs are the most authentic expressions available to culturally minded Africans interested in preserving the dignity and eloquence that characterize their languages. African proverbs are also popular as age-tested knowledge banks, often used to preserve and to enforce societal values and beliefs; to an outsider, therefore, proverbs are a window into the cultural, social, and philosophical functions of a specific people. Since humans often find it hard to digest bitter truth when it is openly thrown in their faces, the witty, short and often sweet and humorous proverbs can be used to convey bitter truth in a veiled, easy to digest medium which is also nonconfrontational. In other words, one can use proverbs to tell the truth but to tell it with a slant to make it digestible and not to offend one's audience, as the renowned poet Emily Dickinson suggested in one of her poems "Tell All the Truth but Tell It Slant."

Additionally, African proverbs are a literary scholar's delight because of their use of figurative language and related poetic expressions; similes, metaphors, personification, overstatements, paradoxes, allusion, irony and other such rhetorical devices abound in these proverbs. As expressions of abstract ideas, proverbs are always open to multiple interpretations, especially if one pays specific attention to the connotations the natives attach to specific words. The use of allusion is also an invitation to the scholar to get more insight into the specific people's sociocultural activities. African writers often purposely pepper their creations with carefully chosen colorful proverbs to showcase the beauty, poetry and dignity of their people and their languages, as well as the wisdom of those people. In his early novels, especially *Things Fall Apart*, Chinua Achebe clearly displays the dignity of the Ibo language and demonstrates his people's philosophical concepts using Ibo proverbs.

Other not so visible epigrams, but which are often heard, especially among school children, are **riddles**, which are frequently used to sharpen minds and cultivate oracy/orality in addition to preserving history and cultural traditions of the people. Africanists in general can learn a lot about the people, their environment and activities from the content in such people's riddles. African literature scholars, in particular, prize these riddles mostly because of the literary techniques employed, including the colorful language used.

Songs are also important in the African oral tradition, and they play a vital role in the preservation of the African people's history and traditions. Many important lessons, historical and traditional events and activities are accurately chronicled in African songs. There is plenty to learn from songs concerning important African people's historical events like famines, wars and discoveries. Rituals of how to wage a successful war, conduct a fruitful hunt, make a livelihood from the rivers and lakes, celebrate the arrival of twins, communicate with ancestors and the creator, organize the second burial, court successfully and have a good and lasting marriage are also chronicled in songs. African writers like Flora Nwapa and Ngugi wa Thiong'o give their readers front seats to a cultural show that walks them through the lives of their people using songs. As the reader listens to these songs, often reproduced in their entirety, one gets to intimately know the singers and their listeners who, most of the time, participate actively in these songs. African songs are also a valuable source of current information in various countries because most lyrics accurately express whatever is going on at the time in the political, social, religious and other arenas, especially when foreign reporters cannot get there and national ones are unable to report from within.

Myths, though not as numerous as other types, play an important role in the African oral tradition. Ali Mazrui argues that humans attribute their existence and sense of being to two myths: the myth of origin and the myth of purpose. These myths propel us to devote ample amounts of time to exploring the nature of our very own existence and seeking responses to the reporter's formula: who, why, when, where, what, and how. Fortunately for Africans, there are numerous myths around them to facilitate this search. Renowned African writers utilize mythological narrations in their works, enabling their readers to get a glimpse into the cultural history of their people. In *The River Between*, for example, Ngugi wa Thiong'o, a writer known for his significant use of oral tradition in his writings, introduces his readers to the Gikuyu people's rich mythological traditions, first explaining their origin in Murungu, their creator; Gikuyu, their father; and Mumbi, their mother. He then goes on to explain the mythological roots of the rivalry between the two ridges of Kameno and Makuyu, and why Kameno surfaced as the leader. The reader also gets a glimpse into the Honia River's mythological importance to the Gikuyu people as a life-giving and life-sustaining entity that reminds the feuding forces in the ridges that they and their quarrels are insignificant in comparison to life's sustaining forces. Like myths all over the world, African myths in various cultures artfully explain the creation of man, the universe and other creatures, the essence of their creator, and the nature of the relationships between these creatures and their creator, as well as the nature of human existence. African myths also serve a more practical purpose; they debunk the religion myth which propelled European missionaries to assume that Africans did not have the concept of the Supreme until the missionaries introduced it to them. The concept of God, and only one God, is central in most African mythologies, demonstrating a clear understanding of who created them and what that creator's plans for them and the environment around them were; the most important plan seems to have been immortality, but the humans themselves foiled that plan.

Legends are also important in the African oral tradition. Not to be confused with mythology, these are human stories, about humans who in most instances are larger than life; these humans perform unimaginable feats like establishing kingdoms single-handedly, winning impossible wars with very little or no help, averting disasters — the list goes on. Legends are set more recently in time compared to myths, and they preserve a people's history through generations; when carefully explicated, legends can be valuable historical narratives. Owomoyela sums up the importance of legends to Africans by stating that a community's history can be pieced together from its legends. For example, the Manding people, although spread in various countries in West Africa, can piece together their common history and reclaim their historical and cultural spaces by reading any version of the Sundiata Epic, especially reader friendly versions like D.T. Niane's *Sundiata: Epic of Old Mali.* This epic is a repertoire of historical information about the 13th century empire of Mali and its social and political institutions, as well as the present day Manding people's ancestors. Many such epics abound in African literature, as can be seen in collections such as John William Johnson, Thomas A. Hale, and Stephen Belcher's *Oral Epics from Africa*, a total of 25 epics from West, North and Central Africa.

The central pillar of the African oral tradition, though, is **folktales**. Most of these tales portray human and/or animal characters who represent the positive human qualities societies want to preserve and enforce, and the negative ones they want to purge. A renowned British author, Edward Morgan Forster, argued at the beginning of the 20th century that in fiction, writers can no longer realistically portray absolute human qualities like good and evil because with the new psychology, that of Freud, we gained an understanding of the complexity of human behavior and how fluid it can be. African storytellers, although they understand Forster's argument, might qualify that sentiment because they can still accurately and realistically portray human virtues such as kindness, obedience, and honesty, and vices such as laziness, greed, and jealousy in their folktales. African writers have also used folktales to set their people's historical records straight and to reclaim their cultural spaces. Probably one of the proudest storytellers who has successfully refocused this genre to redress inaccuracies in his, and probably other people's, history in a dignified way and with an unequaled sense of humor is Jomo Kenyatta of Kenya. "The Gentlemen of the Jungle" is not the folktale our ancestors used to tell, but we recognize the characters and understand the message Kenyatta wanted to convey. The animal characters are lifted out of the oral tradition with all of their corresponding characteristics. The elephant is all powerful, but its power is shortchanged by its lack of intelligence and inability to organize. So in walks the king of the jungle to put the house in order, as well as the fox to outwit the man! Folktales are also used for etiological purposes. We know why a tortoise has a cracked shell, spiders have narrow waists and frogs have no tails, and so on.

The Baganda Oral Tradition

With more than forty-four ethnic groups, each with its own unique language, culture and traditions, obviously Uganda has various rich, vibrant oral traditions which are still influential in people's lives despite the forces of globalization and urbanization. It is amazing to see how well the oral tradition, because of its fluid, dynamic nature and ability to sharpen memory, functions in Ugandan schools. Ugandan students, especially those in rural areas, are required by policy to begin their formal education in their native languages, and to keep using those languages for the first few years. This policy helps these students to acquire and successfully retain a large body of knowledge through the use of their respective oral traditions. For example, through use of *ebitontome* (oral poetry) as an instructional tool, teachers in various disciplines can impart knowledge to students on a variety of topics ranging from traditional historical ones like colonialism to contemporary issues such as HIV/AIDS prevention. A literature teacher can use folktales as a stepping-stone into world literature; the students are able to actively engage into this storytelling, contributing and analyzing their own stories and before they know it, they have conveniently and delightfully meandered into *Romeo and Juliet*.

Our focus in this book, however, is the Baganda people's oral literature. Like most people on the continent, the Baganda people cherish their oral tradition; and they are striving to keep it alive for various purposes, most important of which are entertainment, instruction, and preservation of the language and culture. The oral tradition is of great value to the preservation of Luganda because in these oral pieces, the Baganda have the most authentic, beautiful expressions, which are the essence of their language. Luganda is taught in schools up to university level, and it is one of the languages being focused on for research and teaching in the Languages Institute at the nation's flagship university, Makerere; in 2007, the Luganda faculty at the institute published the most up to date Luganda language *Nkuluze* (dictionary). There are also several Luganda societies in the region, all emphasizing the preservation of the language; these societies have produced several English-Luganda and Luganda-English dictionaries, among other publications, and a Luganda browser is in place to propel the language into the technological age. The oral tradition is the most important tool in all these preservation efforts.

In the Baganda oral tradition, epigrams abound mostly in the form of **riddles** and **proverbs,** to basically inform and sharpen the mind. The Baganda people rely on their epigrams for various purposes, including giving advice on a variety of topics ranging from parenthood to getting rich, pointing out the importance of communal as well as individual responsibilities, cautioning each other, teaching *Kiganda* behavior especially to the youths, and overall capturing and preserving the essence of what makes a *Muganda* (see glossary at "Baganda") person that specific person. Baganda people's **folktales**, which are told by all age groups, generally serve the same purposes as epigrams; they are an invaluable reservoir of these people's values, and they are practically told to enforce those values. Folktales can also be very entertaining. Using **myths**, the most important of which is the story of *Kintu*, the Baganda people are able to explain their origin, how they came to be, who they are, why they die, their purpose on earth, and the nature of their relationships with each other and with all those around them. Through mythology, the Baganda can also account for their origin and that of Buganda, the existence of some of the physical features around them like lakes and rivers; for example, there are known accounts of how their largest lake, Nalubaale (a.k.a. Lake Victoria), came into existence, as well as one of the inland rivers, Namajjuzi. **Legends**, the most important of which is the *Kato Kintu* legend, are archives of Buganda history, traditions, and much more. For example, through legends, the Baganda know when and how they came to be a kingdom, the history of that kingdom through the years, and the origin, nature, purpose and functioning of their most important sociological units, *ebika,* through their legends.

Baganda children learn a lot about their family histories through *okutinta*, which is a brain teaser game during which children quiz each other about their respective families, activities, events, and much more. It is a very fast-paced game, sort of like Jeopardy but faster. One wanting to *kutinta* alerts the audience with this call: *tintatinta.* The expected response from an audience that knows what is coming up is *"ennume tetinta nga ndaawo."* Such a response signals to the caller that the audience is ready for this brain exercise and eager to show off their knowledge in turns. In schools, children acquire and retain a lot of knowledge through *ebitontome*, which is a form of poetic chanting that requires a high degree of memory recall. Children can chant on any topic, but mostly they chant on historical events, inventions, religious teachings and unexplainable wonders and phenomena in their universe. This chanting challenges both the teachers and their students; the teachers have to present materials to their students in a poetic, highly organized, easy to remember, enjoyable format, while the students concentrate on learning the materials and reciting them among their peers and to their relatives in their homes. The author got a chance to listen to some of these students chanting on a variety of topics, and it was a rewarding experience for all present.

Songs also play a vital role in the preservation of the Baganda people's history and traditions. Many important historical and traditional events are accurately chronicled in both traditional drum-based and kadongo *kamu* songs. From these songs one can, for example, learn about tragic occurrences the Baganda people have survived over the years, including their sad and forceful involvement in World War ll. Songs like "*Basajja Bannange Twabonabona*" are a valuable record of how Baganda men were brutally "recruited" for that war. Able-bodied men were often simply kidnapped from their villages and put on lorries. Then they would be taken to collection depots; most of those depots were out of the country, like the one in Nairobi, Kenya. At the depots they would be checked for physical fitness, and then if found to be in good shape, they would be shipped off to war. Famines and plagues are also noted in these songs.

There is also plenty to learn from these songs concerning important Baganda people's rituals and everyday practices and activities. The Baganda are very "spiritual" people in their everyday practices, and there is a lot of information defining their beliefs and activities in songs such as "*Bwangu Bwangu*," which lists several *lubaale* figures and their specific duties. To understand the nature and essence of a *lubaale* figure, one can reference Christian saints who, like some of the *lubaale* figures, were humans that distinguished themselves in specific activities when they were alive. A list of notable *lubaale* figures includes *Ndawula*, who, in songs such as "*Jjajja Tabaala*" and "*Ndawula*," is introduced as a multipurpose figure to approach whenever one needs divine intervention in any circumstance. *Ddungu* is for the hunters who, in songs such as "*Ddungu Ddungu Lubolooga*" and "*Ddungu Omulungi*," is requested to bless and guide the hunters because his eyes can penetrate forests and see farther than any human can. It is believed that he can, therefore, direct the hunters to where animals are and alert them to likely dangerous encounters. *Mukasa*, Guardian of the Lake, is celebrated in "*Amazzi Genyanja*" and is requested to keep fishermen safe.

Many other *lubaale* figures such as *Nalwanga* for fertility, *Kibuuka* for war, *Luboowa*, *Musoke*, and *Kiwanuka* are all celebrated in songs. "In pre-colonial Africa, as everywhere else around the globe before A.D. 1000, people continuously migrated from place to place, conquering each other, assimilating each other's way of life and forming and destroying each other's socio-political administrative systems in the process" (Kizza); there are many Baganda songs that point to these activities, especially the waging of wars. "*Abatabazi Abedda*" and "*Balwaana*" reference such wars, detailing how they were fought, by whom, when, where, how many died or survived, and how to wage a successful war. There are many work related songs detailing the importance of jobs like *okukomaga* (see glossary); in songs like "*Walulumba*," one gets to know the dos and don'ts of *okukomaga*, how it is done, by whom, why, and when. Subsistence farming was a way of life among the Baganda. Each adult male owned a *kibanja* given to him by his father; he was expected to marry and raise a family on that land. Songs like "*Tulime*" enumerate the crops that were normally cultivated, beginning with the most important crop for the Baganda, that being *matooke,* their staple food; *muwogo, kasooli, ndaggu, niina, ntula, butungulu, binyeebwa, bikajjo, miyembe, nanansi*, and many others are also listed.

Expected neighborly behavior is explained in songs like "*Muliraanwa Bwayisa*"; neighbors were expected to help each other in daily activities like brewing beer, harvesting crops, repairing houses, and so on; if your neighbor was happy, you too would be happy. Plenty of advice about love, relationships and marriage is enshrined in songs such as "*Gwenjagalira bbaawe ekyoka kimunyoola*" and "*Nabutono Tembeya.*" Twins are celebrated by the Baganda, and there are many congratulatory songs like "*Nnalongo Weeryowe,*" songs to welcome the twins in the family, like "*Kabikkuse,*" and songs about how to take care of twins, like "*Abalongo Twabazaala Babiri.*" Baganda lullabies are also informative. Calming down a screaming infant is a formidable task that may require creativity; in songs like "*Sirika Sirika,*" the Baganda spotlight their perfected art of handling such situations. In songs one gets to mourn with the Baganda when a loved one dies, and to celebrate the Last Rites during which an heir is appointed to take the place and responsibilities of the deceased. "*Maama* [or *Taata, Jjajja*] *Abaawo*" gives instructions of what should be done early in the morning of the Last Rites day, and "*Mbogo Mbogo*" describes the installation of the heir. Praise songs abound for all kinds of people, especially for parents, lovers and politicians; in such songs one gets to know what the Baganda value in people holding such offices and what they find unacceptable. Informative songs also feature predominantly in very lively people's theatre performances, which in addition to entertaining the participating audience serve practical purposes as well. The popular Theatre for Development highlights contemporary issues and dispenses advice on a wide range of topics including health, relationships, gender, parenting and politics. Overall, songs are a real treasure in Baganda oral literature.

Since songs are very hard to reproduce accurately in translation and to transcribe in prose, especially putting their lyrics into music notes, we do not have many examples of them in this collection, but there is ample information above to engage an interested scholar and even casual reader in the discourse on the topic. In addition, some of the songs discussed above are provided in the appendix to give the reader a flavor of Luganda, and to hopefully prompt researchers to seek for more in-depth information concerning not only those songs but also the topics covered in them. We have also included, in translation, a legend, a myth, a sampling of riddles and proverbs, and ample prose narratives in the ensuing chapters to immerse both the serious scholar and casual reader in a meaningful literary discourse on the Baganda and their oral tradition, literature, culture and history within the larger context of the African oral tradition. As mentioned earlier, in addition to discussing the essence of the pieces themselves and how they function among the Baganda, the author will also focus the discussion on the literary characteristics of these pieces through rhetorical analysis. The storytellers, audience, arguments being made in various pieces, and any other related aspects will be analyzed, as well as the language being used, with emphasis on explicating figurative language.

It is important to note in passing that one of the most important aspects of any oral tradition is the delivery, or performance (if one prefers to use the term), of the material, which puts emphasis on the who (performer, audience), when, where, why and how. In actuality these stories are forever relevant and alive because the storytellers themselves and their audiences are always in the present, visibly there and then. In collecting these pieces, the author was privileged to actually see and hear them being performed by and for a familiar people, and in a familiar language and cultural environment. The audiences' reactions, the performers' appearances and their ability to perform together with their tonal, hand and facial expressions all add greatly to the appreciation of the African oral tradition, and although the author cannot fully reproduce all those significant oral tradition aspects for the reader, every effort has been made to convey those experiences as accurately as possible, especially through rhetorical analysis.

2

The Baganda of Uganda

Located in south central Uganda, the Baganda are the largest ethnic group in the country, making up 17 percent of the total population, which was around 24 million in 2007. But who are the Baganda of Uganda? We can provide a response to that query by investigating two perspectives, one historical, the other mythological.

The Baganda: A Historical Perspective

The migration of Bantu people into what is known today as Uganda originated in the general Bantu migration sparked by two reasons, namely what scholars such as Wallbank have called the disastrous climatic changes between 5000 and 1500 B.C., which produced the Sahara desert as we know it today, and the growth of population. Before those recorded climatic changes, the Sahara is said to have been a humid but well-watered place capable of sustaining plenty of animal and human life. Historians like Basil Davidson describe the Sahara during its good days as teeming with wild game and being populated by people of various occupations, including traders, hunters and farmers. But as the lakes and rivers started drying up and the Sahara became hotter and less inhabitable, it started losing its animal life and finally its people, who are said to have migrated in two directions. One group headed east towards the Nile valley, and they became the descendants of today's Nubians. The other group, most of whom were later classified as Bantu-speaking people, migrated southwest towards the tropical forest. The Bantu were, and still are, primarily subsistence farmers who would settle in areas, clear land, organize themselves in larger units basically for protective purposes, and start permanent settlements. But as their population grew, the Bantu continually migrated further south and east looking for better land to farm and fresh pastures for their livestock. As they migrated and settled into present day central, east, and south Africa, they continuously absorbed and at times displaced the indigenous peoples like the Bambuti and the Khoisans they found in their paths and the places they settled into permanently. This is precisely how one ethnic group of Bantu people now known as the Baganda came to settle in what is south central Uganda today.

There are said to be several versions pertaining to the founding of the Kingdom of Buganda as we know it today because this information was handed down orally. But according to the most accepted version, the south central Uganda area today known as Buganda was inhabited by a considerable number of people long before the famous 1200–1500 great migration. These original inhabitants had organized themselves into several social-political lineage units, still functional today, called *ebika*. Each *ekika* is represented by a totem, which can be an animal, a bird, or any other creature that is not human, from which it derives its name. Before 1300 each *ekika* used to be headed by a leader who had distinguished oneself as capable of ruling one's people, but today that position is hereditary. This *ekika* leader was responsible for, among other things, organizing and leading troops responsible for defending the *ekika* from outside attacks, protecting the *ekika* and its traditions, settling disputes among the *ekika* members, and presiding over general administrative *ekika* affairs. All the *ebika* in a locality were supposed to be equal and independent although every now and then a militarily strong *ekika* leader would capture a number of *ebika* in a region and declare himself head of them all until he was overthrown. Ssemakula names several of those militarily strong *ebika* leaders at that time, including *Sseguku, Bukokoma, Muyizzi* and *Bemba*, whose leadership lasted for significant periods of time ("Buganda").

Legend has it that one of those leaders, *Bemba*, was in charge of six *ebika* in his area, namely *Ffumbe, Lugave, Ngeye, Nnyonyi, Nnyange,* and *Njaza*, when *Kintu*, the credited founder of the kingdom of Buganda, invaded that area bringing with him thirteen *ebika*, and established a reputation as a great warrior. It is also stated in the oral literature that *Bemba* was a very harsh and ruthless leader, so his people gladly welcomed *Kintu* as a liberator. The story of *Kintu*, who he was and where he came from, comes in several versions in Baganda oral literature, some of which even claim that his name was not *Kintu* but *Kato*; that he renamed himself

22

Kintu after conquering Bemba to be in line with Kintu, the mythological father of the Baganda; and that his wife's name was *Nantuttululu*, but that he changed that to *Nambi* for the very same reasons he changed his to *Kintu* (see "Kintu: The Myth" that follows). As to where he came from, most Baganda believe that he was a militarily distinguished *ekika* leader in an area beyond Mount Elgon in northeast Uganda, who, like *Bemba* and others like him, had established hegemony over the other *ebika* leaders in that area. But there are other versions that state that *Bemba* and *Kintu* were brothers who had fought over the inheritance of their father's kingdom, and that *Bemba* had won that fight. After winning, *Bemba* is said to have exiled *Kintu*, who then returned to battle *Bemba* when he had accumulated substantial resources to aid him in that mission. Whatever version one takes, the two versions agree that *Kintu* invaded *Bemba* and succeeded in killing him. After defeating *Bemba*, *Kintu* consolidated his power over all the *ebika* leaders in the area and declared himself leader of the now nineteen *ebika* of people speaking the same language and practicing the same customs, the Baganda people. When he had successfully consolidated his power over the nineteen *ebika*, *Kintu* convened probably the first known constitutional conference in Buganda, to which he invited the *ebika* leaders and elders who, in consultation with their members, openly discussed and formulated the kingdom's first and only "constitution," which has been in operation since that time although it was not put on paper at the time. (For more information on Baganda see Kizza, 29–41.)

Since the founding of the Kingdom, circa 1200, the Baganda have sustained an intricate sociopolitical, hierarchical *ebika* system which is central to the cultural and political functioning of the Kingdom of Buganda; this system is referenced and alluded to often in Baganda oral literature.

The *ebika* assumed specific responsibilities, both political and social, to keep the Kingdom functioning coherently. Over the centuries, the *ebika* grew in number as the Kingdom's population increased both naturally and through conquering and assimilating people from neighboring areas; as of 2009, there were 50 *ebika* in Buganda.

Kintu: The Legend

Just as there are several versions of the founding of the Kingdom of Buganda, the legend of *Kintu* also comes in a number of versions in

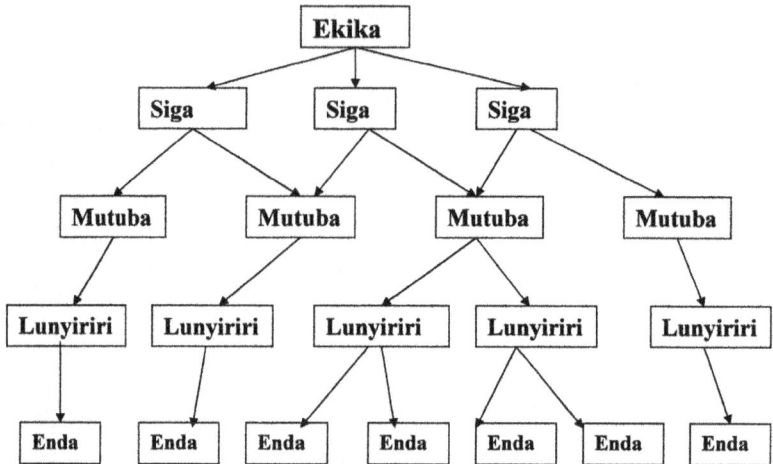

The Hierarchical *Ebika* Structure in Buganda

Baganda oral literature; the one below was transcribed by the author, who collected various narrations from the region.

Once upon a time there were two brothers, *Bemba* and *Kintu*, both in line for the leadership of the Baganda (some sources say that they actually might have been twins). When their father was dying, he willed the throne to *Kintu*, which did not make *Bemba* happy. After the death of their father, there developed a rivalry for the throne between *Kintu* and *Bemba* despite their father's will, and it is said that this rivalry was fueled by their other siblings, who also wanted the same throne. One day *Kintu* got into a very bad disagreement with his brother *Bemba*, and it ended with *Kintu* being overthrown and sent into exile by his brother. *Kintu* gathered a few of his loyal men, and they headed northeast, having decided to seek refuge in a kingdom they had heard of that supposedly was similar to theirs; that kingdom was Abyssinia [which is present day Ethiopia]. Among *Kintu*'s loyalists were three of his most trusted men: *Kisoro*, his aide; *Lukwoto*, his porter; and *Wavumira*, one of his bodyguards. Their journey was long, considering that it was on foot, but eventually they made it to Abyssinia, and to their relief, they were warmly received by the Abyssinian king, who offered them a place to stay as long as they needed it. Since they were exhausted, and they had no immediate plans to confront *Bemba*, they decided to make an extended visit in Abyssinia, an idea which their host fully supported. They lived happily in Abyssinia, but they never forgot their homeland.

After staying in Abyssinia for a considerable length of time, the group started making plans to return to Buganda. In their best scenario, *Bemba* would be dead; but should he still be alive, *Kintu* was prepared to fight for what was rightfully his, the throne of Buganda. After making elaborate plans for their return, the group realized that they had been away for so long that they could not easily retrace their steps back to Buganda. Fortunately for them, their host, the Abyssinian king, had a possible solution. He had an ancestral directional spear that he was willing to give to *Kintu* to help him retrace his steps. *Kintu* was grateful to the king, who not only gave him the spear but also instructed him as to how *Kintu* was going to use it to find a comfortable spot to settle in once he made it to Buganda. He was to head southwest, and whenever he saw a rock, he was to place the spear on it upright. If the spear bent and fell over, he would know that he had not yet arrived where he was supposed to be going; he would then pick up the spear and continue journeying. The spear would remain standing straight when placed on top of the rock at his destination in Buganda.

Armed with the Abyssinian king's directional spear, *Kintu* and his loyalists started their journey back to their native land. They traveled for a while before seeing any rock until they reached Mount Elgon [in present day *Bugisu*], but when *Kintu* placed his spear on top of this mountain, it bent and couldn't stay in place, which meant that they had not yet arrived in Buganda. They departed from Mount Elgon and continued with their journey, passing through *Gabula* before deciding to rest at *Bweramondo* in *Bugerere*. After resting, they resumed their journey, crossed River *Ssezibwa* and stopped to rest again at *Butwala*. However, while crossing River *Ssezibwa*, *Lukwoto*, the porter who was carrying *Kintu*'s stuff, including *Kintu*'s bag that had been filled with the journey's supplies, accidentally dropped that bag into the river and the stream carried it downwards to *Zzinga*. *Lukwoto* did not report the loss of this bag, for fear of his master, until the master asked for something to eat while resting at *Butwala*. As soon as *Kintu* heard about the loss of his treasured bag, he decided to return to *Zzinga* in hopes of retrieving it since it had all his journey's supplies, but he was unable to find it. Filled with rage for the loss of his bag, *Kintu* decided to proceed with his journey up to *Ddindo*. When he reached

Ddindo and saw a huge rock extending for miles, he placed his spear on it and the spear remained straight, which meant that he had finally reached his destination in Buganda.

Kintu started making himself at home in *Ddindo*, where he established an elaborate residence on this rock. After settling in, he married his first wife from the area, named *Nambi*, with whom he had his only child, a daughter named *Nakyejwe*. Later on he got more wives, among whom were *Nantuttululu*, *Nakatonyi*, and *Bakazi Lwendo*. But even though *Kintu* was now comfortable in Buganda, he did not forget his mission, to regain the Buganda throne from his brother *Bemba*, that is if *Bemba* was still alive and the reigning king. So *Kintu* started making inquiries about the leadership of the kingdom. Incidentally he might have stayed in Abyssinia for a very long time because he soon learned that while he was away, the Baganda had increased their numbers greatly, and they had organized themselves into several clans. Each clan was headed by a strong clan leader who was supposedly independent and in charge of his own clan people, but *Kintu* also learned that every now and then, a stronger clan leader could wage war on other clans and, if successful, take control of them all until he was overthrown. *Kintu* was then informed that there was one such leader who had gained control over all the Baganda in the area, and guess who that was? His infamous brother *Bemba*, now living at *Naggalabi* in *Buddo*! *Kintu* was also informed that *Bemba* was a ruthless leader who had earned himself the nickname of *Musota* (snake) because he was so cruel that not only did he behave like a snake and as such was feared by all, but also that supposedly even snakes obeyed him. *Bemba* had killed a good number of his people because he couldn't stand any opposition or disobedience whatever the case happened to be. *Kintu* then ascertained that the Baganda people were more than ready for a change in leadership.

Having gotten such encouraging news, *Kintu* decided to journey to *Ssese Islands*, home to Baganda deities, to ask for permission from these deities to become king of Buganda and save the Baganda from *Bemba*. On this journey to *Ssese Islands*, *Kintu* passed through *Mangira* before resting at *Munywa* in *Bbebe*. From *Munywa*, he went to *Magonga* in *Busujju* from where he proceeded to *Bukasa*, and then to *Kitinda* before traveling by boat to *Ssese Islands*. Once on the islands, *Kintu* was told of a powerful clan leader residing there by the name of *Mukiibi*, who had fled from the mainland because of *Bemba*. *Bemba* had commanded *Mukiibi* to accomplish a task for him, and *Mukiibi* had refused. In response *Bemba* had gotten in a fight with *Mukiibi* and killed one of *Mukiibi*'s sons; the fight ended with *Mukiibi* fleeing for his life to Ssese. Now *Kintu* had an ally against *Bemba*, so he called on *Mukiibi*, who was more than willing to help him overthrow *Bemba*. After receiving permission from the deities to become king of Buganda, *Kintu* journeyed back to *Ddindo* with *Mukiibi* and two of *Mukiibi*'s men by the names of *Nfudu* and *Kigave;* the travelers stopped at *Gobero* where *Kintu* left his boat before continuing to *Ddindo*.

On arriving at *Ddindo*, *Kintu* and *Mukiibi* started making elaborate plans to overthrow *Bemba*. Wanting to be fair and reasonable, *Kintu* decided to send messengers to *Bemba* to negotiate the leadership of Buganda, but *Bemba* killed whoever *Kintu* sent his way. Now *Kintu* was getting frustrated; at this juncture, *Mukiibi* offered his two men, *Nfudu* and *Kigave,* to help *Kintu*, and *Kintu* took up the offer. Of these two men *Nfudu* was the wittiest; he had been nicknamed *Nfudu* because of his ability to make himself look like *enfudu* (tortoise). Because of his wit, *Nfudu* was put in charge of the operation, and he was ordered to go and negotiate with *Bemba* and bring him back alive to *Ddindo*. Should he successfully accomplish that mission, *Nfudu* was to be granted immortality by the then King *Kintu* [the Baganda used to believe that their kings were endowed with godly abilities]. With much excitement in anticipation of such a reward, *Nfudu* and *Kigave* got under way to *Bemba*'s residence in *Naggalabi*. When the pair arrived in *Bemba*'s royal court and *Nfudu* stated their business to *Bemba*, *Bemba* deceived him, telling him that since it was already nighttime, these two should get a good night's sleep and report to him the next day.

Of course *Bemba* had no intention of seeing that message-carrying *Nfudu* alive the next morning, so he ordered his guards to kill him that night as they had done with all the previous emissaries from *Kintu*, but *Nfudu* had one great trick to play on these guards. He was good with making masks, which the guards did not seem to know anything about. Actually, he had been nicknamed *Nfudu* because he had made a very real *Nfudu* (tortoise) looking mask which he used to adorn his head at night to look like a tortoise. Whenever he was under this mask, he would seem headless to the onlookers, and this trick worked wonders for him on what would have been the last night of his life. When the guards approached

Nfudu to kill him that night, they were stunned to see a tortoise instead of a person, and they fled the scene, probably terrified. The news soon reached *Bemba*, who wanted to see this tortoise person for himself. *Nfudu* seized the moment and explained to the admiring *Bemba* that he cut off his head every night to protect himself from his enemies, just as he had done with the guards, and he keeps his head in a safe place until morning, wearing his tortoise mask during the night. He added that because he was so clever and ever ready to protect his head, he was immortal.

Bemba could not believe his luck; since he had enemies in every corner wanting him dead, this was a trick he could not wait to try as it would solve all his problems. *Bemba* made an appointment with *Nfudu* to teach him the trick the following night. As soon as it got dark, *Bemba* promptly arrived at his guest quarters to acquire the knowledge that would make him immortal. He asked *Nfudu* to explain the procedure clearly, and *Nfudu* did so with delight. According to *Nfudu*, all *Bemba* had to do was put his head on a chopping block, and immediately after it fell off him, he would be given his own tortoise mask to adorn himself and every night thereafter while securing his head from his enemies. A great, and yet very simple trick, so thought *Bemba,* and as soon as *Nfudu* finished with the explanation, *Bemba* immediately put his head on the chopping block. Just for effect, *Nfudu* asked *Bemba* one more time if he wanted to do this, and *Bemba* eagerly responded positively. In no time *Bemba*'s head was off, and numerous snakes were seen coming out of his neck as he took his last breath, and he was no more!!! There was rejoicing all over *Naggalabi* when the news of *Bemba*'s demise started reaching the people, and the more the news spread among the Baganda, the more the people celebrated; *Bemba* had been a terror to all. When snakes stopped popping out of *Bemba*'s head, *Nfudu* wrapped it up, with the help of *Kigave*, for the journey back to *Ddindo*.

On arrival at *Ddindo*, *Nfudu* presented *Bemba*'s head to *Kintu*, but although *Kintu* appreciated *Nfudu*'s work, he did not grant him immortality as he had promised. *Nfudu* was supposed to bring *Bemba* alive to *Ddindo*, not dead! But because *Bemba* had been defeated, *Kintu* assumed the *Kabaka* of Buganda title he had earlier gone to seek from *Ssese Islands*. After settling in *Naggalabi* as King of Buganda, *Kintu* organized a more coherent political entity around the clans and their leaders, an entity that is still around, the present day Kingdom of Buganda. *Chwa Nnabakka* inherited the kingdom when *Kintu* disappeared [the oral tradition has no details of what happened to *Kintu*], and thus began a lineage of Buganda Kings up to the now reigning 36th King of Buganda, *Ronald Muwenda Mutebi ll.*

Ddindo: The Physical Location of *Kintu*'s Home

To the delight of Baganda oral literature enthusiasts, there is a physical place located off Kampala Gayaza road known as Kabaka *Kintu*'s rock. This rock is located in *Ddindo, Kasawo*, one of the subcounties of Buganda. The town of *Kasawo* is roughly 39 miles from Kampala city center, and *Ddindo* is about one and a half miles from *Kasawo* town. According to the Baganda oral literature pertaining to *Ddindo* (see *Kintu*: The Legend), Kabaka *Kintu* first settled here on his way back to Buganda from Abyssinia. On the rock, an extensive area of about ten acres, are "interesting" imprints

An overview of the rock at *Ddindo*. Visitors must remove their shoes when walking on the rock as a sign of respect.

29

that are supposed to convince visitors that the first king of Buganda actually lived there with his family. Tourists are welcome to tour the rock and hear intriguing details about the life of the first residents of this place. Visitors first report to a big house by the gate, where they take off their shoes at the front door and they are received in a large room fitted with traditional Baganda multicolored hand woven mats which serve as seats. After getting comfortable, visitors are given a warm ceremonial welcome and briefing by the caretakers of the place who are all women. The welcome includes a typical *Kiganda* greeting from the ladies, all dressed in traditional Baganda women outfits (*Busuuti*), who one by one repeat the same greeting to the visitors, and the visitors respond accordingly. First the men visitors are greeted as a group, and then the women.

LADY: *Tusanyuse okubalaba ba ssebo* (We are glad to see you, sirs).

Men visitors are prompted to respond as follows: *Naffe nnyabo* (We too, madam).

LADY: *Eradde ba ssebo* [an expression sort of like "is all well?"].

MEN: *Maamu nnyabo* [an affirmative response to the above].

LADY: *Muli mutya ba ssebo* (How are you, sirs?).

MEN: *Tuli bulungi* nnyabo (We are well, madam).

LADY: *Mwebale okujja okutulabako ba ssebo* (Thank you for coming to visit with us, sirs).

MEN: *Kale nnyabo* [a positive, supposedly enthusiastic response to the above].

The lady then greets the women in the same way. When this author visited, about 15 ladies greeted the visitors. A casual conversation can follow about the visitors' journey, weather, events, and so on.

After the greetings, the chief caretaker briefs the visitors about the etiquette of the place and what to expect during the two or so hours' tour depending on how curious the visitors are and the number of questions they might have at various locations. If the visitors have any questions before the tour starts, they can ask them. The visitors can also make a donation for the upkeep of the house by placing the donation in a traditional hand woven basket (*ekibbo*). One making a donation is shown the traditional way to put it in the basket, first by kneeling and then placing the donation in the basket using both hands. Now the visitors are ready for the tour, being guided by the chief caretaker. When this author visited, there was also a guide from the Buganda Historical Society to fill in the

Ddindo guides; the author is in the middle (July 2008). The bark cloth (*olubugo*) draped over the shoulders by men and secured around the waist with a sash by women, is a Baganda traditional attire made from the inner bark of a specific tropical tree (*omutuba*). The bark is carefully stripped off the tree without being torn in pieces and it is treated with herbs. It is then malleted in a shed built for that purpose (*ekkomagiro*) to prevent the bark from drying up in the process, until it turns into a soft terra-cotta colored material. The now very smooth material is dried under the sun, and the result is a soft material that was traditionally used as a dress, bedsheets and a shroud. Bark clothes are still being made in Buganda, but on a very small scale, and they are now being used mostly for traditional cultural ceremonies and for making decorations.

31

historical details. Both guides wear the traditional *olubugo*, which is what the king and his people would have been wearing at that time.

The first order of business is to take off shoes as a sign of respect for the place and to emphasize its importance in the history of Buganda. Here are some of the most prominent features imprinted on the rock that the visitor may want to see:

1. A moon, drum and door lock on one of the very first stones at the entrance of the rock. It is said that whenever the full moon appeared during the reign of *Kabaka Kintu*, it signaled the beginning of a period of happiness, and the king began the ceremonies by playing that specific drum using that door lock. This tradition is still being practiced by whoever happens to be the chief caretaker of the rock when the full moon appears.

2. A stone in the form of a cow, also a few meters from the entrance. This hornless cow was the only one the king had, and its milk could only be taken by *Nakyejwe*, the king's only daughter.

3. A stone in the form of a boat which the king used to go fishing.

4. An imprint of the king's bed. The oral tradition states that this bed used to have four stands but that when *Edward Muteesa II* died in exile in 1969, three of the stands automatically broke off and only one remained, probably foretelling the end of the Kingdom which had been instituted by *Kintu*. (Although *Muteesa I*, the then reigning king of Buganda, had warmly received the explorers Stanley and Grant into his kingdom in 1875, Buganda became an integral part of Uganda during colonialism as opposed to being an independent political entity, and it was weakened in the process. *Muteesa I*'s successor, *Muwanga II*, was forced to negotiate an agreement with the British in order to survive, and the following kings all struggled to keep the Kingdom going, but only succeeded to do so within the limits of the British policy of Indirect Rule until Uganda gained its independence in 1962. Unfortunately, the first president of Uganda after colonialism, Milton Obote, clashed with the then reigning king of Buganda, *Muteesa II*, and he abolished all traditional kingdoms and local governments in Uganda in 1966. Obote then sent *Muteesa II* into exile in London, where he died in 1969, and forbade the Baganda to bring the king's body back to Uganda for traditional

burial ceremonies in the royal tombs at Kasubi; little wonder then that *Kintu*'s bed shed three of its stands when *Muteesa ll* died. The Kingdom of Buganda ceased to exist in 1966 until it was reinstated in 1993 with the coronation of *Ronald Mutebi ll* as the 36th King of Buganda.)

5. *Engule*, the king's crown, just a few meters from the imprint of the king's bed.
6. *Omweso*, a board game that the king used to play.
7. One of *Kintu*'s giant footsteps. Supposedly he was a huge person.
8. *Olukiiko*, the king's parliament. Within the imprint of the king's parliament are two identical stones called *abalongo ba kabaka* (the king's twins), and two fish like stones. The oral tradition asserts that the king used to treat his subjects to a fish meal first before any *lukiiko* session could start. There are also imprints of other stones in the form of stools on which the subjects used to sit during the sessions.
9. *Nambi*'s footsteps, supposedly on her way to the kitchen.
10. The kitchen with an eternal flame. In the kitchen is an imprint of a rack (*akatandalo*) above the fireplace (*ekyoto*) onto which *Nambi* used to place the kitchen utensils and banana leaves (*endagala*). (The staple food of the Baganda is green bananas [*amatooke*], which are peeled and wrapped as a bundle in banana leaves, then secured using banana barks [*ebyayi*]. This bundle of bananas is then placed in a pot that has been cushoned with *emizingonyo,* and a slight amount of water is added to the pot. The pot is then covered with more banana leaves and it is placed on three blocks [*amasiga*] around the fireplace. Firewood is put into the fireplace and a fire is started and kept going until the bananas are steamed to softness. The softened bananas are then mashed, just like potatoes, and served with stew such as beef, fish, and so on. Traditionally, there is supposed to be a rack just like *Nambi*'s in every Muganda [see glossary definition of "Baganda"] person's kitchen, for storing utentials and banana leaves.)
11. The king's iron box, also found in the kitchen.
12. A trench-like depression called *eryato*, about four meters away from the kitchen; the king used this depression for making a local brew

known as *omwenge*. (The Baganda make a traditional beer-like drink, *omwenge*, from bananas, which they ferment in *eryato*. Traditionally, the Baganda have extensive banana plantations in which are found several types of bananas for different uses; some are for cooking, some for eating when ripe as fruits, some for roasting, and others for making *omwenge*. The green *omwenge* bananas are put on a rack above the fireplace [*ekibanyi*], or in a specifically dug pit, then covered with banana leaves and dirt until ripe. Usually they ripen within seven days. They are then peeled by hand, placed in a trench lined with smooth young banana leaves or in a wooden canoe-like object with a small opening [*eryato*], and mashed. Water is added, and the mixture is poured in *eryato* where it is mixed with sorghum and the *eryato* is covered overnight to allow the drink to ferment. The next day, the fermented drink is sieved and the resulting liquid is the Baganda's traditional beer, *omwenge*.)

13. Two knee-like depressions, and a black-looking stream down the rock. This is supposed to be the birth spot of the king's only child, *Nakyejwe*.

14. Four small saucepan-like depressions, *ebyogero*, in which *Nambi* used to bathe baby *Nakyejwe*. (Traditionally, the Baganda gather several specific herbs when a baby is born, and they boil all of these herbs in a pot of water called *ekyogero*; they then bathe the infant in that water. This mixture cleans the baby and keeps the baby's skin smooth. The herbs are frequently replaced with new batches, and the water is changed each time the baby is bathed; baby can be bathed in this mixture for about a month.)

15. Two bed-like stones. These represent *Nambi* and *Nakyejwe*'s beds. Besides these bed-like stones is a drum-like stone known as *akagoma ka Lubendera*. *Nambi* used to comfort *Nakyejwe* whenever she was crying by playing on this drum and singing to her. Baganda women can still be heard comforting their crying babies by singing: *Kano ke kagoma ka Lubendera bwaba akaaba, kenkubako nasirika* (this is Lubendera's drum, and whenever he is crying, I play it and he calms down).

16. Two knee-like depressions where *Nambi* used to kneel when sharpening her knives. Baganda women sharpen their knives on stones.

17. Two stones where *Ddungu*, deity of the hunters, used to rest and roast his hunted meat.

18. The king's well, which is said to have dried up at one time, but came back on its own. The oral tradition states that people used to dump garbage along the shores of this well. They would swim in it as well, but, according to the tradition, one time a child drowned in the well. Also, as one man was dumping rubbish along its shores, his fingers were cut off by an invisible force, and this marked the end of these activities at this site.

19. A front yard where the king used to hold his ceremonies. This area is still used for the same traditional functions by people needing *Kintu*'s blessing. Often such people make sacrifices to the king and others give gifts in thanks for whatever the king has given them. The gifts are often cattle, sheep, chicken, goats and so on. When-

The king's well at ***Ddindo***.

ever guests come to this hill for a visit, they are treated to a traditional meal of roasted bananas and roasted meats of chicken, cattle, sheep and goats given as gifts. (According to Baganda tradition, guests must be fed regardless of reason and length of the visit.) *Kintu*'s children have to be fed whenever they visit him in *Ddindo* or each other's homes. The guests can also be entertained with *Kiganda* drums, songs, and dance courtesy of the caretakers, and they are always invited to actively participate by singing, clapping, drumming, and dancing as well.

In addition to tourists, this rock area also attracts scholars interested in the study of various disciplines, including the history of the Kingdom of Buganda and its rulers, the African oral tradition, and geology because the physical attributes of this rock are unique and challenge universal theories of rock formation.

Rocks at *Ddindo* which might be of interest to geologists.

The Baganda: A Mythological Perspective

Although mythology is an integral part of almost all cultures, it is not equally valued in all of them; the Baganda, however, are among those cultures that place great value on theirs because they believe it is the key to their very existence. For example the Baganda treasure the *Kintu* myth featured below, because they believe that it documents, among other things, their origin in *Kintu*, a mythological figure who is culturally recognized as the father of the Baganda people. This narration also highlights the nature of their human existence, the creation of their universe, the essence of their supreme, and why they have to die.

One of the admirable features of oral narratives is their fluidity; griots, including notable ones like the narrator of Niane's version of the epic of Sundiata, have praise for this fluidity; it does not solidify the story and make it inaccessible and/or unattractive to generations far removed from the origin of such a story. It does not "stiffen and dry up its subject" as Joseph Ki-Zerbo points out. Because of that fluidity, there are several versions of the significant mythological story of the Baganda we are going to read below.

Despite the various versions, the central story of any mythological narration always remains intact; it is the presentation of that story that is constantly adapted to the audience, and its rhetorical nuances depend on the specific storyteller's ability to engage one's audience.

In this Baganda mythological story, *Ggulu*'s daughter gets married to *Kintu*, and they start a family. But along the way, the couple attracts *Walumbe*'s attention and he ends up taking residence among their children on earth.

This story is fascinating not only because of its mythological significance to the Baganda, but also because it parallels the Bible's Adam and Eve story, a version which the Baganda were probably not familiar with before the onslaught of Christianity in the late 18th century. The rhetoric is also worth commenting about to facilitate the reader's engagement with this story.

This translated version is compiled from several oral versions collected by this author and assistants from various narrators around the Kingdom of Buganda.

Kintu: The Myth

Once upon a time there was a very powerful, wealthy man living in the sky by the name of *Ggulu*; he had many sons and only one daughter. Down on earth in Buganda there lived a very lonely man called *Kintu*, whose only possession, which also doubled as his companion, was a cow. *Ggulu*'s children used to come down to earth riding on a rainbow and play all over; they thought it was an empty place, until one day when they came down and landed in a place they had not been to before. This was Buganda. They were shocked to see a man all by himself in the whole of Buganda, tending his cow, only one cow. They had all kinds of questions for him: who are you?; where do you sleep at night?; what do you eat?; how long have you lived here?; where did you come from?; and so on. The man answered all their questions pleasantly, which fascinated *Ggulu*'s oldest child, the only girl of *Ggulu*, by the name of *Nambi*, and she decided to get to know this man better.

After such an exciting visit with *Kintu*, the children returned to the sky, but *Nambi*'s heart stayed in Buganda. One day, she decided to come down all by herself and pay this man a visit, but it was going to be a challenging journey since she had never made it alone before, without her

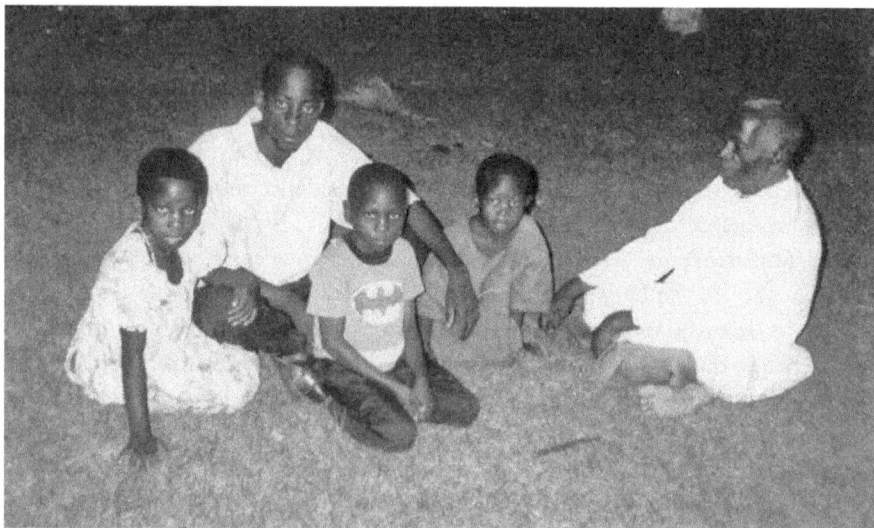

An elder getting ready to narrate the story of Kintu to a curious audience.

38

brothers. There was no road to follow, but as usual, the rainbow readily appeared in the sky and it brought *Nambi* speedily to earth. Once she reached her destination, the rainbow disappeared, but that was not a problem for *Nambi* because she liked the man and even felt sorry for him because he was so lonely. She had a solution: since all the young men living with her in the sky were her brothers, why not get married to *Kintu* and become his companion! Brilliant idea, but before they could live as man and wife, *Nambi* had to introduce her prospective husband to her father and get his approval. *Kintu* agreed to the plan and the two of them, together with the cow since they had no where to leave it, set out to go to the sky and meet *Nambi's* father. (The Baganda perform a very elaborate introduction ceremony during which the bride-to-be introduces the groom-to-be to her parents; some think that this ceremony has its origin in this story.) As luck would have it, the rainbow that *Nambi* thought had disappeared was at their service when they needed it, and in no time, they were in the sky.

Once in the sky, *Nambi* excitedly introduced her prospective husband to her father, reiterating her plan to get married to him to keep him company. The father was hesitant at first; after all, he had only one girl and she was proposing to go live on earth! But eventually he came around. Before he could give his approval though, *Ggulu* had to make sure that *Kintu* was indeed the right man for his daughter, so he devised various tasks for *Kintu* to test his intelligence, wit, stamina, endurance and temperament. The first night, *Kintu*, who had been given a room in a small guest house on the premises, dreamt that his first task the following day was going to be eating a large amount of food. And sure enough, as soon as day broke, *Ggulu's* servants started bringing dishes of food to the guest house, and as expected, they informed him that he had to eat all of that food if he wanted to become *Ggulu's* son-in-law. The more dishes the servants brought, the more disheartened *Kintu* became. By mid-afternoon, the house was near capacity with food dishes, and *Kintu*, who had started eating in the morning, was about to declare defeat. But as soon as the last servant left, *Kintu*, because of his strong belief in destiny and that a person cannot be given a task one cannot handle, succeeded in devising some magic tricks of his own and started making the food disappear in a hole that he miraculously discovered in the middle of the room. By nighttime, all the dishes were empty, but although *Ggulu* was impressed, he was not yet done testing *Kintu*. He came and wished *Kintu* a good night because day two was going to be more exciting than day one had been.

It was soon day two, and *Kintu* woke up to find *Ggulu*'s servants in the living room after they had placed one large empty tank on the verandah; one of them held an empty basket. *Kintu* was soon to hear that *Ggulu* wanted him to fill the empty tank with water from a well about a mile away, using that basket. Panic set in as *Kintu* thought of possible ways to accomplish this task. Once left alone, *Kintu* started walking towards the well, basket in hand, but at that time with no clue as to what he was going to do. When *Kintu* was lingering around the well wondering what he was going to do, a friendly spider came to his rescue and weaved an invisible web around the basket; now *Kintu* was in business, and by sunset, he had filled the tank. Once again *Ggulu* was impressed, but once again he was not ready to give away his daughter, so he wished *Kintu* a good night and promised to call the next day. Since he was totally exhausted, *Kintu* slept soundly, and it was soon day three.

Early in the morning of the third day, *Kintu* was once again woken up by *Ggulu*'s servants. This time they had brought him an axe, and they explained that *Ggulu*, who used rock pieces as firewood, wanted him to chop such pieces from a solid rock using the axe they had brought, and that he was not supposed to chip that axe. After chopping the pieces, he was to tie them up in a bundle and take both the bundle and axe back to *Ggulu*. Quite a daunting job, but probably not so much for *Kintu*, who, on spotting the rock he was supposed to chop, invoked his magic. By noon he had the pieces all tied up in a bundle as he had been instructed to do, and he delivered both the bundle and the unchipped axe to *Ggulu* by early afternoon. "Very well done," commented *Ggulu*, "but I have just one more surprise for you. Go and enjoy the rest of your day, and I will be in touch tomorrow." On the fourth day, *Ggulu* himself joined *Kintu* for breakfast and told him that the two of them were going to take a walk to *Ggulu*'s cattle pasture. As soon as they got there, *Ggulu* informed *Kintu* that his final task was to find his cow from *Ggulu*'s look-alike herds, after which *Kintu* could return to earth with *Nambi* as his companion. Fortunately for *Kintu*, a wasp, visible to him only, led the way through the animals and landed on the horn of *Kintu*'s cow. *Ggulu* was so impressed when *Kintu* identified his beloved cow from so many others that he immediately gave *Kintu* permission to marry *Nambi*.

Arrangements were made for the journey back to earth. *Nambi* was told by *Ggulu* to take a male and female type of each plant and of each living creature to populate the earth for her, her husband and their children's use. *Ggulu* warned his daughter to pack carefully, to make sure that she had all she needed and was supposed to take with her because it was going to be a one way journey; *Nambi* was never going to return to the sky. This was not because *Ggulu* did not want his daughter to ever visit; it was for her protection from her very nasty twin brother, *Walumbe*, who was intentionally kept out of these arrangements. *Walumbe* was sent on a mission far away from home when *Ggulu* first heard of *Nambi*'s plans because *Ggulu* knew what *Walumbe* was capable of doing and how unstoppable he was. *Walumbe* was not even told that *Nambi* was getting married for fear that he might want to go with his sister down to earth and cause problems for the couple. When all the plans were in place, the rainbow appeared as expected, and *Ggulu* said his good byes and wished *Nambi* and *Kintu* a good life in Buganda.

The journey was a very good, smooth, quick one, and the couple were happy to get home. On arrival, *Nambi* started unpacking to plant the seeds timely, but she realized that she had forgotten the seeds for the chicken food. There was no way *Nambi* was going to live without her chickens, which were not going to survive without their food, so she decided to return to the sky. *Kintu* reminded her of her father's warning and pleaded with her not to go, but she would not hear of it. *Nambi*, disregarding her father's very stern warning, returned to the sky. There she found *Walumbe* searching for her in every corner; after all they were twins!! "Where have you been my dear sister," *Walumbe* wanted to know, but *Nambi* tried to keep him out of her way with no success. "Now that I've found you, I will not let you get out of my sight. I cannot imagine a life without you," said *Walumbe* in his annoying scratchy voice. As soon as *Nambi* found her seeds, she started down to earth, with *Walumbe* in tow! That is how *Walumbe* came and made a home on earth.

It is important to point out here that *Walumbe* and *Nambi* were the first twins on earth. Once on earth, *Walumbe* made himself at home, built his own place near *Kintu* and *Nambi*, and life went on smoothly. Within a year, *Nambi* and *Kintu* had become parents; needless to say there was joy and celebration all over. *Walumbe* too joined in the celebrations, happy to get a nephew, whom he thought would be his companion since *Nambi* and *Kintu* had each other. But things did not work out that way; the young parents kept their son to themselves. "Not to despair," thought *Walumbe* to himself. "There will soon be another one of those!" And a year later, there was another one of those, but once again, the baby was not given to *Walumbe*. "Probably I will have better luck next time," thought *Walumbe*. Then came baby number three, and number four, and still the parents would not give any of their kids to *Walumbe* to keep him company. When the fifth kid was born, *Walumbe* went straight to his relatives and stated his case plainly: "Please give me a kid to keep me company and to do chores with; I am so lonely." But *Kintu* and *Nambi*, heeding *Ggulu*'s warning about *Walumbe*, adamantly refused to give him a kid, and they made it clear that no matter how many kids they got, they would never give any to *Walumbe*. *Walumbe* left their house with no comment, but he was quite upset! And guess what happened next!!

That very night, when the *Kintu* family was deep in sleep, *Walumbe* entered their house and claimed one of the kids as his own! On seeing their kid lifeless the next morning, the parents, who until then had never known *Walumbe*'s work, thought the kid was deep in sleep! They tried to wake their baby up, but to no avail. Mockingly, *Walumbe* informed them that the baby would never wake up; he was now *Walumbe*'s possession! *Kintu*, *Nambi* and the remaining four kids wept for days, rubbing and shaking the baby constantly but to no avail. They eventually dug a deep hole, wrapped up the baby's body in bark clothes and buried their baby! But not before they threatened to expel *Walumbe* from earth! An empty threat — right?

After several months of grieving and waiting for an apology from *Walumbe*, which was not forthcoming, Kintu gathered enough courage to go and face *Ggulu*, apologize for *Nambi*'s disobedience and his failure to prevent her from returning to the sky, report *Walumbe*'s despicable actions, and ask for *Ggulu*'s help in handling *Walumbe*. After reminding *Kintu* of his very stern warning about *Walumbe*, *Ggulu* agreed to give his children a second chance, and he sent one of his other sons, who was known to be a problem solver, to go to earth with *Kintu* and help them to return *Walumbe* to the sky. *Kayikuzi*, the son sent on earth to help, was given instructions to first use persuasion to return *Walumbe* to the sky. "Should *Walumbe* refuse to be persuaded, use any means, including force, to bring him back here with you," instructed *Ggulu*.

42

Once on earth, *Kayikuzi* went to work. "My dear brother, you must be so lonely here, and you do not look happy, busy, or even respected and loved as much as we love you in the sky," beseeched *Kayikuzi*. "Why don't you come back to the sky with me? Father misses you greatly and so do we all. Since you are an image copy of *Nambi*, we all need you to help us keep our memories of our dear sister alive in the sky! And father relies on you for many operations; please do come with me!" *Kayikuzi*'s pleas fell on deaf ears! "I am not ever going to return to the sky. I love my life here, and I think I have found a way to gain respect down here! Who cares about being loved?" was *Walumbe*'s cold response to *Kayikuzi*. After giving thought to *Walumbe*'s words and ascertaining that *Walumbe* was not likely to leave earth voluntarily, *Kayikuzi* resorted to plan B, which was to capture *Walumbe* and return him to the sky by force. And the pursuit was on. Once *Walumbe* ascertained what *Kayikuzi* was up to, he made himself scarce, kept out of sight, and ran swiftly whenever his brother neared him. *Kayikuzi* tried to capture *Walumbe* day after day, but with no success. One day *Walumbe* was cornered, but he thought of a plan very fast; since his foot was so powerful and he tended to leave gaping holes in his path, he was going to disappear under the earth! As soon as *Kayikuzi* made his move, *Walumbe* stamped his foot on the ground and disappeared in the hole he had formed by stamping. After pinpointing the exact location of that hole, *Kayikuzi* dug deeper all around it until he spotted *Walumbe* hiding way down under, but *Walumbe* slipped through *Kayikuzi*'s hands before *Kayikuzi* had gotten a chance to tighten his grip on him, returned to the surface and made another hole just as *Kayikuzi* was resurfacing from the first one. The pursuit continued with *Walumbe* disappearing under ground every now and then, and *Kayikuzi* digging him out each time, and *Walumbe* escaping each time. [This hide and dig activity might have lasted a long time, because there is a place in Buganda called *Ttanda* (see *Ttanda* page 45) with over 240 identical holes that traditionally are said to be those that *Kayikuzi* dug in pursuit of his brother *Walumbe*.]

By now, *Walumbe* had perfected his skill of hiding underground. Not wanting to concede defeat, *Kayikuzi*, who by then was getting exhausted, devised one more plan. He asked *Kintu* and *Nambi* to keep their kids indoors while he went underground one more time to unearth *Walumbe*. *Kayikuzi* added that the kids should be indoors because he did not want them to make noise on seeing *Walumbe*. He wanted *Walumbe* to feel secure on the surface to give him (*Kayikuzi*) a chance to sneak up on *Walumbe* and capture him. And as before, the pursuit was on, with *Walumbe* disappearing underground, and *Kayikuzi* digging his way there and getting hold of *Walumbe*. The two of them struggled, and *Walumbe* slipped out of *Kayikuzi's* hands and surfaced! But guess who was out playing when *Walumbe* appeared above the ground? *Kintu's* kids!!! They screamed on seeing the muddy, scary looking *Walumbe*, and once again *Walumbe* disappeared underground. *Kayikuzi* was more than frustrated; he was furious with *Kintu* and *Nambi*, who once again had failed to do what they had been told to do. *Kintu*, feeling totally embarrassed and not wanting to look any more wimpy than he already was, put on a brave face and thanked *Kayikuzi* for his efforts. *Kayikuzi* returned to the sky, and *Kintu* swore to continue the fight with *Walumbe*. *Kintu's* plan of action was simple and nonconfrontational but quite effective, and it has been in use since then. Whenever *Walumbe* took any of *Kintu's* children, he would get more, and he resolved to keep on getting children so that his children would never be wiped off the face of the earth by *Walumbe*.

Walumbe and *Kintu* never resolved their differences; *Kintu's* descendants continue the fight with *Walumbe*, and underground is officially known as *Walumbe's* abode, where he is kept company by *Kintu's* children whom he takes by force.

Issues for Discussion

There is a substantial number of issues to engage a critical reader in this story, and also give one insight into, or incentive to research, some historical and cultural issues and traditions of the Baganda, such as:

- Baganda religious practices
- Comparisons and contrasts with the Bible story of Adam and Eve
- The discourse on Christianity in Buganda
- Themes/lessons implicit in the story
- Rhetorical devices and questions
- Baganda premarital introduction ceremony
- The significance of the tasks *Kintu* had to perform

- Character analysis
- The significance of the names in this story to the Baganda

It is important to remember that one is "reading" a translated version put together from various oral sources, a version which may even sound simple and in places seemingly trivial, but to a Muganda person, all the details in this story such as the tasks *Kintu* has to perform in the process of wooing his wife to be, the names of the characters, and the *Kintu* family's encounter with *Walumbe* have intrinsic meaning; they are an integral part of a Muganda person's life. Simple as this story may seem to be, it is the yolk of Baganda culture.

Ttanda: The Physical Location of *Walumbe* and *Kayikuzi*'s Battle

One of the fascinating places in Baganda oral tradition is *Ttanda*, known among the Baganda as *Walumbe*'s abode. This place is about 35 kilometers west of the capital city Kampala, off Kampala-Mityana Road.

According to Baganda mythology as narrated above, *Walumbe* is said to have come down on earth following his twin sister, *Nambi*. But since *Walumbe* got nasty when *Nambi* and *Kintu* refused to give him any of their children, *Kintu* went to the sky and asked *Ggulu*, Walumbe's father, for help. *Ggulu,* who knew how nasty and dangerous his son could be, sympathized with *Kintu* and his daughter, *Nambi*, and agreed to send his most ingenious and physically very powerful son, *Kayikuzi*, to remove *Walumbe* from earth. But when *Kayikuzi* came down to earth to persuade his brother

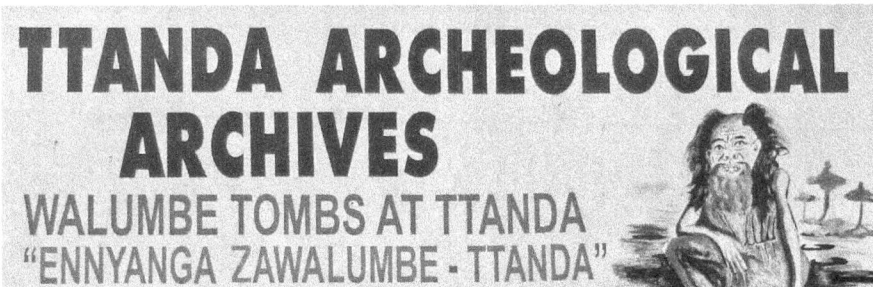

TTANDA ARCHEOLOGICAL ARCHIVES
WALUMBE TOMBS AT TTANDA
"ENNYANGA ZAWALUMBE - TTANDA"

A sign on a main road directing visitors to *Ttanda*.

Walumbe to return to the sky with him, *Walumbe* flatly refused. *Kayikuzi* then resorted to using force hoping to corner and capture *Walumbe* and eventually journey with him back to the sky. As told in the *Kintu* myth, this was a great undertaking for *Kayikuzi*, but he embarked on the task eagerly and started chasing *Walumbe* to catch him. *Kayikuzi*'s strategy was to chase *Walumbe* until *Walumbe* could run no more, and since the place where they were living, *Ddindo* (see "Ddindo: The Physical Location of *Kintu*'s Home"), was all rock, *Walumbe* would have had nowhere to hide after getting exhausted, so capturing him would have been easy. Soon the chase was underway, and after circling *Ddindo* for several days and finding no hiding place, but all sore and with bleeding toes from running on rock, *Walumbe* decided to head southwest and *Kayikuzi* followed him. When they arrived at *Ttanda, Walumbe* was pleased to find himself in this area because it had soft ground and was, therefore, friendly to his bare feet. But more important still, *Walumbe* noticed that he made sizeable holes wherever he stepped.

The entrance to *Ttanda.*

One day, when *Kayikuzi* was about to capture the exhausted *Walumbe*, *Walumbe* realized that he could disappear in the holes made by his feet and hide from *Kayikuzi*, so he disappeared into one. When *Kayikuzi* spotted the hole in which *Walumbe* had disappeared, he began digging it to widen it and eventually get *Walumbe* out. But since the ground was soft, *Walumbe* made an underground tunnel and surfaced from a new hole while *Kayikuzi* was still busy digging the first hole. And when *Kayikuzi* too surfaced and spotted *Walumbe* above ground, *Walumbe* disappeared under hole number two, and this time *Kayikuzi* followed him into it instead of spending some time digging it. But as before *Walumbe* escaped through a new tunnel he had dug and surfaced on the other side of the hole he had disappeared in; *Kayikuzi*, too, surfaced in pursuit. Eventually, *Kayikuzi* gave up the chase and returned to the sky, but *Walumbe* is said to have stayed underground where he would occasionally come from and grab one of *Kintu*'s children; he felt safer there because he knew how hated he was

One of the holes at *Ttanda*.

by *Kintu* and *Nambi* and all their descendants. Up to this day, *Walumbe's* abode is underground (*Ttanda*), but he frequently surfaces to take more of *Kintu* and *Nambi's* descendants by force.

The digging and hiding under holes and surfacing at different spots might have lasted several days and maybe even nights; there are an estimated 240 holes (*Nyanga*) at *Ttanda*. Visitors to *Ttanda* can still see some of these holes, which are surprisingly deep and similar in appearance, with mechanically high-precision circular entrances, but no one knows for sure how deep they actually are.

It is amazing, though, to see how precisely arranged these holes are in a straight line and in powers of two.

Since it is believed that *Walumbe* resides underground in those holes, sometimes sick people visit *Ttanda* to appease *Walumbe* by placing black

A hole covered with three *Embugo* at *Ttanda*. The black one contains Walumbe's power; the terra-cotta one in the middle is the common traditional cloth; while the white one on top is for culturally significant people like kings and, of course, the all powerful *Walumbe*. Spears guard the covered hole.

pieces of materials (*embugo*) on top of those holes. It is also believed that *Walumbe* is so powerful, but that his power can be contained underground if the hole is covered first with a black *olubugo*, then a terra-cotta one and then topped with a white one. *Kintu* and *Nambi* wrapped their dead children in those same materials (*embugo*) and buried them underground. Traditionally, the Baganda used to wrap their dead for burial in *embugo*.

Also found at *Ttanda* are shrines for various Baganda deities such as *Musoke*, *Kiwanuka*, *Ndawula*, and *Mukasa*, all erected by people who say they dream that they should go to *Ttanda* and put up such shrines. People visit these shrines to solicit various kinds of help from these deities.

Ttanda is also a popular tourist attraction which in 2008 sometimes averaged fifty visitors a week.

3

Epigrams

Introduction

Epigrams are prominent in the Baganda oral tradition, and their reputation is in part due to their length, authentic nature, rhetorical value, availability, entertainment potential, and the meanings and messages implicit in them. Since epigrams are short, they are easy to commit to memory verbatim and very easy to reproduce. Also, because they are short and easy to remember verbatim, epigrams are the most authentic Luganda expressions available to Luganda language scholars, students, and the culturally minded Baganda people interested in preserving the dignity and eloquence that characterize their language. Most of these epigrams have been handed down through generations intact, and they remain so despite centuries of Luganda language growth and acquisition of words, phrases and other various expressions resulting from contacts with foreign forces. Epigrams are also the most rhetorical masterpieces in Luganda, and engaging in an analysis of their rhetorical characteristics such as tone, setting, and, most important, figurative language has been for decades, and continues to be, scholastically rewarding. Epigrams are also numerous and readily available, and if the leading party turns out to be as witty as the epigram(s) one is reciting, the audience can be thoroughly entertained. For the Baganda, not only are epigrams language-preserving, entertaining, and rhetorically viable pieces, they are time tested pieces of conventional wisdom. As pointed out in the introductory chapter, the Baganda people rely on their epigrams for various purposes, including giving advice on a variety of topics ranging from parenthood to getting rich, pointing out the importance of communal as well as individual responsibilities, cautioning each other and keeping people safe, teaching *Kiganda* behavior — especially to the youths — and overall capturing and preserving the essence of what makes a Muganda person that specific person.

Below is a sampling and discussion of the most popular epigrams in Luganda: the riddles and proverbs.

Riddles

Riddles are important literary pieces in Africa, and of particular practical interest, mostly, to the youths who use them for various purposes including the following: to challenge each others' knowledge of their societies, to strengthen their capacities to listen, to acquire, analyze and internalize new knowledge which they are expected to use, and to think fast and critically using this art form. Riddles are great brain exercises. Unlike stories, riddles can be made up on the spot and told by anyone, anywhere, mostly for entertainment or to just pass time; students often exchange riddles walking to and from school to challenge each other, to pass time and to quicken the pace of their journey. Children generally engage more in this riddling than adults do. Since the content of riddles is derived from the riddlers' environment, and is composed of objects, names, activities, and so on familiar to a specific group of people, Africanists, in general, get a glimpse into these people's "world," while African literature scholars, in particular, are attracted to the rhetorical situations and colorful language of these pieces.

The Baganda, like most African ethnic groups, have various types of riddles, but here we are going to identify two popular ones. The first type is a call-response riddling known as *ebikokkyo*. These are brief call statements, each with a specific one-word or one-phrase response. The audience (numbering anywhere between one and twenty at times) will know that they are being challenged to figure out such statements because the challenging party opens the session with a familiar call that prompts a response. The caller will say: *kkoyi kkoyi* (here the audience is being recognized for their knowledge; you do not *kkoyi kkoyi* people whom you know don't have the desired responses). Kkoyi kkoyi is a brain wake-up call; the caller is asking the audience to activate their memory and to put on their thinking and imagining caps in preparation for the quick-paced brain challenging activity coming up. The audience confidently replies: *lya* or *ddya* (literally translated as eat). This is followed by the caller asking the audience what he should be eating: *ongamba okulya ndye ki?* (literal translation: you are telling me to eat, what should I eat?), and the audience replies: *lya olulimi lwo* (eat your tongue). This last statement is a metaphor prompting the caller to engage one's tongue uttering words of wisdom.

The caller then proceeds to probe the audience for knowledge using familiar statements, objects, animals, names, and so on, and the audience is expected to give specific one-word responses. If the audience cannot provide the expected, commonly accepted response, they have to acknowledge defeat and "pay" for their ignorance. In such a situation, the caller asks the audience to give him a famous, rich, distinctive village (*ekyalo*), other than the caller's own village of course. (Villages are the second smallest sociopolitical units among the Baganda people, next to the family. A village can be made up of anywhere between ten and one hundred families, and the village chief is an important person.) So in asking for a village, the caller is asking for chiefdom, and the audience has to offer their caller a distinguished village. If the caller accepts the village offer, he can tell the audience the answer and the game continues. Even if this riddling is not a real prize competition, no one wants to display lack of such common knowledge when playing it, especially among peers (mostly youths).

The role of the caller is not exclusive though; anyone in the group can take over at any time, but whoever takes over has to signal the audience with *kkoyi kkoyi*. Here is an example:

CALLER: *kkoyi kkoyi*: AUDIENCE: *lya*.

CALLER: "*Nnina mukazi wange atambula azina*" (I have a wife who dances as she walks). If the audience is mostly adults, the caller says, "I have a wife who..."; this preface is gender neutral — it does not matter whether the caller is a man or a woman. However, if the audience is of children, the caller will say, "*Nnina omwana wange*" (I have a child who). Referencing wives and children in these riddles signifies how precious they are among the Baganda, and the caller is acknowledging that the knowledge coming up is also as precious. Also, children relate better to the riddles and benefit more from the information given when the caller addresses them and the content is on their level. The expected response for the example above is *ekisanyi* (a certain soft spider-like insect which makes a dancing motion as it moves).

Below are some more examples in translation:

CALLER: I have a wife (or child) who lives in a palace: AUDIENCE: A tongue [the tongue is comfortably guarded by the mouth and teeth just as a king is guarded by his men in his palace].

CALLER: I have a wife whom I married while she was all black, but in old age she has turned all white: AUDIENCE: Hair.

CALLER: I have a wife who simply swallows her food, never chews it: AUDIENCE: Chicken [these are common domestic birds in Buganda].

CALLER: I have a wife who walks facing both sides (back and front): AUDIENCE: a bundle of firewood [traditionally, the Baganda people used to collect firewood from forests, tie it up in bundles, and carry it home on their heads].

CALLER: My wife comes every morning and leaves every evening: AUDIENCE: Sun.

All *ebikokkyo* are not prefaced with the above wife/child phrase, however; some are simply just phrases or clauses emphasizing familiar objects, situations, and so on, as clues; here are some examples:

CALLER: A dwelling that is built by many people, but cannot be inhabited by more than one person: AUDIENCE: A grave.

CALLER: A double-door with one supporting frame: AUDIENCE: Nose.

CALLER: All the women in that home wear clothes of the same color and size: AUDIENCE: Edible white ants.

CALLER: Since I've seen you, you will have to take me with you to your home: AUDIENCE: *Ssere* [a very annoying weed seed that sticks on people's clothes].

CALLER: A murderer whom all love: AUDIENCE: Fire.

CALLER: No matter how much it rains, this place cannot flood: AUDIENCE: Ocean.

CALLER: It makes a good sound; too bad it eats people: AUDIENCE: Hyena [during the early days when people were just setting up homes in previously uninhabited areas, hyenas used to be in plenty, and people used to fear them because of their people eating reputation].

CALLER: A place with three fireplaces: AUDIENCE: Sky with moon, sun, and stars.

CALLER: Head south to see an all white tree: AUDIENCE: A stripped fig tree [the bark of this tree is used to make traditional clothing; when this bark is carefully removed from the tree, the remaining trunk should be all white].

CALLER: An item that is impossible to repair: AUDIENCE: A gourd [repairing a broken gourd is a very difficult task that is performed by skilled people; if you break one, you must look for one of those people to help you, but not all broken gourds can be repaired regardless of skill].

CALLER: It was wearing coats long before the king of Buganda had one: AUDIENCE: A wasp [traditionally the Baganda hold their king in high esteem as one endowed with specific powers from their creator].

CALLER: Hoes that do not shrink no matter how much they are used: AUDIENCE: Teeth.

CALLER: A house standing on one pole: AUDIENCE: A mushroom.

CALLER: It is a clan of old people: AUDIENCE: A gathering of frogs [all of them are wrinkled like old people].

CALLER: It is all bones on the outside and all meat inside: AUDIENCE: Egg.

CALLER: It looks beautiful when seen from a distance: AUDIENCE: A hill [if you see one from afar, it might look gorgeous, but it may not appear that gorgeous when you near it and you realize that you have to go over it on foot as the Baganda people used to do].

CALLER: It is always kind in the morning and evening but quite brutal at noon: AUDIENCE: Tropical sun [it often feels so good in the morning and in the evening, but it can be scorching in the middle of the day].

CALLER: Two equally huge bodies: AUDIENCE: Heaven and earth.

The second popular type of riddles among the Baganda is made up of more elaborate scenarios, each ending with a question which can be literally stated or implied. Those being challenged have to listen very carefully to the scenario, paying specific attention to the details and the figurative language being used, and then respond to a specific question following that scenario. This kind of riddling requires no introduction like *kkoyi kkoyi*. Some scholarship characterizes these riddles as puzzles or dilemma stories (see Finnegan, for example). Here are some examples (feel free to identify each as a dilemma story or a puzzle depending on what you are familiar with):

SCENARIO: Three people come to a river wanting to cross it. One sees the water and crosses the river without getting wet. One does not see the water, and that one too crosses the river without getting wet. The third sees the water, crosses the river, and is drenched. Who are these three people? RESPONSE: A Pregnant woman crossing a river with a baby on her back.

SCENARIO: While taking a leisurely walk one evening with an arrow and bow in hand, a man sees a very beautiful tree with many colorful guinea fowls in its branches and he decides to use his arrow and bow to shoot at them. Before aiming, though, he first counts the guinea fowls, and there are twenty-three. *What fun!* he thinks to himself. Immediately he shoots and kills three of them. How many guinea fowls stay on the tree for the next round? RESPONSE: None, birds fly away when one starts to shoot at them.

SCENARIO: God planted seven trees on one of his creatures. Two trees dried immediately; four grew up and remained fresh, and one simply shrank in size and became unmanageable. Which one of his creatures did God plant his trees on, and what are these trees? RESPONSE: He planted the trees on a cow. The two trees that dried up immediately are its two horns; the four shriving trees are its four legs, and the unmanageable shrunken tree is its tail that the cow wags all the time.

SCENARIO: A man leaves his village by walking through a very thick forest following a popular footpath, and he goes for a long visit far away. After several years he decides to return home, but the path he used to cross the forest many years previously is now overgrown and he cannot see it. There are very dangerous animals and snakes in the forest he has to cross, so he cannot simply walk all over. He has no idea where the new path is or if there is even a new one, and there are no people in the forest who can help him out. It is hot, very hot, midday! How can he get across? RESPONSE: He puts the area on fire. A footpath used over a long period of time is likely to be visible once one clears the area, because not much can grow on a very much used footpath unless it is dug and fertilized over time.

SCENARIO: You are traveling on foot on a very hot day and you have a very long way to go when you spot a tantalizing orange tree covered with ripe, succulent oranges and your mouth begins to water. When you near that tree, you realize that you cannot get any nearer because it is being guarded by a very nasty, dangerous madman. How do you get hold of those oranges? RESPONSE: You pick up stones and start throwing them at the madman. If you are lucky, the madman will pick the ripe oranges and start throwing them at you — lucky you! Simply gather your oranges and run like an Olympian.

Proverbs

One can safely say that proverbs are the most intriguing literary pieces in the African oral tradition because they are brief and to the point, seductive in tone, and rhetorically enchanting; and as age-tested expressions of wisdom, they always serve a purpose, and they are generally accepted as statements of "truth." Unlike stories and riddles that can be told at any time for entertainment, proverbs are always prompted by the situation at hand; they are message and knowledge laden statements that just do not get told unless they are needed at a specific time and place. Proverbs are statements giving advice or warning or just knowledge, and they are often used in difficult situations or when there are problems among the people, which can be solved using the traditional wisdom these proverbs convey.

Like other African proverbs, the Baganda proverbs (*engero ensonge*) are a literary critic's delight because they are rich literary expressions relying on rhetorical devices such as allusion, personification, paradox, simile, metaphor, connotation, sound, and many more to convey meaning; there is plenty to engage a literary critic. Rhetorical devices signal an invitation to the scholar to look deeper into the lives of the people such pieces originate from because it is difficult to fully comprehend the messages imbedded in such devices if one is not familiar with the cultural background and overall mind-set of the people uttering those expressions.

The Baganda, like many other African ethnic groups, treasure their proverbs because they are functional in several aspects: proverbs are trusted expressions of wisdom that help to keep society functioning properly; they preserve the dignity and eloquence of their language; and they keep the culture alive. Not all Baganda people are equally eloquent when it comes to proverbs, so those who can convey such expressions with grace are admired.

Baganda proverbs can come in several styles ranging from simple clauses like *okwerinda sibuti* (being prepared is not a sign of weakness), to elaborate pictorial sentences like *ekita ekitava kussengejjero kibuna enkindo* (a gourd that is always at the beer brewing place gets covered with stitches). But the most popular style is a two-part statement, with the speaker giving the listener the first part and the listener signaling an understanding of how to complete the given statement by shaking one's head or audibly supplying the appropriate part. In the Luganda proverbs cited below, a dash will be used to signal the break between the two parts. Here is an example: *Obusungu mugenyi — akyala naddayo* (Anger is a visitor — it comes and it leaves).

One good reason for citing the proverbs in Luganda is to give the reader a chance to visualize the untranslatable rhetorical devices like breaks and sounds such as alliteration, assonance, consonance, and so on. Here is an example: *Akawuka akaali kakulumye — bwokalaba okadduka* (If you see an insect that bit you in the past — you run away from it). Notice the use of alliteration and assonance in that statement. Implied metaphors also abound in Luganda proverbs; for example: *Omukisa mpewo — nobwoggalawo guyingira era gufuluma* (Good luck is [like] air — even if you close your door, it can get in and out freely). Rhetorical questions are also popular, always assuming that the listener knows the answer, and these questions too will be visible through punctuation; here is an example: *Akutemyako oyagala wa mbazzi?* (Do you want one alerting you to danger to wave an axe in your face?). Although minor variations of tone, verb tenses, poses, and so on can occur depending on the individual speaker's expertise, proverb knowledge and ability to use the language, the content words are fixed and constant, known and expected by the audience.

The richness of proverbs lies in their ability to economically express multiple meanings, so the author will not attempt to fully explicate the examples given below. Actually no one can claim to fully explicate a proverb, as such a claim would negate the very nature of these dynamic, literal, living expressions that are always relevant because their meanings are closely attached to the context in which they are used and the intended audience and purpose at that moment. To gain a total appreciation of a proverb, though, one must explore all literary aspects of such a piece, including the piece's literal meaning, the contexts in which it is likely to be heard, and possible associated meanings intended for the audience. To that end, the author will provide that information to the reader so that the reader can use it as a starting point to actively participate in the intended discourse, which is actually not difficult to join and contribute to because the overall focus is on our humanity.

Since we cannot exhaustively explicate these proverbs, we realistically cannot claim to categorize them fully either, but the following sample categories give the reader a glimpse into the Baganda people's value system and overall cultural psyche. The Baganda frequently address significant sociocultural issues such as those relating to friendships, self-reliance, property, parenthood, old age, honesty, strangers, beauty, relatives, providence, patience, knowledge, community, fairness, and caution; consequently, the sample proverbs below are divided into these popular categories.

Friendships

Friendships are important in any culture, and the Baganda are no exception in valuing them, along with giving pertinent advice as can be seen below.

Egindi wala — ngateli mumanye. (A place is far only if there is no one you know.) According to the Baganda, a friend never lives far. If you say that such a place is far and therefore you cannot go there, it is translated as meaning that you do not know anyone there or that you do not care for the people you know who live there.

Omukwano gutta bingi. (Friendship resolves many issues.) Friends are more likely to forgive each other. This proverb, therefore, promotes friendships as a means of achieving peaceful coexistence; the more friends you have around you, the more forgiving you will be.

Alima ne bba — taba munafu. (A wife farming with her husband cannot be lazy.) You cannot be lazy if you have the support of a loved one; additionally it is assumed that you cannot fail when you are in the company of one who cares about you.

Akusubiza — akira akumma. (A promise is better than a denial.) Promises sustain hope; one who promises to think about your request and get back to you is a more caring person and a better friend than one who simply refuses outright, without even taking time to think about it. The former indicates a willingness to devote a portion of one's time to a friend.

Akwatulira — akira akugeya. (One who tells you the truth is a better friend than one who talks about you behind your back.) Underlying this proverb is the notion that in friendships, openness is better than keeping secrets; if one is a friend, that person will tell you the truth even if such truth will hurt, instead of talking about you behind your back.

Abataka abagalana — bebalima akambugu. (Elders in a good relationship can cultivate an area of hard weeds.) *Akambugu* is a quick-spreading, very destructive weed with deep roots that requires a lot of energy and resources to kill. This proverb implies that friends working in harmony can overcome any difficulties and triumph over life's trials.

Omukwano butiko—tebukkatirwa. (Friendship is [like] fresh mushrooms, you do not squash them.) This metaphor emphasizes the delicate nature of friendship by comparing it to fresh mushrooms; if you want a friendship to last, you must handle it with care.

Akulabako akatono—akira alagiriza. (One who visits you regularly, even if it is for a very short time, is a better friend than one who regularly sends greetings but rarely visits you.) True friends should make time for each other, real physical time.

Akwana—akira ayomba. (One who makes friendships is a better person than one who quarrels a lot.) Implicit in that proverb is the idea that friends do not quarrel with friends; consequently, the more friends one has, the fewer quarrels one will get involved in.

Namwatulira—taba namikwano. (A person who prides oneself in constantly pointing out to others what is wrong with them or their behavior cannot have friends.) It is important to tell a friend the truth, but there are always going to be things a friend shouldn't point out to a friend to spare one pain or embarrassment; true friendship means having judgment as to what you can and cannot say to a friend.

Omuganzi—takola kibi. (A loved one does no wrong.) This proverb of course cannot be taken literally, but it implies that when a friend does something wrong, that person's friend(s) should forgive that person, or stand up for that person, or help that person get out of a difficult position; friends shouldn't pass judgments on friends!

Oguzzibwa omugamzi—omukyawe yaagumala. (When a beloved does something wrong, the one not so loved pays the price.) This is another proverb that can be explained like the one above; a loved person cannot do anything wrong; people go to great lengths to protect their friends.

Obuyisi bwomu—nsega yebika. (A loner's death is announced by vultures.) If a person has no friends, when that person gets in trouble or finds oneself in a dangerous situation, there many not be anyone to help. Even if that person dies, no one may get to know except by vultures feeding on his body; once people see vultures circling a place, they automatically know that someone, or something, dead is in that spot being circled.

Waggumbulizi kaaba nako — kaawa munywanyi we. (Whatever a big rat has, that is what it should give to its friend.) Friends share regardless of how much or little one has, and one's friends cannot complain that they have been given little.

Ssentamu nkadde — togiteresa munno. (You do not store your old pot at a friend's house.) If you want a friendship to last, avoid doing things that might cause trouble between the two of you.

Mbulira gwoyitanaye — nkubulire empisa zo. (Tell me who your friend is — I will tell you what your behavior is like.) Even though stereotyping is not a positive, reliable identification, still people have a tendency to assume that not only do opposites attract, but so do resemblances. In this case, the proverb cautions to choose one's friends wisely because those seeing you are going to assume that you have something in common with those you call your friends.

Self-reliance

There are many proverbs among the Baganda people that stress the importance of self-reliance, and self-reliant people are admired. Parents and extended family members stress these proverbs to their children, and so do friends among themselves.

Atalukutambulire — akusibira y'amenvu. (A person not making the journey for you packs ripe bananas for your snacks and meals on the way.) The traditional mode of transportation among the Baganda was walking, and people would walk very long distances, for days, so you can imagine if one packs ripe bananas for a journey likely to last anywhere from a week to three months. This proverb is suggesting that one should be actively involved in planning one's activities instead of simply delegating; the person trusted to do the planning might be naïve of what is actually required or simply malicious; either way, you should be fully involved in the planning because nobody knows your needs better than you.

Omuggo oguli ewamunno — tegugoba ngo. (A stick at a neighbor's house cannot be relied upon to chase away a leopard from your house.) In other words, you should always have your own ways of protection instead of relying on a friend's. This proverb is a reminder that you should always be prepared to solve your own problems, especially those seemingly improbable ones.

Olwoya lwomunnyindo — olweggya wekka. (You are responsible for plucking your nose hair.) Even though the sense of community is very strong among the Baganda, self reliance is still emphasized because there are some things that one must do for oneself with no outside help. It also reminds people that personal problems must be solved by the affected individual; such a person should not wait for others to solve that person's problems.

Omugabi teyeseera. (One in charge of distributing stuff should give oneself a portion equal to everyone else's.) Being generous is great, but you do not want to be over generous at your own expense; you are responsible for your self; therefore, generosity should begin at home, and making such a distribution is also respected as a sign of good judgment.

Omunaku kaama — yelandiza yekka. (An orphan is [like] a yam; no one helps a yam to wrap itself around a tree in order to grow.) This is a hard-work ethic and self-reliance promoting proverb prompting people, especially those with no one to take care of them, to take charge of their lives instead of simply sitting around whining and feeling sorry for themselves.

Ennaku bwekusanga ogigumiranga — ekikere kisula kisitamye. (When bad luck comes your way, you must endure it; a frog has to sleep squatting.) The Baganda people believe in an individual's will power to survive whatever might befall that individual; there isn't anything that one cannot endure if one accepts the condition. In other words, learn to endure what you cannot change.

Eyesitukidde — tanywa matabangufu. (One who physically goes to the springs to collect one's water never drinks dirty water.) While delegating is a good strategy, there are people who tend to overuse it or simply misuse it by rarely bothering to lift a finger, and always expecting perfection. In other words, "If you want something done right, do it yourself" or at least have some input!

Kange kakira akaffe. (Mine is better than ours.) It is better to depend on your own resources than depending on those of a group. One should have more pride in what is one's own than a group's property.

Mazzi masabe—tegamala nnyonta. (If you keep on requesting people to give you water to drink, you can never quench your thirst.) Begging is not a problem solving strategy; it simply postpones your needs and often leaves you thirsting for more. This proverb encourages people to work hard for what they want instead of depending on others.

Ow'akamwake—yakagerera ennoga. (The owner of a mouth is the only one who can decide how spicy one's food should be.) No one can tell you how much you can or can't do; making that kind of decision is a personal responsibility, and should be done by the one affected.

Property

Property ownership complements self-reliance; in other words, acquiring property and taking very good care of your possessions facilitates self-reliance.

Kanyama katono—okayana kali munkwawa. (Have your piece of meat in hand first and then complain that it is too small.) In other words, do not refuse an offer simply because it is too little, too small, or not quite up to your standards; first accept whatever you are given and then proceed to negotiate for better terms.

Ettuufu ligwa wala. (What is good is always far away.) If you want something good, you have to sweat for it; it is not always easy to get good stuff.

Atabubira nsiko ye talira. (A person who does not protect one's property cannot benefit from it.) Although jealousy is not a virtue, one needs to protect one's property, relationships, and so on. Always take very good care of what is yours. You cannot lay claim on whatever you leave unprotected.

Buli wa mamba—awana yiye. (Every catfish owner praises one's own.) People should take pride in what is theirs and praise it; you cannot always wait for others to point out how or what is so good about your possession(s).

Omukadde—akwatira ku mmere ye. (An old person uses their food to get what they want.) A person with property cannot fail to get whatever that person needs.

Oguweddeko entonto — ennyonyi ziguyita ttale. (Birds have no respect/use for a fruit tree when all its fruits have been finished; they think that tree is a wasteland.) It is important for people to protect their property and not squander it or make it available to all because once all one's property is gone, that person will no longer be of use or even get respect from those who used up that person's property; a person with no property is considred a wasteland.

Atunda ayolesa — yatera okumazawo amangu. (One who advertises one's merchandise is more likely to sell it all in a timely manner.) If you have a good product you intend to sell, you should package it attractively and make it very visible so as to attract buyers. Also, one with good qualities who wants to be noticed should display them to get credit; in other words, do not hide your valuable attributes.

Kyerondera — taba mubbi. (One who picks up discarded property cannot be called a thief.) Take great care of whatever you own; once you neglect your property and someone else takes it, you cannot cry foul or reclaim it.

Kiridde bwami — tekibulwako mikwano. (A chief cannot lack friends.) In other words, people value and respect those with valuable attributes; if you want to be loved and respected, you must have some attractive talents and treasures.

Okuwola n'okwazika byebitta emikwano. (Lending and borrowing others' property spoils friendships.) This proverb cautioning against lending and borrowing, especially among friends, is popular in many cultures.

Akezimbira — tekaba kato. (One with property/home cannot be called a child.) Once a person acquires property or builds oneself a home, that person cannot be treated like a child; respect is given to such a one.

Parenthood and Parental Responsibility

As pointed out in "*Kintu*: The Myth," the Baganda treasure parenthood, which is regarded as crucial for the survival of the ethnic group, their clans, and their families; it also guarantees each individual's immortality. But the Baganda are also keenly aware that this treasure comes with a variety of responsibilities, so they dispense plenty of parental advice, as can be seen in the following proverbs.

Azaala ekibi — akiwongerera. (One who begets a bad child has to pay the price.) Parenting is a big responsibility, and the Baganda place the blame for whatever wrong a minor does on the parents, not on the minor! If you do not bring up your kids properly, you pay dearly for their delinquencies. There is also another explanation, simply that one is responsible for one's actions.

Omuto tayonona — omukulu yayonona. (A child does not cause damage, an adult does.) As with the proverb above, this one also reminds parents that if one's child causes damage to someone or to someone's property, the parent of that child is responsible for that damage. Damage-causing children are thought to be badly brought up children.

Azaala omulalu y'amumanya — Ensenene zigwa kwa kikome. (A parent of an unruly child is the only one who can know what that child is going to do and when. Grasshoppers rest in cool weather.) Parents are held responsible for their children's behavior as explained above; they are supposed to know their children and predict what might happen or what one's child might do in any given circumstance. The grasshopper reference makes a good point because one would have thought that people work in cool weather and rest when it is hot, not the other way round.

Mwana mubi — avumya nnyina. (A badly behaving child brings blame to the mother.) Whereas the first three proverbs above divide parental responsibility equally between parents, this one stresses a tendency among the Baganda to give mothers more responsibility for child rearing than fathers; so if a child behaves badly, the mother is the first parent to be blamed. It is also a reminder that there is a tendency to trace a child's bad habits to that child's parents, beginning with the mother.

Akabwa keweyolera — kekakuluma entumbwe. (A dog you groom is one that bites you.) You must put effort into bringing up your children properly because if you fail to groom them appropriately, they might become your worst enemies. Bad people are not a danger only to outsiders, but to their family members as well.

Okuzaala kuba kuzukira. (Parenthood makes one immortal.) The Baganda people share a belief with many other African ethnic groups that a parent does not die; one lives on in one's children. Consequently, if one does not have children, that one will go into oblivion when one dies, and will be totally forgotten.

Omuze gufiira kumugumba. (A habit of a childless person ends with that person's death.) The Baganda people believe firmly that children learn from their parents; both one's good and bad habits resurface in one's children.

Akuba owuwe — akuba awumba engalo. (Punishment given to a loved one is never severe.) Parents are reminded not to be abusive when punishing their children; those punishments are supposed to be given in a spirit of love, and they should be corrective, not injurious.

Enda mawogo — ezaala abalungi na'ababi. (A womb is [like] a cassava tree; it can produce both good and bitter cassava roots.) Cassava is a popular root food item among the Baganda, and you can harvest anywhere between five and ten roots from any one tree, but you cannot assume that all the roots harvested from one tree are going to be equally good or bitter by simply tasting one; each root comes with its own taste. This metaphor is applicable to parenting, cautioning that each child has their own character traits, and parents, as well as other people, should avoid stereotyping children by simply basing their conclusions on those children's siblings' behavior.

Anakuggya ennimi — ageya nnyoko ngowulira. (One interested in prompting you to fight says bad things about your mother in your presence.) Among most African peoples, a mother is supreme and sacred, and one's children are always ready to defend their mother's honor.

Ekitezaala — tekyaala. (A species that does not replicate cannot increase its population.) One of the reasons parenthood is encouraged among the Baganda is to enlarge one's clan. The Baganda people are organized in patrilineal units called clans (see "The Baganda: A Historical Perspective"), and each clan's striving for survival and claim to prominence, influence and cultural and physical spaces are facilitated by the strength of that clan's numbers.

Emiti emito — gyegiggumiza ekibira. (Saplings sustain life in the forest.) A society without young people cannot survive.

Oba nomuliika — n'akuwonyeza abaana. (It does not matter how much you have to pay a person so long as that person helps your children when they are in trouble.) Expense is not an issue when it comes to taking care of one's children.

Akaliba akendo — okalabira kumukonda. (You can predict that a sapling pumpkin will make a beautiful drinking gourd as soon as it sprouts.) There is a belief inherent in this proverb that parents can predict their children's future from an early age; likewise, this proverb prompts parents to monitor their children's behavior as they are growing up so as to intervene as soon as the parents sense something not going right.

Akuweera omwana — akira nakwagadde. (One who gives good things to your child is a better friend than one who simply always proclaims their liking for you but pays no attention to your children.) In other words, if you want to befriend a parent and retain that relationship, you should pay special attention to that person's children, if one has them.

Mwaana mugimu — ava ku ngozi. (A healthy looking baby is one who gets good care from the moment of birth.) This proverb prompts parents to take great care of their babies from infancy to ensure their good health in the future.

Omuzadde tagulwa. (One cannot buy a parent.) This one is for the children. First, this is a value-ridden proverb; simply put, parents are precious; no amount of money can avail one of a parent. Second, children should know that they have no choice when it comes to who their parents are; it is, therefore, advisable to respect and be proud of one's parents regardless of who they are or what they have or what they give you. Additionally, children are reminded to take great care of their parents when the parents cannot take care of themselves, for whatever reason, because parents cannot be replaced no matter how rich one might be.

Omusika taba nnyoko. (An heir cannot replace your mother.) The Baganda have a cultural tradition of installing heirs for dead adults; for example, if a mother dies, an heir for her is chosen from her brothers' or male cousins' female children, if she did not choose one in her will. That heir is supposed to perform all the cultural activities a mother does for her children, but as this proverb points out, parents cannot be replaced; an heir is an heir, not a parent, no matter how much one tries to fill that parent's shoes.

Gwosenvuza mubuto — akusenvuza mubukadde. (The child you teach to walk in infancy helps you to walk in your old age.) Parental responsibility is rewarding, especially in old age. If one brings up one's children lovingly, that person will be taken good care of in old age by those children.

Ogula ngatto kwewonya maggwa. (You buy shoes to protect yourself from thorns.) Parents are reminded of this proverb, meaning that bringing up one's children well is like purchasing an insurance for old age because one is assured of good care then by one's children.

Omulundira wala — alabira kumanyi. (One tending a flock at a distance senses trouble through the level of one's strength.) This proverb refers to parents keeping track of what is going on with their children when the children are far from home. A parent can discern that a child is in trouble if one gets a weak feeling.

Respect for Old Age, Authority, and Property

The Baganda people, like many other ethnic groups on the continent, place emphasis on respect, especially for elders and for authority and for others' property, as can be seen in the proverbs below.

Kaami katono — okagayira mitala wa mugga. (If you want to show disrespect to a not so great chief, do so from across the river.) Baganda people urge respect of authority and its boundaries; you cannot show disrespect to an authority figure, regardless of how little physical power that figure has, when in the presence or vicinity of that person; an authority figure must always be respected. Likewise, you cannot show disrespect to a person when you are on that person's property.

Akakadde kawano tekayomba — ngobuziina bwako wekabuleka wekabusanga. (An old relative does not quarrel if such a one's personal belongings are always in exactly the same position as one left them.) The elderly are expected to be dignified, problem solving, loved, peaceful and valued libraries, among other things. They are not expected to initiate fights except in very trying circumstances, and disrespect of them and their space would be among such circumstances. This proverb overall encourages respect of personal property and privacy to avoid conflicts. If you respect each other's property and privacy, you can share premises peacefully, and sharing space is important among the Baganda.

Eriso ly'omukulu—awaddugala wewalaba. (The dark spot in an old person's eye is where sight is.) Baganda, like many other Africans, revere old age as a source of wisdom. This proverb is a reminder that old people's wisdom is enhanced with age; that their age is an asset, and not a liability. Old people are thought to have insight into what may seem problematic to those around them despite their failing physical strength.

Twenkana oli mukkubo. (We are equal only when we are walking along a public road.) Whenever a Muganda says that to a person, the speaker is prompting that person to be respectful. People must be respected when one is in their home or place regardless of the relationship between the two parties. Even if you are one's boss, you must respect your employee once you are within the boundaries of that employee's property. A visitor cannot claim equality with a host at any venue belonging to that host, which means that one of the few venues where one can claim equality with another is on a public road, or any other public space for that matter.

Ezenkanankana n'ebisiki—tezaaka. (Two equal pieces of wood side by side cannot make a fire.) This proverb reminds people to acknowledge authority wherever one might be—home, work, school and so on—in order for society to function properly. There must be a leader in any situation involving more than one person if we expect harmony, civility, security, productivity, accountability, and many other related outcomes, and that leader must be acknowledged and respected as such for the good of all.

Omukulu takulira mpya bbiri. (One cannot be chief of two homes.) There can only be one chief in each situation, and that chief must respect fellow chiefs when one is in their spaces, and not behave as if they themselves are the only chief. In other words, power has limits that must be observed for the good of all.

Honesty

Not only is honesty an abstract concept, but it is also a practical guide to solving some of life's problems, as the Baganda point out in the proverbs that follow.

Ow'ebbango — bwotomuwemukirira tewebikka. (When sharing a bed with a hunchback, do not hesitate to point out that he is taking all the coverings or else you will sleep in the cold.) Always be honest; do not withhold the truth simply because it is unpleasant or you do not want to hurt one's feelings; if you do, you may end up paying for the consequences. Always have the audacity to make your case no matter how difficult or troubling it happens to be for the other party.

Akwatulira akira akugeya. (One who tells you the truth is a better friend than one who withholds it to protect you.) A friend should tell you the truth no matter how bad or hard to take that truth may be.

Amazima — tegebulizayo. (Truth cannot be hidden.) Honesty is always the best policy because if you tell a lie, the truth soon or later surfaces.

Strangers

In Luganda, there is no word for "strangers" as we know it; such people are called "visitors." The Baganda encourage hospitality to all, not only to those they know, and the two proverbs below provide some insight into their reasoning.

Ensisinkano — teba yalumu. (Coincidences do not happen only once.) This proverb cautions people not to mistreat strangers; you never know when, where, how and under what circumstances you will run into the same person again. Also, if a stranger needs help, you are encouraged to help that person if you can because you might run into that very person when you yourself need help.

Mu nnyumba temuba kkubo. (There is no road going through a house.) This is an important proverb demonstrating the Baganda people's hospitality. Since there is no road going through your house, anyone coming to your door should be treated like your visitor. Young couples are reminded of this proverb as they set up their homes.

Beauty

The concept of beauty might be an individual judgment since beauty is in the eyes of the beholder, but common advice on the subject is in abundance in every culture. The Baganda too have their say as follows:

Abalungi ndagala nnamu—teziggwa mulusuku. (Beautiful people are [like] new banana leaves — there will always be some in the banana plantation.) Bananas are the staple food of the Baganda, so they tend to have large banana plantations, which makes the above metaphor easy to understand (the translation is a simile for clarity, but the Luganda version is a metaphor). The proverb points out that if you lose your lover, do not despair that you've lost the only beautiful person in existence as there will always be other beautiful people to love, just as there will always be new banana leaves in the banana plantations. This proverb also advises those who think that they are beautiful not to flaunt their beauty. Incidentally, beauty is not that rare!

Bwotava kumulungi—ofa owoza. (If you cannot part with a beautiful person, be prepared to spend all your life being defensive.) There is a belief that beautiful people are trouble and have a tendency to be careless and at times even destructive. In this case, the proverb cautions those willing to befriend beautiful people to be prepared to defend their lovers. One may also be forced to protect or to defend one's beautiful partner physically, in which case such a person might be sued by that person's potential attackers. It is also a warning to people who love beautiful things so much; once again, the desire for beauty may land one in hot water.

Abalungi mbwa zanamaso—bwetabba eyigga. (Beautiful people are like prized dogs — they either steal or go hunting for themselves.) Once again, a warning about beautiful people being trouble and unmanageable. Partners of such people find themselves in the same position as prized dog owners; they do not want to believe that their dogs can have bad habits, but beauty does not prevent bad habits. Beautiful people, just like beautiful dogs, can have bad habits that can cause their partners or owners to cease loving them.

Obulungi si ddya. (Beauty does not sustain a marriage.) This proverb is advice to beautiful people that they need other good qualities, in addition to their beauty, to have successful relationships. Beauty by itself is no guarantee that one will have a lasting relationship; beautiful people's marriages can fail just like any others.

Ekyagaza omubi — omulungi takimanya. (A beautiful person cannot know why anyone would love an ugly person.) Beauty is more than skin deep, which means that there may be plenty to love in a supposedly ugly person which cannot be seen by onlookers. Also, beauty is in the eyes of the beholder, so it is difficult to agree on what constitutes beauty.

Obulungi bukira obugagga. (Beauty is better than riches.) Most people have to work very hard to get rich, whereas there is a tendency to reward beautiful people simply because they are beautiful. Such awards might eventually make a naturally beautiful person rich without that person putting in a lot of effort. Additionally, riches come and go; they are unpredictable, but a person's natural beauty is more permanent.

Omulungi tabulako kamogo. (Beauty is not faultless.) This cautions people not to equate surface beauty with inner goodness; beautiful people can have faults just like other people.

Relatives

Extended families, which are very popular among the Baganda and indeed all over Africa, can be both a blessing and a challenge, and because of that, there are several proverbs addressing familial relationships as can be seen below.

Oluganda kulya — olugenda enjala terudda. (Food sustains kinships — a kin who leaves your home hungry will not revisit you.) This metaphor stresses the importance of sharing among relatives and taking care of each other by comparing such activities to eating, which is essential for survival.

Aboluganda nsuwa — zikonagaana naye tezatika. (Relatives are [like] clay pots — even when they knock against each other, they never break.) This metaphor (simile in translation) compares kinship relationships to delicate and fragile clay pots, stressing the importance of handling such relationships with care, but also reminding relatives that they can fight, but they cannot damage, split, or disown each other. Outsiders are also cautioned to stay out of kinship quarrels.

Kabbo kaabuko — kagenda kajjudde kakomawo kajjudde. (A basket to the in-laws is taken full and returned full.) In-laws are revered; one cannot go to visit one's in-laws empty handed. Likewise, the hosts are expected to return the favor. Giving and receiving among in-laws is expected to be a two-way sign of respect.

Atakwaalize nganda — akulaga bifo. (One who does not want you to have extended family relatives shows you places instead of introducing you to these places' owners.) The Baganda thrive in extended families, and they value kinships, so it is important for one to know as many of one's relatives as possible. Also related to that explanation is advice to parents to introduce their children to as many of their relatives as they possibly can before such people die. It is not good to show your children places where their relatives used to live but such relatives are no longer there, let alone taking them for funerals of relatives they never knew they had.

Nyoko abanga omugwira — nakuzala mukika. (It is better to be born within a clan even if your mother is a foreigner.) The Baganda people are organized in sociopolitical groupings known as *ebika* (clans); every Muganda is born into a clan, which gives one identity and a sense of belonging. Since the family structure is patrilineal, even if one's mother is an outsider, the child will be a Muganda belonging to the father's clan. This proverb underscores the importance of belonging to a clan as the essence of being a Muganda.

Owennyimba mbi — ayimbira mubabe. (One with a bad voice sings only when in company of relatives.) Relatives are expected to support their own in all circumstances.

Providence

The Baganda have a keen sense of their creator (*Katonda*), and they put a lot of trust in him, as can be ascertained from the following proverbs. There are also several Baganda names originating from these people's relationship with their creator, some of which are also below.

Katonda bwakuwa—nennume ezaala. (If God wills it for you, even a bull can have a calf.) You can have whatever *Katonda* wants you to have.

Tosekereranga ajeera—ffenna omugabi yomu. (Never laugh at those less fortunate than you because we all have the same provider.) This is caution against arrogance as well as a reminder of how transient material things can be. Since we all have the same provider, we can be lucky today and totally unlucky tomorrow, depending on our mutual provider's plans for each of us.

Katonda kyakuwa—togaana. (You cannot refuse to take whatever God gives you.) This proverb expresses the Baganda's belief in destiny; accept whatever *Katonda* gives you instead of trying to change or exchange it. *Kyakuwa,* a gender and clan neutral name among the Baganda, originates from this proverb.

Katonda kyaterekera omulamu—tekivunda. (Whatever God has in store for a person cannot rot no matter how long it takes one to get it.) Another comforting, destiny-accepting proverb reminding people not to worry about the passage of time; according to this proverb, whatever is meant to be will be, regardless of how long it takes. The gender and clan neutral name *Kyaterekera* is a reference to this proverb.

Lubaale mbeera—nganembiro kwotadde. (God helps those who help themselves.) Although the Baganda people believe in destiny, they remind people not to just sit around and wait for that destiny; it has to be prompted, and people must be active participants in their destinies, whatever that happens to be.

Patience and Persistence

Africans are globally known as patient people, and the Baganda are no exception; they are constantly reminded, especially through proverbs, of the benefits of both patience and persistence.

Amawolu galiibwa mujjukiza. (Leftovers are eaten by those who remind the cook that such food exists.) The essence of this proverb is that persistence can be rewarding; you should never shy away from reminding people to keep their promises to you or to give you what you want, no matter how often you have to remind them before they act.

Addingana amawolu—yagaggyako omukutto. (Those who persistently eat leftovers eventually get their fill.) This proverb is the usual "practice makes perfect" tinted with "persistence can be rewarding." It also reminds us that endurance is rewarding.

Akwata empola atuuka wala—nawolovu yatuuka kukibuga. (Patience and persistence will take you far—a chameleon made it to the city center using that strategy.) This proverb encourages us not to give up on desired goals, because the process of achieving them is slow and tedious; the reference to one of the slowest creatures known to man achieving its goal because of patience and persistence explains it all.

Ekiyita waggulu otega wansi—empungu terya bire. (Set your trap on the ground for whatever is soaring in the skies—an eagle does not eat clouds.) This proverb encourages people not to give up on what they want simply because it seems out of reach at the time; if you devise a good strategy and practice patience, sooner or later you get what you want. Eagles are proud and soar high, but if you want to catch one, place its desired food in its sight because no matter how far it goes in the skies, it eventually will come down looking for one of life's necessities — food.

Ekibimba kikka—empungu terya bire. (Whatever goes up comes down — an eagle does not eat clouds.) Another variation on the above proverb stressing that there is no need to strain oneself trying to get whatever seems to be temporarily out of reach; if one practices patience, such an item comes within reach sooner or later.

Okulya eggi—kwesubya miwula. (Eating an egg is giving up on chicken.) If one wants to get ample satisfaction from a product, that individual must be willing to wait for that ultimate prize; in other words, good things come to those who are willing or able to wait.

Oyita ewala—notuuka emirembe. (It is better to take a longer route and arrive safely.) People are cautioned about shortcuts. Sometimes a shortcut can be a good idea, but if such a route sounds too good to be true, chances are it is not practical, in which case you should always opt for the longer one.

Mpolampola — ayiisa obusera. (One who takes time cooking millet porridge eventually succeeds in getting it ready.) Making a good serving of millet porridge is a slow process that requires patience, but one who devotes ample time to this task gets amazing results. In other words, if you want good results, you must be willing to spend ample amounts of time on the task involved.

Nezikokolima — gaali magi. (Crowing cocks were once eggs.) If you wait long enough for something to materialize, you often get good results; in other words, good results take time. There is also another interpretation that focuses on great things originating in little ones, but once again stressing patience.

Kamukamu— gwemuganda. (One by one makes a bundle.) Do not be discouraged by slow processes; if you are patient, you can eventually reap a good harvest from a slow process.

Knowledge and Wisdom

Searching for, acquiring and keeping knowledge are not easy tasks, but they have to be done; below are some pointers from the Baganda.

Oluyitayita — lukira olulira kunkoligo. (A free wandering creature eats better than a tethered one.) Although the Baganda value guidance, they leave room for individuality and encourage personal initiatives and adventures. The above proverb encourages parents, mentors, teachers and so on, to leave room for individuals under their care to experience and explore various environments, gather their own knowledge, and make their own initiatives in the belief that sometimes, experience can be a very good source of knowledge. Also, the more people one meets, the more knowledgeable one may become by acquiring knowledge from those one meets along the way.

Embulire — tefa yonna. (A knowledgeable creature does not perish). This proverb prompts people to seek, value, and share knowledge because the more you know and share, the more valuable you are going to be. And because people will always value knowledge, even when one who is a source of knowledge dies, that person cannot be forgotten because that one's knowledge will be around.

Amagezi muliro — bwegukuzikirako okima ewamuliranwa. (Knowledge is [like] fire — if yours goes out, you can rekindle it at the neighbor's place.) This metaphor (Luganda version) comparing knowledge to fire stresses the necessity of knowledge as a life-sustaining element and indicates its availability as a communal sharable product just like fire used to be in the olden days. This proverb encourages individuals to always seek knowledge. Since knowledge is sharable, it can never be exhausted or in short supply; all one has got to do is seek it from one's neighbors.

Amagezi luwombo. (Knowledge is like sauce prepared in banana leaves.) Traditionally the Baganda make their most delicious dishes in tender, delicate banana leaves. When you are served sauce in such banana leaves and you finish what you can see at the top, you can check under the layers for more. In other words, knowledge is layered and you must check all layers to get the whole truth. Also, knowledge is precious and it should be handled with care, which is why it would be stored in tender bananas leaves. Last, tender banana leaves used as dishes are not supposed to leak, so one cannot lose one's knowledge if it is stored safely.

Omuweesi akyamuzimbya kukkubo — kulagirirwa. (The reason an iron-smith built his business near a road is to get advice from passersby.) Iron-smiths used to be very respected for their ability to turn shapeless chunks of iron into beautiful, carefully shaped items. But according to this proverb, even these seasoned professionals needed advice. Realistically, no one can claim to know all there is to know about one's profession; there is always room for more input and advice.

Ndi mugezi — ngamubulire. (I am knowledgeable means I seek advice.) This proverb encourages people to seek knowledge; if one is willing to listen to others, one can be very knowledgeable. This proverb also stresses the communal nature of knowledge among most Africans; knowledge should be shared liberally when one asks for it.

Gakuwebwa munno. (Knowledge is acquired from those around you.) This proverb advises people to seek for and listen to advice given by those in one's company because two heads are better than one. It also reminds us that we do not have to go to great lengths to acquire knowledge; it can be acquired from a neighbor.

Nomugezi awubwa. (Even a person with a lot of knowledge can err.) This proverb reminds people to be humble and accept advice, because as humans, we are fallible; also, no one can know it all.

Togayanga kyama kyamuto. (It is not wise to belittle a child's advice.) The Baganda value knowledge in all forms and from all sources, so this proverb cautions people to listen to all advice no matter how unimportant the person giving it is. You never know, the advice you disregard simply because the person giving it is not at par with you or does not meet your expectations might turn out to be crucial information.

Negwozadde akkubira engoma nozina. (You can dance when your child plays the drum.) This proverb, like the one above, reminds people that children can have valuable knowledge and skills, so they should not be marginalized when it comes to giving ideas and suggestions.

Amagezi amayigirire — gassa Wakayima. (Imitation cost br'er rabbit his life.) Whereas getting knowledge from others is a respected activity, wholesale blind imitation of others' activities is not. This proverb advises people to be alert, intuitive, critical-thinking, active learners who take time to thoroughly digest the information given by or copied from others before utilizing it.

Amazina amayigirire — gamenya omugongo. (An imitation dance can break your back.) This is another variation of the proverb above. While learning and borrowing from others can be a rewarding experience, the Baganda caution that wholesale imitation of others' actions or ways of life can be hazardous.

Community

Like many other African ethnic groups, the Baganda have a very keen sense of communal responsibility and the benefits of being a member of a community. Here are some reasons why.

Agali awamu — gegaluma enyama. (Teeth can chew meat because they work together as a group.) Each individual tooth cannot chew meat by itself, but as a group, teeth can effortlessly chew even the toughest meat. This proverb emphasizes the benefits of working as a group, especially when the task in front of you is formidable.

Abangi webasimba olunwe — we kyabikira. (A wound bursts at the spot indicated by the majority.) This proverb emphasizes the importance of collective wisdom; it parallels the English saying of "two heads are better than one."

Omulya mamba aba omu— n'avumaganya ekika kyonna. (One bad act done by an individual person brings blame to the whole clan.) The Baganda are organized in several sociopolitical groupings, one of them being a clan. Clan members have a responsibility to protect their clan's reputation and promote its integrity among the other clans. The better the clan's reputation and sense of integrity, the greater influence that clan is going to have in the whole ethnic group. In such a competitive atmosphere, competing especially for influence, an individual vice is considered a group vice, bringing shame and disrepute to that whole clan, therefore lessening the clan's pride and influence. This "one bad apple spoils a bunch" proverb is very important to the Baganda.

Birungi sibirungi — ngomwana afananye mulirwana. (Good but not so good is when one's infant resembles the man next door.) The Baganda value children, and whenever one is born in a community there is joy all around, but that joy becomes bittersweet if the baby was conceived in adultery, and the security often felt in a community is undermined by such news.

Musajja gyagenda — gyasanga banne. (A man finds friends wherever he goes.) This proverb illustrates the Baganda people's belief that all humans are inherently good and communal creatures; therefore, one does not have to fear or be apprehensive going to unfamiliar places because there are no people there one knows. One should be able to find friends wherever one goes; the word "stranger" is not in their language.

Abayita ababiri — bejjukanya. (Traveling in pairs mitigates boredom.) The traditional mode of transportation was walking, and people used to travel far on foot, often walking both day and night. Not only is loneliness boring, especially in a situation like this, it can also be dangerous; so this proverb advises people to always seek others' company. There is comfort, strength and safety in belonging to a group.

Omulirano — gwokya bbiri. (Whatever happens at your neighbor's happens to you.) People are advised to be good neighbors and help each other, especially in times of trouble.

Fairness

The Baganda promote being fair at all times and under all circumstances as an individual responsibility that has far-reaching consequences within the group. Below are some proverbs to stress that point.

Enkima tesala gwakibira. (A monkey does not pass judgment over forest disputes.) Since monkeys depend on forests as their habitat, they would find it hard to be impartial in matters affecting their vital space, so they should keep out of such disputes. This proverb is a warning against getting involved in situations that might compromise, influence or, worse still, distort one's sense of fairness. In other words, people should avoid getting involved in what might be called conflict of interest situations.

Tosala gwakawala — ngatonawulira gwakalenzi. (Do not pass judgment based on the lady's side of the story before hearing the man's.) This proverb emphasizes fairness. Traditionally in domestic conflicts, a woman is often the first to approach her in-laws with her complaints, and there is a tendency to feel sorry for her or to be swayed to her side before the in-laws get a chance to hear from the husband. This proverb warns against passing judgment before thoroughly examining both versions in a conflict; since there are always going to be two or more sides to each story, one should hear all versions before taking action.

Caution and Pertinent Advice on Various Subjects

This is an inclusive category to highlight sample proverbs that do not readily fit in any of the specific preceding categories.

Konoweeka — tokalinda kuvulubana ttaka. (Do not let a baby you will carry on your back get soiled.) Traditionally, Baganda women carry their babies on their backs so as to free their hands for other chores. According to this proverb, if you have a task to perform or a situation to confront or a problem to solve or a decision to make, you should do it in a timely manner, before it gets unpleasant or harder. Do not let the mess you can clean up today become tomorrow's hard to clean stain; respond to challenges promptly.

Gwossussa emwanyi—omusanga kunyanja ngayawungula. (The person you skip when handing out hospitality coffee beans is the one you find manning boats at a river crossing.) Traditionally the Baganda show hospitality to their guests by giving them roasted coffee beans to chew on as soon as they are seated. This proverb reminds people to be hospitable and pleasant to all who come to one's door, regardless of status, strangers included, because you never know, a person you mistreat or discriminate against today might turn out to be the only one capable of getting you out of a tight spot or even saving your life one day.

Zolaga omulungi—tezirwa. (A promise made to a loved one is never far off.) Time flies when you are expecting something good; just be patient!

Ekimyumu ekingi—kyaleka emmese obuwulu. (Too much partying cost a mouse its spouse.) An adult single male is considered a "boy" among the Baganda, and he is not given respect, so spouses are cherished. But again, losing one's spouse because of a situation one could have easily controlled is taken as a sign of immaturity, irresponsibility, and lack of judgment. So, sure, have fun, but not in excess; doing anything excessively can be costly.

Asiika obulamu—tazza mukono. (A person fighting for his life cannot relax.) One cannot be lax or complacent when confronted with a survival issue; life is a treasure we must guard with all we have.

Omumpi wakoma wakwata—ensolosozi eruma atudde. (Short persons cannot add height to their stature—red ants must be content with biting only those sitting down.) This is a friendly warning not to aim higher than you can realistically reach; ambition is good but being overly ambitious can be dangerous, especially if the desired goal is beyond your physical capabilities. Just be satisfied with what you can comfortably accomplish.

Gwakanga misana—kakiro tabulamu. (No matter how bright moonlight is, it will always have a tint of night in it.) It is not wise to assume that a "good" person cannot do anything bad. The Baganda people believe that since evil is embedded in human nature, just as moonlight is an integral part of the night, one should always be cautious, even when dealing with apparently "good" people.

Bandaba — yasuubwa omukira. (One who assumed that he was visible to all, including to the one giving out tails, ended up with no tail.) There is a folktale among the Baganda that recounts why frogs do not have tails, based on this proverb. When all creatures were called to get tails from their king, the frogs simply sat in one place and assumed that since the king was their uncle, he would definitely reserve the best tails for them. But before they knew it, all the tails were gone! This very common proverb is used to prompt people to be proactive, to put effort into what they want to achieve and not to rely on self importance, status, family ties, and so on to get results. It also cautions against arrogance.

Gyotega amaggwa — gyebakugobera. (The path you fill with thorns might end up being the one you are forced to take when escaping from your enemies.) This proverb cautions against malicious plotting, trapping and scheming supposedly aimed at one's adversaries, competitors, and any other people one is not on good terms with. One should be aware of the consequences of those actions should one end up trading places with those "other." Better still, always be careful with whatever you do, it might come back to haunt you.

Bwogoba essajja — olekamu aganadda. (When chasing a formidable enemy, remember to reserve energy for the return trip.) This proverb reminds people to pursue huge ventures cautiously, reserving enough room and energy to backtrack in case such a need arises.

Gwebakwatira mukituli — yaaba omubbi. (Whoever is caught in the act is the one who gets the blame.) This proverb reminds people that they are responsible for their actions, so they should not simply act because of peer pressure, or without knowing exactly what it is they are doing.

Atya omusana — talya bwami. (One afraid of heat cannot become a chief.) Being a chief is revered, but it requires real and hard work, especially during the old days when chiefs had to travel on foot through their constituencies, wherever they happened to be. One must also be physically and mentally prepared to face and solve difficult problems, including dealing with difficult people. So if one is not ready for the challenges and hardships related to one's desired position, especially one of leadership, one should not pursue that position. In other words, one who cannot stand heat cannot be in a kitchen.

Wova toyombye — wotera okudda. (You are more likely to return to a place you left peacefully than to the one you left because of a dispute.) It is important to remind people to try not to burn their bridges as they journey through life; you never know, you might find yourself again in the place you left sometime back in shame, having fallen out with its residents. This proverb encourages us to persevere and to be patient no matter how badly we are being treated at a certain location so that when we leave that kind of place, we can return to it when such a need arises.

Asuubira — akira aloota. (Hoping is better than dreaming.) This philosophical proverb preferring hoping to dreaming encourages people to maintain a positive attitude in times of adversity. A person who maintains hope keeps alive the possibility of getting what one wants as opposed to one who regards such desires as dreams. Dreaming is more passive since dreams are elusive, fleeting subconscious activities, whereas one has to be totally awake, active and in control to keep hope alive.

Ennaku musana — tegwokya omu. (Suffering is [like] the sun's heat; it affects all equally.) This metaphor likening suffering to heat is of comfort to those suffering; although it does not take away their pain, it reminds them that they are not alone in their pain or totally responsible for it. Suffering, like the sun's heat, is universal, and is unpleasant, humanly difficult or even impossible to prevent from occurring.

Kitta akimannyidde — enyanja etta muvubi. (Overconfidence kills — a lake can take the life of a fisherman.) The Baganda love fishing, so this proverb is necessary to remind them that one's life is always in danger when one is fishing. But in particular, it urges people to always be cautious, regardless of how familiar they are with whatever they are doing. Overall, this proverb cautions people not to be overconfident, especially in situations they cannot physically control; one must also remember that experience is not a substitute for caution.

Akutwala ekiro — omusiima bukedde. (The reason to appreciate one who forces you to journey in the night becomes apparent at daybreak.) This proverb urges people to appreciate all favors regardless of how untimely, inconvenient or out of place a favor may seem to be at the time it is done. At a more opportune moment, one might recognize that favor for what it was meant to be, a real favor.

Ogutateganya — teguzza nvuma. (You cannot get the desired results if you do not put in effort.) Hard work pays; you have to work hard to get what you want.

Okuwummula — sikutuuka. (Taking a break does not mean that you have arrived.) A very good proverb, especially directed towards teenagers who have a tendency to quit while the work is in progress; breaks in work are good but they should not be mistaken for a task accomplished.

Owekikye talemererwa — enjovu telemererwa masanga gaayo. (One cannot fail to carry what is naturally one's own — an elephant cannot fail to carry its tusks.) This proverb is an encouragement to those whining that their responsibilities and tasks are too heavy for them to accomplish single-handedly. Such people are reminded that God cannot give you more than He knows you can handle. It also cautions people to always take care of their own.

Atanayitayita — yatenda nnyina okufumba. (One who has not been around the block thinks that one's mother is the best cook.) The Baganda people value experience as a basis for making sound judgments and decisions, and one way to gain experience is to venture outside of one's comfort zone; mother is in many ways synonymous with comfort.

Bweyinda — sibwetonnya. (Heavy thunder is not always a sign of heavy rain.) This proverb cautions people not to equate appearances with reality or quantity with quality. We know that empty tins can make very loud noises and vice versa.

Ekimala empaka — kusirika. (Keeping quiet stops an argument.) If you see that an argument is getting out of hand, simply stop talking and remain quiet. Arguing is a two-way process; no one can argue alone, so there is a better chance of an argument ending if one of those arguing stops talking. One can also avoid making regrettable remarks during an argument if one says very little or, better still, says nothing.

Ekiri muttu — kimanyibwa nnyini kyo. (No one else can know what is in one's package except that package's owner.) Simply put, do not say or do anything that you do not want other people to know about you; you are responsible for your privacy.

Eryokanga netonnya — netulaba ensisira bwe zenkanya emyoyo. (You cannot tell how sturdy a hut is if there are no heavy storms to pound on it.) Tragedy is a test of a person's temperament, perseverance and overall character. The Baganda believe that you cannot claim to truly know a person if you have never been with that person in extreme, trying circumstances; these bring out the best and, unfortunately, the worst in people.

Okuddiza guba mwoyo — nowuwo akumma. (Giving is a virtue that even your relatives can lack.) This proverb reminds people to be grateful when given things, regardless of quality or quantity, because giving is an act that comes from deep within one's heart; it is not an obligation but an act of love.

Ekibi — kikira engoma okulawa. (Bad news travels faster and farther than the sound of drums.) This proverb cautions people to avoid putting themselves in compromising situations, because if one does something bad, "the whole world" gets to know of it.

Ekijja omanyi — kinyaga bitono. (Preparedness mitigates loss.) This is reminding people to always be prepared for life's uncertainties and disasters. However good life may be at any given moment, it is safer to always be prepared for whatever can go wrong, because that is our reality. The better prepared you are, the less you lose or have to pay for when the unexpected happens.

Kambukire baaba wabukidde — kwekugwa muntubiro (Let me follow in my elder sibling's footsteps is the sure way to land you in deep waters.) This proverb cautions against following blindly, thinking that since you are related to a specific individual, you can do or be all that individual can do or be, or that you will not be held responsible for doing what a relative has already done. While it is often advised to heed advice and to follow in an experienced relative's footsteps, this should be done cautiously, because by nature you are two different people and that relative may not be the best role model for you at that particular time. Such a relative might have less or more ability to accomplish that task. Also, you are reminded that you are responsible for whatever you do, so avoid blind imitations that can land you into trouble.

Okwerinda — si buti. (Readiness is not a sign of fear or weakness.) The Baganda emphasize the need for being prepared at all times. As another proverb above points out, you minimize your losses if you are prepared for uncertainties.

Gunsinze — aliwa bitono. (One who says sorry in a timely manner pays less in fines.) This proverb is a prompt to accept responsibility for what has gone wrong on your watch and apologize promptly instead of waiting to be investigated and punished accordingly.

Kyotonalya — tokyesunga. (You cannot count on what you do not have in hand at the time.) This is the equivalent of "a bird in hand is worth more than ten in the air."

Tekiwomera matama abiri. (What is tasty for one mouth may not be that delicious for another.) This proverb reminds us that we are unique individuals so we should avoid generalizing and stereotyping when dealing with each other.

Obwayiise — tebuyolebwa. (Poured millet is difficult to collect.) Millet seeds are so tiny and delicate that if they are accidently poured anywhere they are impossible to collect. This proverb encourages people to move on in cases of unrecoverable losses, and to recognize that some losses are unrecoverable so that they do not waste time trying to do the undoable. In other words, know when to quit. This proverb is literally the equivalent of "do not cry over spilt milk."

Ekyazze — tekizzibwayo. (You cannot undo what has been done.) This proverb echoes the one above cautioning people not to cry over spilt milk. The emphasis here, though, is on bad or tragic situations; once such a situation arises, it is advisable to put effort into dealing with it as opposed to spending valuable time complaining about it or asking unanswerable questions. So if something happens to you, and you hear people saying "*ekyazze*," they are implying that there is nothing you can do to undo what has happened.

Nyanja eradde — tebulako jjengo. (A sea is never without a ripple no matter how calm it may appear on the surface.) This proverb reminds people to be cautious and tread apprehensively, especially when all seems to be calm; things are not always what they appear to be. In other words, if something is too good to be true, it probably is not true.

Wosanga enkofu — tewaba jjinja. (There may not be a stone where you find a fowl.) This proverb reminds people to always be prepared in case something good but unexpected comes along, and one needs to take action there and then.

Awoza — akira alwana. (A person who takes one's case to the authorities is better than one who resolves situations by fighting.) Traditionally, the Baganda are supposed to settle their disputes in front of their elders; it is not advisable to simply fight when wronged, let alone taking matters in one's hands to get restitution.

Bwolwa munnyama — supu awola. (When you spend a lot of time eating pieces of meat, you miss out on the hot soup.) If one has two tasks to perform and wants equally good results, one should divide the time equally between these tasks, and perform both promptly.

Nantabulirirwa — asabala bwa bbumba. (One who does not heed advice goes sailing in clay boats.) People are advised to seek advice and heed it when given. Ignoring other people's advice might land one into trouble.

Kusitukiramu — ngeyatega ogwe kyayi. (You have to move immediately, like one who used banana fibers to set a trap.) This proverb is told to emphasize the need for urgent action; if one wants you to take action immediately, the speaker can use this proverb, and it is self-explanatory. If one sets a banana fiber trap and the trap catches the intended object, that person has to take action immediately because banana fibers are fragile and often quite easy to unfasten!

Emirembe ngalo — buli gumu gusinga kugunagwo. (Generations are like fingers; each one has its own length and size.) A very good proverb, especially directed to parents who often clash with their children along generational lines; no two generations are the same. It is also a caution against stereotyping since no two people can be exactly the same.

Ewagwa enkuba — tiwagwa njala. (There cannot be famine where there is rain.) This is literally a reminder that if it rains frequently, one cannot claim that one has no food, as that will be a sign of laziness. But it is also a warning that if the conditions are enabling, one has to perform as expected, whatever the task happens to be.

Nva nnungi — tezirwa kugaga. (Good source goes bad very quickly.) This proverb prompts people to take action as soon as they encounter favorable conditions because nothing good lasts forever. It also cautions people, especially parents, not to over-shower their children with praises because there is a possibility for such children to get out of control as a result of those praises.

Nsibambi — edibya mukene. (Bad packaging devalues fish.) A well-packaged product sells quickly; if you want to get good results and quickly, you must make the deal attractive. This proverb is also valuable advice for people wanting to ask for favors or those seeking jobs to remember to be polite and present themselves attractively.

Akafa omukutto — tikaluluma. (One who dies because of overeating cannot haunt anyone.) This is one of those proverbs that remind people to take responsibility for their actions; obviously you have no one to blame if you hurt yourself.

Kyeyagalire — bbwa lya njola. (One who gets a tattoo should not blame anyone else when that tattoo becomes a wound.) Once again, people are reminded that their actions can have unintended consequences, and they should be prepared to accept or deal with those consequences.

Omukambwe kigere kya mbogo — okyegezamu nga evuddewo. (A strict person is like a buffalo's footprint; you cannot measure your footprint against a buffalo's unless the buffalo is not around.) Try to avoid messing around strict people's property; if they catch you, it might get ugly for both parties.

Ebiddawo tibyenkanankana — ewava okugulu wadda muggo. (A replacement cannot be the same as the original; a wooden leg in place of a leg is still a piece of wood.) Just a reminder that no matter how good a replacement is, it is still a replacement. This proverb cautions people to be careful with other people's property because originals can never be fully replaced.

Ekiwuka ekitaluma — yente yabato. (An insect that does not bite is the children's cow.) In Buganda, as in many other parts of Africa, children can help with tending cows. Cows can be great toys for children to play with because, despite their size, they are totally harmless. This proverb advises people to be approachable regardless of how important or big they feel they are in their communities. If you are an important person, but harmless, you will have a devoted audience for your activities.

Kumbaga tekubula musiwufu. (There is always a badly groomed person at any wedding.) No matter how joyful or elegant an event is, there is always the possibility of someone spoiling it if the hosts do not monitor their guests carefully. In other words, trust humans but cautiously.

Okulirana enyanja — sikuliira. (Being in the vicinity of a lake does not mean that one will always have fish whenever one wants to.) Being near something does not imply automatic access to the benefits associated with that item. This is a good proverb to tell people who think that simply because they are related to an important person or share space with that person, they have a right to that person's property and belongings. It also cautions people not to take things for granted. Because something is accessible does not mean that it is easy to appropriate or yours to have as and when needed.

Akanafa — tekawulira ngombe. (One that will die does not hear the train's whistle.) This proverb expresses the Baganda people's belief in fate or destiny. Whatever will be will be, regardless of what others may or may not do to prevent it. In a way, such a proverb helps people to deal with tragedies without dwelling on regrets such as "If I had been there, this would not have happened" or taking responsibility for happenings beyond their control, saying things like "If I had done this or that, this would not have happened."

Atalina manyi — tagwa ddalu. (One without enough energy does not become insane.) This proverb reminds people of their responsibilities for their actions; it is the equivalent of "bite only what you can chew." It is an appropriate proverb to tell people trying to shun their responsibilities towards their spouses and or children.

Kyofa togabye — walumbe yakigaba. (What you do not give away when you are alive will be given away at your death.) This proverb advises people to be generous if they can afford it so that they can be appreciated. If one dies and leaves a lot of property lying around, it automatically gets distributed arbitrarily and of course one never gets thanked for it. It is also a subtle reminder to make wills.

Abomugumu baba bakaaba — ngabomuti baseka. (When relatives of a self-declared fearless person are weeping because the person is dead, those of a fearful one can be having fun.) This proverb is directed towards people who have a flair for bravado when in actuality one is as vulnerable as the person next door. Although heroism is a tempting idea, this proverb reminds people to always play it safe and to always proceed cautiously instead of wanting to be heroes in dangerous situations.

Emmwanyi gyewesiga— tebamu mulamwa. (A coffee bean you put your trust in may turn out to be hollow.) This proverb cautions people not to put all their trust in one person or plan; one should always have a second plan just in case the trusted route turns out to be thorny.

Atamukutte yagamba— nti kwatira ddala onyweze. (Only one not in the ring can demand that the one holding a wrestler should tighten one's grip.) This proverb cautions people to be wary of cheerleaders prompting them to play heroes when such cheerleaders are looking on from a safe distance. In other words, people should avoid urging others to do what the cheerleaders themselves cannot do. It is difficult for a person to know what is required, or to what extent, to accomplish a task one is not involved in. This is a situation that requires a person to walk in another's shoes before judging that other person's actions.

Mukomuwulu— taba n'amatu. (A bachelor's wife never has ears.) Obviously one with a wife cannot be a bachelor, but this proverb draws attention to how people who are not in one's situation can afford to be generous with advice, just as is pointed out in the proverb preceding this one. "If that was my wife, I would have cut off her ears" is the kind of advice more likely to come from a person who has no wife to begin with. People are cautioned to think through advice given to them, especially if it is coming from people who have no knowledge or experience of the situation the one they are advising is in.

Akuwaliriza okulinnya— bwogwa akuyita kaddu wannema. (One prompting you to climb high is often the first to laugh and call you names when you fall.) The Baganda value advice and recommend people getting some whenever they can, but at the same time, they caution not to simply accept other people's recommendations without scrutiny. Humans are not as good as they should be; one can intentionally dish out dangerous advice and get pleasure out of seeing the victim sweat. So before embarking on a recommended activity, make sure that it is within your means and strength.

Oguliko omusesa — teguzikira. (A fire that has one tending it cannot go out.) This proverb can be interpreted two ways, depending on the context in which it is used. On the one hand, it is good advice cautioning people that things cannot go wrong or get spoilt when there is a caretaker. On the other hand, though, if one, for example, starts a nasty rumor about you, you are advised to confront the offending party promptly because it is the only way you can put out such a fire.

Okubwesoka — sikubulya. (Being first in line is no guarantee that you will get what you want in the end.) This proverb reminds people not to assume that if one succeeds at the front end, one is subsequently guaranteed success; early success is for sure encouraging, but one should not become complacent because of it.

Nditwala kinene — afa tatuse kubuko. (One waiting to take a huge gift to one's in-laws can die without ever going to visit them.) This proverb advises people not to postpone doing whatever it is one has to do, waiting for perfection, because perfection never happens. Also there is no such thing as enough, so do not wait until you have enough time, enough money, and so on to do what you want to do; a person who waits for perfection or "enough" ends up accomplishing nothing.

Omulimba — asanga mukkiriza. (There would be no liars if there were no people to believe those lies.) Do not encourage bad habits! If a liar believes that people eat up the lies, then one cannot stop lying.

Olya kuntono — netalumira. (It is better to eat a palatable small amount of food than to fill up on distasteful food.) This is a good proverb to remind people that quality is often better than quantity. Also, one would rather have less and have peace of mind than have plenty and be restless because of the burden that goes with having plenty.

Kamaanyi — kalibwa nambiro. (A sizeable hunt cannot be gotten without sweat.) Big rewards cannot be achieved without due effort; if one desires something sizeable, one must be prepared to work hard to get it.

Abantu balamu magoma — gavugira aliwo. (People are like drums; they entertain you only when you are in the vicinity.) People are more likely to support you when you are around as opposed to simply responding to messages requesting their support. If you want help, it is better to ask for it in person.

Ekkumi — terikyawa omu. (Ten people cannot all hate one particular person.) This is a belief in collective wisdom; if a sizeable number of people accuse one of doing wrong, chances are that person is guilty as charged. This proverb also reminds people that it is not wise to say bad things about a person when in a crowd, assuming that since the person being talked about is not around that person will never know that he was talked about badly; there is always a chance of the absent person having a friend in that crowd.

Entasiima — ebula agiwa. (A person incapable of saying thank you soon runs out of people to give them things.) People want to be appreciated for their good deeds; it is, therefore, important to show gratitude whenever one receives a favor, gift, and so on. People one does not thank are not likely to keep on giving that individual things or even to help them.

Gwotoyise naye — simuzibu kulimba. (It is not difficult to lie to a person you haven't been traveling with.) Although trust is held in high regard among the Baganda, they also caution that one should not accept all one hears at face value; trust but verify.

Amaaso g'omuganda gali mungalo. (A Muganda person's eyes are in the fingers.) This is another variation of trust but verify. A Muganda person needs to touch and feel before believing. If you want to be convincing, you should think of tangible evidence or examples to help you make your case to the listeners.

Abantu balamu bitooke bisalire — tibyekwekebwamu. (People are like trimmed banana trees; you cannot hide among them.) This proverb reminds people to always remember that humans can expose one's secrets anywhere, anytime, that we should always be cautious when revealing ourselves and our secrets to others. Trust people, but cautiously, knowing that there is always a possibility of your trust being betrayed.

Omugezigezi — akuguza ekibira. (A crafty person can sell a forest to you.) Just like the previous proverb, this too cautions people to be alert, especially when dealing with crafty individuals capable of making anything look and sound better than it actually is.

Omulalu wakuwera — wotwalira. (You must instantly take whatever valuable item a mad person gives you.) Although taking time to examine whatever one is given before taking it is a great idea, the Baganda advise people to immediately take possession of whatever valuables they are given because people can change their minds instantly.

Okalya dda — kadda dda. (What you eat today comes back later to haunt you.) Be careful in all you do because anything you do today might resurface tomorrow when you are anywhere anytime.

Gwosenvuza mubuto — akusenvuza mubukadde. (This proverb has two translations, depending on the context in which it is said. On a positive note, it can mean that the child you help to crawl will help you crawl when you are old and need help to get around. But it can also be interpreted negatively as meaning that the child you make crawl will make you crawl in your old age.) People are reminded to help those in need if they expect to be helped when they also find themselves in difficult situations; it is a variation of "*Okalya dda — kadda dda.*"

Kola ng'omuddu — olye ng'omwami. (Work like a servant to eat like a king.) You always reap what you sow; if you want a great harvest, you must sweat planting the seeds. If you want to be comfortable, you must work hard to become comfortable; hard work has its benefits.

Ogutateganya — teguzza nvuma. (A hassle free task is not likely to be rewarding.) This proverb is of the same essence as the one directly above; if you do not sweat, you cannot expect to reap rewards. One who wants great rewards should not complain about the size of the workload.

Kabwa kabbi — kagumya mugongo. (A thieving dog must make its back strong.) This proverb cautions people not to get involved in risky behavior unless they are strong enough to stomach the consequences.

Akayaana ennyo nomulalu — afa awoza. (One who frequently argues with an insane person dies defending oneself.) This proverb cautions people not to get involved in shouting matches, quarrels, disagreements, and other such unbecoming activities with people presumed to be unreasonable, because unreasonable people are not likely to concede, which means that the activity would go on forever. Also, those passing by or listening or in the vicinity may not be able to tell the difference between the two shouting parties; the supposedly reasonable person might be forced to defend oneself against insanity charges.

Tolumba mulalu—ngatolina jjinja. (Do not invade a mad person when you have no stone.) In other words, be prepared to fight the battles you initiate; have the means and strength you might need to fight such battles, otherwise you will find yourself in a vulnerable position.

Bwoyita n'omubbi—nawe bakuyita mubbi. (If you befriend a thief, you will be called a thief.) Be careful about the company you keep; people have a tendency to determine one's character based on the character of one's friend(s).

Enkumbi terimba. (A hoe does not lie.) The Baganda are traditionally subsistence farmers, so they put a lot of emphasis on farming as a means of making a living. So long as one uses one's hoe as it is supposed to be used, that individual will live comfortably.

Ennongosereza—etegula omutego. (Over-perfecting a trap can end up setting it off.) Perfection is good but rare; therefore, an obsession with it should be avoided because not only can it be futile, it can also be costly.

Awali omulema—tofunyirawo lunwe. (One should not bend one's index finger in the presence of a cripple.) This proverb reminds people to be sensitive about other people's feelings, not to do or say things that might make others uncomfortable. If, for example, you bend your index finger in the presence of a cripple, the cripple might think that you are making fun of him. Also, be aware of the company you are keeping before making a joke; there is a time and a place for everything.

Omweyogereze—takusuuza kayanzi ko. (A jester should not make you throw away your cricket.) You should not abandon or feel ashamed of what you value simply because a jester has made fun of it; someone's garbage might be another person's treasure. Be assertive and always defend what is of interest or value to you.

93

Amamese amangi — tegesimira bunnya. (Many rats cannot dig their own holes.) Although many hands make for light work, there are times when one has to be weary of numbers; sometimes when people are in a crowd, they may not perform as well as they would do if left to themselves.

Emmeme etefumba kigambo — ekwogeza munno kyatalyerabira. (One who does not weigh one's words before uttering them can make an unforgettable statement in the presence of a friend.) It is always important to think before speaking to avoid making embarrassing or offensive, unforgettable remarks.

Kyerabirwa mugambi. (The speaker can forget what one said, but the person to whom it was said cannot forget what was said.) This is another proverb like the one above. Be careful when talking to others; you might say something to someone and forget it, but often the listener retains what is said, especially if it concerns that listener.

Gwomanyi enfumita — tomulinda kugalula. (Do not let a bad shooter fire the first shot.) This proverb is primarily for hunters; it is not a good idea to allow a terrible shooter to fire at the animal or bird first because if that shooter misses, the target will get away. But it also cautions people to be alert to potential problems so as to prevent them from happening.

Embiro — tezimala musango. (Running away does not resolve disputes.) It is better to admit when one has done something wrong, and not simply run away, because sooner or later such a person is going to be found and made to pay for whatever they did. Running away simply postpones punishment; it does not replace it, and it can actually make the situation worse for the offender, resulting in an even bigger punishment.

Omusango teguvunda. (A misdeed does not decay.) This proverb is the same as the one above, reminding people that a bad deed does not become less bad over time or forgotten or even simply disappear; it is better to deal with such a situation right away.

Nakalyako ani?— abula gwakkusa. (One who refuses to exclude some people when distributing something small ends up satisfying no one.) A person wanting to please all the people all the time may end up pleasing nobody at any time. Sometimes, one has to choose whom to give something to when there is not enough for all.

Contradicting Proverbs

In the body of scholarship on proverbs, there is scanty information on contradictions often found in any people's proverbs, but it is a noticeable issue. Rhetorically, contradicting proverbs are valuable because they remind the reader or scholar that proverbs are context oriented; they are prompted by the situation at hand, often told as a response or remedy to that situation. I would also add that these contradictions found in the proverbs mirror the contradictions and uncertainties which are an integral part of real life. We should embrace and respond to contradicting proverbs just as we embrace and respond to the multipurpose and multifaceted nature of our lives. Contradicting proverbs, therefore, challenge us as well as shake us out of our complacencies by forcing us to critically examine our knowledge of who we are and of the environment that surrounds us. Below are sample pairs of Baganda contradicting proverbs to ponder:

(a) *Abikka ebibiri — tabojja.* (One wanting to collect delicacies from two sources simultaneously may taste neither.) According to this proverb, it is difficult to do two tasks simultaneously and have time, energy, resources and even enthusiasm to do both well. This is a popular warning against multitasking; it is assumed that it is wiser and eventually more profitable to complete one task before embarking on another. This proverb is also a friendly warning against greed. But then, it is in direct contradiction to the advice of the proverb below:

(b) *Atega ogumu — talira.* (One who sets only one trap at a time does not get meat.) This proverb encourages multitasking, advising that doing several tasks simultaneously is rewarding, and it may be the only way to get the desired results.

(a) *Munkyamu mwemuva engolokofu.* (We learn from our mistakes.) Although making mistakes is not encouraged, this proverb encourages people not to give up simply because they made a mistake; making mistakes is normal, and mistakes should be seen as a challenge to achieve the desired results, not as a defeat, or reason to give up on something or someone. This proverb is often directed to despairing parents with fears that their good-for-nothing children will grow up to be good-for-nothing adults, and this is where it is in direct contradiction with the one below:

(**b**) *Akakyaama amamera — kaba kazibu okugolola.* (That which bent when growing up cannot be easily straightened when it comes into its own.) The literal reference is to trees, but the metaphor is clearly to children. This proverb is often directed to parents to pay attention to their children's upbringing because whatever bad habits they acquire in youth might be hard to drop when they turn into adults. Conversely, when one does not want to deal with an unruly teen who is not one's child, the individual can quote this proverb.

(**a**) *Bbugubugu — si muliro.* (Excessive speed is not fire.) This proverb encourages patience, and warns that excessive speed does not always produce desired results, but it contradicts another very popular proverb, below:

(**b**) *Omwangu yatta enswa.* (A quick person is the one who gets the edible ants.) *Enswa* are seasonal delicacies mostly from anthills, and they are collected only after rainstorms, and then only for a brief moment. This proverb urges people to speedily "grab" whatever they need as soon as it becomes available to them, and so does the one below, both in contradiction to the one above.

Linda kiggweyo — afumita mukira. (This proverb has its origin in hunting: A hunter who waits for the whole animal to come within sight spears the tail.) Despite all the proverbs hailing patience, this one advises quick action. One is advised to grab whatever one wants as soon as such an item becomes available. A hunter who waits for the whole animal to appear instead of spearing the head as soon as he sees it spears only the tail, which means that such an animal can get away.

Ennindiriza — yamezza ssemitego. (Hesitation cost a wrestler a match.) This is another proverb running contrary to those advocating patience; this proverb encourages people to take action as soon as an opportunity avails itself, because hesitating can be costly.

Conclusion

As stated in the introduction to this chapter, this has been simply a sampling of Baganda epigrams, intended to persuade the reader to join in the ongoing dialogue and inquiry into these people's complex, yet often marginalized, artistic creations. It is important to remember that these epigrams are not static, historical documents meant to be archived for future generations; they are living, breathing literary creations that are continuously being cautiously reworked to prevail as current, relevant and practically valuable guides and responses to each generation's critical issues and situations while retaining the essence of their traditional rhetorical appeal. Syntactically brief but rhetorically laden, supposedly simple in meaning but semantically expansive, Baganda epigrams have been and still remain a scholarly rewarding, but still wide open, formidable subgenre of oral literature for Africanists and the Baganda people themselves to probe.

4

Prose Narratives

Introduction

Prose narratives are a significant feature in the African oral tradition, and they come in various forms often depicting specific ethnic groups' cultural heritage. But whatever forms these narratives take, they are significantly different from myths in content, purpose, focus, and even narrative context. Prose narratives are purely fictional narratives that should be entertaining as well as rhetorically viable to attract audiences. Although most of these narratives are classified as morality and character building tales in that they convey specific messages to the listeners, and some of them serve etiological purposes, they are often not taken as seriously as myths, and their narrative contexts are not as somber as those of mythologies. Most of these narratives are extended, more elaborate and entertaining versions of proverbs whose content, language, narrative technique, and other such rhetorical features can be altered to fit the occasion, the purpose, and, above all, the audience physically present at the time. In the context of prose narratives, the audience is invited to listen and participate by adding pieces, singing if there happens to be a song in the narrative, and prompting and correcting the narrator as needed. The audience, therefore, plays a crucial role in the actualization of a prose narrative; unfortunately this is another valuable aspect of the African oral tradition that cannot be reproduced in a translated, written version. Also, since prose narratives are always audience friendly and age group focused, even children can be effective narrators, which is not always the case with mythology. Overall, there is often more room for creativity in prose narratives than in mythology.

African prose narratives are often valuable human stories, comparable to usual western literature narratives in many aspects. They are ever current because they feature familiar everyday events and characters, often alleviating the audience's fears of such events and characters or simply highlighting what makes us human. Since storytellers and their audiences are familiar with the characters (animals, people), they can imitate such characters amusingly, add to the content to suit the audience, correct each other and so on. What is being highlighted is these people's reality, although presented figuratively through personification mostly.

It is unfortunate, though, that most people familiar with African prose narratives tend to classify them as simply folktales or, better still, animal stories mostly featuring universally known animal characters like hare, elephant, lion, tortoise, and many others; because of that fact little attention is paid to the human elements in those stories. True, there are many narratives featuring animals in the African oral tradition, but these animals are used partly to highlight a significant issue that is often overlooked or simply marginalized in the western narratives, and that is that Africans care about the coexistence of species who share the same physical space. However, when collecting these narratives, the author was made increasingly aware, and sadly so, that animal centered narratives are waning, especially among young people, who were more inclined to narrate more human-featuring narratives than animal-centered ones. This trend can be attributed to globalization and urbanization, both of which are surging with no end in sight. Also imagine, if you can, the author's surprise when a Luganda version of Cinderella was included among Baganda prose narratives. These trends highlight the possibility of losing the African oral narratives as we know them today, which makes the Baganda prose narratives in this volume and other similar African collections timely and scholastically very valuable.

Although animal-centered narratives abound in the African oral tradition, there are many ethnic groups on the continent who also put emphasis on narratives centered on human and supernatural beings. The Baganda are in that category, as will be seen from the sample *enfumo* (Baganda narratives) below. Traditionally for the Baganda, as is the case with many other African ethnic groups, animals and humans were meant to coexist peacefully sharing the same physical space; consequently, animals and humans interact as viable characters in that space in a number of narratives.

It would be presumptuous to assume that one can explicate any narrative completely; there is always room for more dialogue about any one piece, which in itself makes them great literary pieces! Background information, though, always helps to enrich such dialogues, so the author will provide some pertinent information with the Baganda narratives featured in this volume.

Storytelling among the Baganda people is a very entertaining, participatory activity, just as it is in most parts of the continent. To that end, a Muganda storyteller invites the audience to join in the storytelling with these words: *olwatuuka ngambalabira*. This is an invitation that catches attention, because literally translated it is "once upon a time I saw." After uttering what is clearly an incomplete statement, the storyteller stops. If the audience wants to know what the storyteller saw, they must acknowledge that they are paying attention and ready to hear and participate in the storytelling by replying: *nobulabibwo* (with your very own eyes). Then the storyteller can start narrating. *Nobulabibwo* is a very important response from the audience because it indicates that the audience recognizes the sto-

A storytelling session.

ryteller's ownership of the story, which gives the storyteller the authority one needs to tell the story from the perspective of an active observer of the events in that story. Armed with that authority, the storyteller is free to improvise as needed, making the story relevant to that particular audience as well as more enjoyable and plausible.

The following tales, arranged in eight culturally significant categories, are a very tiny portion of the repertoire of Baganda narratives available among the people, but they are a fair representative sample of that cultural heritage.

Etiological Tales

"Why" is a crucial question for which humans are ever seeking logical responses even when there are apparently very few, if any, to be found. This is when etiological tales enter the picture to explain the logically inexplicable phenomena of our human existence without making us doubt our sanity or even negatively affecting our mental capacities.

Why Cocks Crow at 3:00 A.M.

Once upon a time there was a very powerful king of Buganda whose name was Ssonko. King Ssonko had many riches, including all kinds of domestic animals like goats, cocks, cows, and pigs. He loved all these animals very much and treated them very well.

As he grew older, King Ssonko started falling sick often. One time he became very, very sick and he knew that he was about to join his ancestors, so he called his beloved animals and addressed them as follows: "My friends, my days are numbered, but when I go to join my ancestors, I would like one of you to announce the end of my earthly journey, not only on the day I will depart, but every single day thereafter until the end of time. Who is willing to do that for me?" All the animals kept quiet, maybe out of fear or sorrow or because it was such a gigantic task, one likely to become a burden; but after a while, Cock gathered enough strength and said, "I will do it, Sir." The king thanked Cock profusely, after which he dismissed the animals. A few days later, the king went to join his ancestors at 3:00 A.M. Immediately Cock started announcing the king's depar-

101

ture: "King Ssonko is gone to join his ancestors," he crowed. Cock continued to make this announcement until it was his time to go too, and he passed the torch to his descendants who, up to now and supposedly until the end of time, will keep announcing King Ssonko's departure from Buganda at 3:00 A.M. every single day.

Frog, Dear, Where Is Your Tail?

Once upon a time, all the animals had no tails. One day, their king thought that his animals would look cute if they all had tails, so he called a meeting to be attended by one animal chosen by members of its kind to receive tails on their behalf. Very early in the morning all the animals gathered at the appointed *kisawe* (a village sports and gathering area), and the king soon arrived. He greeted all these eager creatures pleasantly and immediately started distributing tails, starting with the biggest. Whenever he held one tail up, all the animals, with the exception of Frog, would clamor for it: "Please, do give that one to me, please," and one by one the tails started disappearing from the huge container in front of the king. As the tails continued disappearing, Frog's friends asked him why he was not participating in making requests, and he laughed at them, claiming, "My friends, the king is my uncle; for sure he will reserve a very good tail for me; I do not have to shed any sweat for one." In no time, all the tails were gone. As the king was preparing to leave the *kisawe*, Frog approached him, saying, "Uncle, where is my tail?" "And what do you mean, your tail? I do not have any left; why didn't you ask me for one as all the others here did?" amusingly asked the king while climbing into his chariot. As soon as the king was comfortably seated, he went his merry way. Frog couldn't believe his eyes and ears for that matter.

The Baganda have a proverb related to this story, specifically warning people not to have *kojja andaba* (uncle sees me) and related attitudes because Kojja *andaba kyasubisa Wakikere omukira* (uncle sees me prevented the frog from getting a tail).

Monkeys Sure Love Trees

Once upon a time, Monkey and Tortoise were great friends, but Tortoise was very, very lazy. He could not plant seeds, weed or grow any kind of food, but that was not a problem for him because he used to buy all his food from his neighbors. Monkey, on the other hand, was very, very hard working and he grew all his food on his own property, and he always had extras to sell to lazy bones like his friend Tortoise. One time, though, Tortoise ran out of money; yet he had a son to feed, so he went to his friend Monkey and asked him to sell him some food on credit. Tortoise did not tell Monkey that he was broke; instead he said: "My friend, give me some food; I did not travel with money today but you know me; I will bring the money to you tomorrow." "Sure, my friend," replied Monkey, and he gave Tortoise all the food Tortoise needed.

The next day Monkey did not see Tortoise, neither did Tortoise appear on the second, third, fourth, and fifth days; actually, Monkey did not see Tortoise the whole week. After a week of patiently waiting to see Tortoise with no results, Monkey decided to pay Tortoise a visit and retrieve his money. Early in the morning, Monkey arrived at Tortoise's house and knocked at the door. When Tortoise realized who his honored guest was, he put on his coat and opened the door, weeping. "I'm so glad to see you my friend," said Tortoise, holding back tears, "but you found me on my way out. My father passed away last night and I am going for the funeral." "So sorry to hear that my friend," replied Monkey consolingly. "Please convey my condolences to the family, and have a safe trip." Monkey did not even mention his mission for the trip, and he returned home.

Two or so weeks went by, and again Monkey returned to Tortoise's house for his money. This time Tortoise had a different emergency situation: "My good friend, my brother might not live through this night. I've just received word that he might be gone by the time I get there." "So sorry my friend. I will keep your brother in my prayers; have a safe journey," and Monkey returned to his home. And once again two or so more weeks went by with no Tortoise in sight. All that time, Tortoise was busy thinking of plans to buy time to get Monkey's money together, and eventually he came up with a brilliant one. After finding a very good round millet grinding stone and hewing a huge circular hole beneath it, Tortoise sat down his only son and instructed him as follows: "Whenever I see or hear that Monkey is at my door, I will turn this millet grinding stone upside down and sit in this circular hole I have hewed under it. You will then tape me in as quickly as you possibly can. After securing me under the stone, you will turn the stone over and pour some millet on it and begin grinding gently; all of this will have to be done speedily. Then you will temporarily cease grinding the millet and hurry to open the door for Monkey, and when Monkey asks you where I am, you will tell him that I went to visit your aunt or uncle or cousin, whoever will come to mind. I will remind you to turn the stone over and untape me as soon as Monkey leaves my compound." The son understood the plan, but although he wondered why his father had devised it, he did not dare ask.

A few days after Tortoise had completed his plan and gone over it with his son, the son spotted Monkey approaching their compound, and he immediately told his father, who stuffed himself quickly in the circular hole. After securing his father under the stone, the good son turned the stone right side up, poured some millet on it and started grinding gently so as not to hurt his father. When Monkey knocked on the door, the son stopped grinding the millet and hurried to open the door with a grin on his face. "Hello little one, where is your father?" inquired Monkey. "He is not here. He went to visit my aunt," replied the cute little son, still grinning. Monkey, who was already frustrated, got even more frustrated, and in great anger he lifted the grinding stone and threw it in the branches of the nearby tree through the back door. He then made himself comfortable in the house, claiming that he was not going to vacate the premises without his money. Once in the tree branches under the stone, Tortoise carefully untaped himself, got down from the tree slowly with his stone in hand, hid it nearby, and quickly hatched a follow-up plan, then entered his house noiselessly and surprised Monkey: "So good to see you my friend. I was going to bring you your money as soon as I came back; sorry it has taken so long, but I am sure you understand how busy we all can be at times." Monkey was relieved to hear that he was going to get his money at long last. Tortoise pretended to look for the grinding stone: "Where is our millet grinding stone, son? See, my friend, I kept your money securely taped under that stone so as not to lose it. I wanted it kept in that secure place until I got time to bring it to you." Monkey could not believe his ears. He had started smiling, but the smile froze on his face! "Did you say the money, my money, is taped under the millet grinding stone that your son was using when I arrived?" inquired Monkey. "Sure my friend," replied Tortoise, "but now I cannot find it; where might it be, my son?" Before Tortoise's son could open his mouth, Monkey confessed that he had thrown the stone in the branches of the huge tree in the back out of frustration. "I am sorry, but I was really angry and thought that you were playing tricks on me," added Monkey. Tortoise immediately burst into tears and started wailing loudly: "Oh my friend, you've destroyed me. I was actually keeping ALL my money under that stone, not only yours, and now you tell me it is in the tree? How will we get it down?" "Easy, my friend; you are in luck because I am quite good at climbing trees," replied Monkey as he made his way up the tree. Once up there, Monkey searched for the stone, but he could not find it, so he called in reinforcement by his relatives and friends to help him look for Tortoise's grinding stone. But still the stone was nowhere to be found. Monkey and his relatives and friends decided to continue the search as long as it would take, and since then Monkey and his relatives and friends spend ample hours in the trees each day looking for Tortoise's millet grinding stone. But they have never, and definitely will never, find it, but they don't know that!

The Baganda have a pertinent proverb to this story: *eyaakusinze akukubisa gwokutte* (One cleverer than you can beat you with your own stick)!

Why Some Animals Are Prettier Than Others

Long, long ago all the animals — well, nearly all — had the same appearance, a dull and monotonous appearance, but there was one exception! Peacock had many very pretty feathers, especially his tail feathers, as can still be seen today, but most of the animals did not know Peacock then. One day, Zebra ran into Peacock when both were looking for food in the forest, and on seeing how pretty Peacock's spread feathers were, Zebra asked Peacock where he got those pretty colors. "Well, my friend," replied Peacock, "you too can get these pretty colors." "What can I do to get them?" asked Zebra anxiously. "Well, if you want to be almost as pretty as I am, listen carefully to what I am about to say." "I am all ears, my friend," replied Zebra enthusiastically. "When you get time," continued Peacock, "go into the forest and kill a very big animal, any big animal you can kill will do. Take the carcass into your house, but do not eat any of its meat. Keep the meat in a warm room until it rots and maggots appear all over it. Once it has all rotted away and you see only maggots everywhere, come for me." Zebra hurried to his task and in no time, he killed

105

a relatively huge animal. The meat was really, really appetizing, but Zebra kept Peacock's orders and resisted the temptation to eat any part of it. As soon as the meat was all maggots, Zebra informed Peacock accordingly. Peacock called his friends and they headed to Zebra's house, where they found the best looking maggots they had not seen in a while. Peacock and his friends had a great feast and they thanked Zebra profusely. "Very early tomorrow morning," said Peacock when he was leaving with his friends, "come to my house and I will decorate you and you will be nearly as pretty as I am." Very, very early the next day, Peacock mixed some wonderful colors and got ready for Zebra. Soon after sunrise the following day, Zebra arrived at Peacock's house and Peacock decorated him so nicely with very colorful black and white stripes. "Now, my friend, walk to your home very carefully and go and sit in the sun until the stripes dry on you," instructed Peacock. "It is still quite early so you will be able to dry completely before bedtime, but be careful not to spoil the stripes before they dry," stressed Peacock.

Zebra followed Peacock's instructions to the letter, and by sunset, he was completely dry, and, oh, yes, very pretty. Immediately after drying, Zebra went into the forest to show off his beautiful stripes. All the animals marveled at his beautiful colors and begged him to tell them where he had it done so that they too could go and get the same. The joyous Zebra liberally spread the information: "Go to Peacock; he is the one who made me this pretty." No sooner had Zebra finished his story than Leopard jumped up and went to visit Peacock. Peacock gave Leopard exactly the same instructions he had given Zebra. Leopard was told to go and kill a huge animal and bring the carcass to the house. He was warned not to eat any part of that animal; instead he was instructed to keep all of it in a warm room until it was all maggots. Then he was to go and inform Peacock that the meat was now all maggots. Leopard hurried to his task just as Zebra had done, and in no time, he too killed a relatively huge animal. The meat was really, really, really appetizing, and the more Leopard tried to resist the temptation of eating some of it, the harder the task became. When he could not control himself anymore, he ate one of the limbs, which lessened the number of maggots when the meat had all rotted, but there was an ample amount of maggots around. When the remaining meat was all maggots, Leopard informed Peacock accordingly. Peacock called his friends and they headed to Leopard's house, where they found the maggots, but they were not as many as those they had found at Zebra's residence. Peacock and his friends had a good feast, but not as great as Zebra's. When Peacock and his friends finished eating, Peacock invited Leopard to his residence in the afternoon of the next day. "I will then adorn you as I did Zebra," said Peacock. The next day in early afternoon, Leopard arrived at Peacock's residence, who this time had not yet finished mixing the colors. By the time Peacock finished mixing the colors and adorning Leopard, the sun was about to set. "Now my friend, walk to your home very carefully and go and sit in the sun until the spots dry on you," instructed Peacock. But no sooner had Leopard sat down to dry than the sunset. He dried somehow, but not as completely as Zebra had; therefore, he was not as pretty as Zebra when day broke. But he was still proud enough to hurry to the forest and show off his spots to his friends. On the way he run into Hyena, who had not yet heard the story. "You look pretty, my friend; who gave you those beautiful spots?" Leopard pointed Hyena to Peacock's residence, and as soon as Peacock saw Hyena, he repeated the instructions exactly as he had given them to both Zebra and Leopard.

Hyena embarked on the task of finding that huge special animal, and in no time, he had it. But you know Hyena when it comes to meat. Poor creature!! He tried so, so hard to resist the temptation of eating the meat, but to no avail. Before sundown, Hyena had eaten one of the limbs; the next day, he ate a second one. By the end of day two, he had consumed all the limbs. Sure, he kept some meat and it turned into maggots in due time, but there were very, very few. When Peacock saw how few the maggots were, he thanked Hyena and invited him to get to his residence after sunset. Peacock did not waste any time preparing good colors for Hyena, who couldn't control his appetite just this once. The next day, when the sun had set, Hyena appeared at Peacock's residence and Peacock simply splashed the ugliest color ever on him. By the time this color splashing was over, it was getting dark, and Hyena headed straight to bed. The next day when Hyena woke up, he had some color, but definitely not as beautiful as Zebra's and Leopard's.

The Baganda people use this tale to point out that one who cannot control one's appetite often gets the short end of the stick, and justifiably so.

Parenting Tales

Parenting is a unique profession in several aspects, but probably the most fascinating is job performance. Ponder the situation: under qualified or totally unqualified individuals are charged with bringing up, taking care of, nourishing and cherishing an already delicately manufactured product that does not come with a manual. These individuals must tread softly, though, because as time goes by, the product develops its own mind and starts to voice its own opinions; but the parents are held responsible for whatever happens to, or is made to happen by, this product. These individuals' reputation is eternally entangled in this product's behavior; they are praised or rebuked or looked down upon depending on how well or how badly this product performs in the world. Little wonder then that there is plenty of advice, solicited or otherwise, on how to handle this product, and some of the best can be found in the Baganda prose narratives, samples of which are available below.

Maama Siife Nze

Once upon a time there was a woman who got married to a very poor man. They worked hard and eventually accumulated wealth. When they had accumulated a good amount of property, the husband felt that this woman was no longer good enough for him in his new status, so he decided to divorce her and marry a new one. The poor woman was sent far away and given absolutely nothing to start a new life for herself.

Once in "exile," she discovered that she was pregnant by her now ex-husband. She tried to get messages to him but he would not hear of it; after all, he now had a new life with a "fitting" wife, servants, and plenty of property. The poor woman carried the pregnancy to term and gave birth to a very, very beautiful baby girl. Once again she sent messages to her ex-husband, and once again the ex-husband ignored those messages. He did not go to see the baby, and he did not send any help to either the baby or the mother. The poor woman took it all in stride, named her baby *Kirabo,* and started working hard to sustain herself and her baby. She eventually succeeded in making a home for the two of them; and although this home was not as luxurious as she would have had with her ex-husband, it was decent enough. For a while, the woman and her daughter were happy, but not for long. When the baby was able to walk, word reached the ex-husband that the baby looked exactly like him; and his relatives and friends as well as unrelated villagers all started nagging him to take care of that woman and her baby because it was a shame that both mother and daughter lived in such poverty while he was swimming in riches. Rumors started flying around the man's village that he was not as good a person as they had thought he was because of his neglect of the mother of his child and of the child. As the man's reputation got spots all over, he thought of how to remedy the situation.

After much thinking, the man came up with a solution, a very cruel solution to his nagging problem: kill the baby!! Not only did this man want to have nothing to do with this baby, he now wanted the baby dead, so he sent two of his servants to accomplish the job any way they saw fit. By the time the servants arrived at the woman's door, she had already heard the news; she was so scared for her baby, because the ex-husband was a very powerful, above-the-law person! When the poor woman heard the servants knocking at the door, she started crying loudly, asking for help from neighbors, but the child calmed her down with a very sweet song:

> *Maama siife nze, olw'obujogero* (Mother, I will not die because
> of my father's spite).
> *Abagenyi banirize* (Welcome the guests).
> *Emmere fumba balye* (Prepare food for them to eat).
> *Maama Nayiga ekiwero kikino* (Mother *Nayiga*, here is a piece of
> cloth [*Nayiga* was the mother's name].
> *Amaziga sangula* (Wipe away the tears).

As the child sang and danced for the "guests," their hearts melted: what a beautiful, kind child! The servants could not bring themselves to kill such a child, so they ate the food and, after thanking both the cook and the entertainer, they bid their hosts good-bye. The child sent a message with them to give to her father, whom she had never seen, that she really wanted to see him; she invited him to pay her and her mother a visit. On returning to the master, the servants explained what they had seen: a very happy, kind, healthy, beautiful, great singer and dancer child, a miracle baby, in other words, whom they could not kill. They assured their master that even if he had been the one sent to do what they had gone to do, he wouldn't have had the nerve to do it. You can imagine how furious the master was! The two servants lost their jobs immediately!

The following week, the master sent three servants, claiming that two people can very easily reach an agreement, but not three. However, the results were the same as before; the three servants could not harm that child. Now getting more angry, the master sent four servants, but these too came back without having accomplished anything. And what about five — all five cannot be such sissies!! But they were put under the same spell on seeing that happy, kind, healthy, very beautiful, singing, dancing child. And every time, the child sang the same song and sent the same message to her father.

What does one do when all the people around him he had always counted upon to do his will turn out to be useless nincompoops; those were the exact master's words! Despair was getting him no results and his reputation was getting worse every passing day, so he decided to go and put an end to this scandal himself. On seeing the father, the child was overjoyed and she burst into her usual song, this time with more gusto than she had ever done before, knowing very well that this was her last chance for survival! She danced, jumped, and ran into her father's arms, all the while singing and dancing:

> *Maama siife nze olw'obujogero*
> *Taata wuno azze* (Dad is here).
> *Abagenyi banirize*
> *Kamula omubisi banywe* (Squeeze fresh juice for them).
> *Emmere fumba balye*
> *Maama Nayiga ekiwero kikino*
> *Amaziga sangula*

"And you fools, why are you all just standing there," shouted the master to the servants he had brought with him. "Run back to my home and bring the finest linens you can find there to make this child's clothing, and bring some for the mother, too." The man denied having sent those servants, and he constructed a palace for the mother and daughter, who lived in unimaginable luxury the rest of their lives. The miracle baby saved herself and her mother.

The Baganda people have a proverb for this story: *Okuzaala kuzukira,* literally translated as "parenthood is immortality."

Njabala

Once upon a time, a man married a very hard working woman, and together they made a great home. For a while the couple lived in ecstasy, so happy together. But after a reasonable length of time, it became clear to them that they could not have children, or at least that is what they thought, since they had lived together all that long without producing a baby. But they bounced back from their sorrow and started visiting each and every medicine person recommended to them far and wide, but still without any luck. Eventually they stopped attempting to have a baby and resigned themselves to a childless life; all the neighbors pitied them!! But one day, just like that, the woman found herself pregnant, and oh, how they rejoiced!!! The nine months flew by, excitement amounting to a feverish pitch by the end of that period, and they were blessed with a very, very beautiful baby girl, whom they gave a lovely pet name: Njabala. To say that they loved this girl very much would be an understatement; this couple adored their daughter and treated her like a queen. The mother made sure that the little princess did absolutely no chores as she was growing up. Every morning, the mother would wake up early enough to prepare Njabala's breakfast; then she would go to cultivate and Njabala would stay sleeping. Halfway through the morning, the mother would return home to wake up Njabala and feed her. She would then return to the garden and Njabala would stay outside enjoying the morning sun until the mother got back to make lunch. Then the mother would serve the lunch, wash the dishes and prepare supper. In between, she would find time to give Njabala her evening tea.

The girl grew up to be the village's — no, let's say the whole region's — beauty, and of course all in the region took notice. In no time, potential suitors started showing up at the girl's home, asking for her hand in marriage. At first, the mother discouraged them with explanations like "She is still quite young" or lies like "She gets sick often, you cannot manage to have her as a wife," and so on. But she soon ran out of such excuses, and the girl, now approaching 18 years of age, was ready to get married. Eventually the mother agreed to let her daughter go. In no time, Njabala was engaged to an equally handsome man from one of the most famous families in the region; of course Njabala's parents wouldn't have accepted any nobody into Njabala's life. The future in-laws performed all the traditional pre-wedding rituals in style, with a lot of pomp. They brought so much stuff for the introduction ceremony that Njabala's parents could not fit all of it in their house, big as it was, so they called their neighbors to share the bounty. The girl was beside herself with excitement; in a few months, she was going to be the wife of the most sought after bachelor in the region. Needless to say, Njabala was now the envy of all the young women around. But aren't we forgetting something? Njabala had no clue what it meant to be a wife, a homemaker, let alone a famous man's wife, who was expected to be an extraordinary homemaker. Surely it was time for the mother to start teaching her before she ties the knot! But the mother kept on postponing this task. And so Njabala entered into marriage green as a banana! But, what a wedding it was!! The people in the region swore that they had never seen a wedding so lovely! Unfortunately, Njabala's mother died suddenly just a week after Njabala's wedding!!!

Soon after settling into her new home, Njabala discovered the true meaning of marriage, what it really means to be a wife. Unfortunately, she was unable to do anything right: she couldn't cook properly; she couldn't keep her house clean; she couldn't do their laundry, either. Difficult as all these tasks were, they were nowhere near her biggest challenge: cultivation. Ideally, Njabala's husband would have had to take care of the coffee plantation while Njabala tended to the banana plantation and grew vegetables. But Njabala couldn't do her part. Once in the garden, she would hold the hoe in her delicate hands and try to cultivate, but she couldn't. Fearing that her in-laws will soon find out how hopeless she was, Njabala resorted to crying and cursing her now dead mother: "Mother, you did a disservice to me. Why didn't you force me to work? I do not know how to clear the ground and plant vegetables; I cannot look after that huge banana plantation given to me by my mother in-law! I cannot cook; I cannot clean. Why did you bring me up this way, mother? What am I going to do? If you hadn't died, you would have helped me." And she cried some more! To her delight, after having cried so hard for days, the ghost of her mother appeared and started clearing the site for her, digging and leveling the area to be planted. As the ghost did the work, it sang to Njabala:

> *Njabala mwanawange, Njabala tolinsanza omuko, Njabala*
> (Njabala, my child, I do not want my son-in-law to
> catch me here).
> *Abakazi balima bati* (Women cultivate like this) *Njabala*
> *tolinsanza omuko*
> *Nebatema nebawala* (They dig and turn the soil) *Njabala*
> *tolinsanza omuko*
> *Nebanjala nebasiga* (They smooth the soil and plant)
> *Njabala tolinsanza omuko*

Nebasiga ebinyeebwa (They plant nuts) *Njabala tolinsanza
   omuko Njabala*
Nebasiga ebiwande (They plant beans) *Njabala tolinsanza
   omuko Njabala*
Njabala Njabala Njabala tolinsanza omuko Njabala
   (sung twice)

On that first visit, the ghost cleared a huge area and left before she could be seen by the in-laws. When the husband stopped by to thank and encourage his bride, he couldn't believe how hard working she had become! "Wow, Njabala, we are going to be so rich in no time; thank you so much," said the proud husband who, though he had had doubts about his bride's ability to work in the fields, was now convinced that indeed he had a truly beautiful treasure!! The next day, Njabala again called on her mother, and again the ghost did the same, and once again, the husband was delighted. This routine went on for a while! Njabala would wake up eager to go to work in one of her fields or banana plantation where she would call on her mother on arrival, and the ghost would do all the work while Njabala stood around stretching herself, enjoying the sun and all the while listening to her mother's smooth voice singing. But all good things come to an end!

One day, Njabala's husband decided to surprise his wife at work by taking her a cold drink. Since he filled the glass to the brim, he had to tread softy so as not to pour the juice, so he arrived unnoticed by both the ghost and his wife. You can imagine the shock as this man watched his deceased mother-in-law singing, dancing, and cultivating while the good daughter sat around relaxing in the sun! The ghost and the daughter were too caught by surprise, and as soon as they both realized that Njabala's husband had joined them, the ghost fled, and the daughter, who was by now paralyzed with fright, faced her husband alone and in great shame. Since the husband was at a loss for words, he said absolutely nothing, and he headed home in silence but with Njabala in tow. On getting home, the husband packed Njabala's stuff and took her back to her father. He could not imagine a life with a ghost of a mother-in-law doing his wife's work, and all the people in the region also agreed that returning Njabala to her home was the best thing to do.

Njabala lived a very long, lonely, shameful life, and long after she has been gone, her name reminds parents, especially mothers, of their duties towards their daughters. The same name still conjures nightmares for young husbands and instills enough fear in girls to make them eager to learn how to do their chores to avoid Njabala's fate. All we can say is that, thanks to Njabala and her mother, Baganda women make very good wives and extraordinary homemakers!!

Namulindwa

Once upon a time, a man married a good wife, and they made a good home. The woman soon became pregnant, and they both rejoiced; but unfortunately the man died before their baby was born. Now the woman stayed alone, and eventually gave birth to a very beautiful baby girl whom she named Namulindwa (one we've been waiting for). Unfortunately, the mother died when the girl was still an infant, just starting to crawl, so Namulindwa's paternal aunt by the name of Namunono took her in her home and started nurturing her. Namunono took very good care of Namulindwa when she was an infant, and when the child was old enough she taught her how to do chores and to behave well. Namulindwa blossomed into a very beautiful, kind, hard working and polite young lady. But once again tragedy struck, before Namulindwa had come of age. Namunono fell sick suddenly and she was diagnosed with a terminal disease, the very disease that had killed her brother earlier! Namunono knew for sure that she would be dead in less than a month, so she started preparing Namulindwa to take care of herself when she was gone. Namulindwa learned as much as she could from her dying aunt, and she worked tirelessly making sure that her aunt was as comfortable as she could be in her last days on earth.

One evening, Namunono called Namulindwa to her death bed and counseled her thusly: "My dear child, my days are numbered, but if God takes care of you, as I am sure he will, and you reach marriage age, never accept any marriage proposal before seeking my permission." "How will that be possible aunt since you will be dead?" Namulindwa wanted to know. The aunt had saved a very neat looking wooden stick, and she now gave it to Namulindwa with instructions: "Whenever a potential suitor comes to propose, you will ask him to wait in the house while you come to my grave to seek permission. On getting to the grave, you will strike it three times with this stick, and we will have a conversation that will be heard

114

by only you and me! Do not fear; I will be looking after you." Since our ancestors are always around us looking after us, Namulindwa did not question her dying aunt any further; she promised to do as she had been told.

Soon thereafter, Namunono went to join the ancestors and Namulindwa found herself all alone in the house, totally orphaned at such a young age. But since her aunt had brought her up very well and she was very hard working, and polite too, the whole village set out to look after her and to protect her. The more she matured, the more beautiful she became and the harder she worked. Every eligible bachelor started eying her, and eventually suitors started arriving at her house. The first one was the village chief, a young handsome man who had just been installed in that position. Namulindwa was pleased that an important person had shown interest in her, but she remembered her aunt's instructions just in time before giving her consent. "Please, do excuse me while I go to seek permission from my aunt; she told me never to get married before getting her consent," explained Namulindwa. The guests readily obliged her because they knew the significance of such a directive.

Namulindwa went to her aunt's grave with the stick in hand, and she struck the grave with that stick three times as she had been told to do. After the third strike, Namulindwa felt prompted to address her aunt in song, and so she started singing:

Bazze okuntwala Namunono (sung twice) (They've come to take me),
Maama Namulindwa (Mother Namulindwa).

Immediately the aunt responded, also singing:

Ani oyo azze Namunono (sung twice) (Who has come to take you?),
Maama Namulindwa.

And Namulindwa replied:

Omwami w'ekyalo Namunono (sung twice) (The village chief),
Maama Namulindwa.

The aunt's response was short and to the point:

Ogende ogaane Namunono (sung twice) (Go and refuse his proposal),
Maama Namulindwa.

The girl was happy to have communicated with her aunt, but quite sad that she could not get married to that handsome village chief. She went back to the house and gave the potential suitor the news, and the guests left.

The following week another suitor visited Namulindwa; this time it was the village tycoon. After welcoming her guests, Namulindwa informed them of her promise to her aunt, and she headed to her aunt's grave with the stick. On feeling prompted, Namulindwa opened the dialogue in song as she had done previously, and the aunt also did the same, and as before, Namunono told her niece to go and refuse the proposal. Many other suitors came along, including important people like the sub-county chief, the county chief and the prime minister. Imagine! The prime minister!! But each time the aunt gave Namulindwa the same response: *Ogende ogaane Namunono*. Namulindwa was getting more and more frustrated with each visit because the visitors' status improved each time; but each time, the aunt told her to turn them down. She even started worrying: "What if my aunt wants me to die alone, to never marry?" But since she was a good obedient girl, she kept seeking advice from Namunono.

One day, a prince, yes, a real prince, the one next in line to be king, came knocking! Chariots adorned in gold, servants by his side! Oh, my! Namulindwa could not believe her eyes and neither could the villagers! What, a prince coming in person to propose marriage to one of his subjects? They (the royal family) simply send messengers to do the asking on their behalf. But Namulindwa, being the polite, obedient girl she was, as usual told the prince's entourage to wait in the house while she went to seek advice from her aunt. She opened the conversation in the usual manner, singing:

> *Bazze okuntwala Namunono* (sung twice),
> *Maama Namulindwa*

And as usual the aunt replied:

> *Ani oyo azze Namunono* (sung twice),
> *Maama Namulindwa*

And Namulindwa responded:

> *Omulangira wensi Namunono* (sung twice) (The prince),
> *Maama Namulindwa*

To Namulindwa's surprise the aunt said:

Ogende ofumbe Namunono (Go and get married);
 Ogende ozaale Namunono (Go and bear children);
 Ogende osanyuke Namunono (Go and be happy),
 Maama Namulindwa.

Namulindwa thanked her aunt profusely while jumping for joy, and she raced all the way back home, where she immediately accepted the prince's proposal. A very, very, very elaborate wedding was planned, one fitting the prince, of course. The villagers were sure they had never seen such a wonderful wedding and a more beautiful bride! Namulindwa became the people's princess, a very rich, kind, polite people's princess. She had many children and they all grew up happy and strong. Every now and then Namulindwa would return to the village to weed around her aunt's grave and to clean it, but above all, to thank her for having made her wait for the prince. Namulindwa, the prince and their children lived happily thereafter in the palace!

Baganda parents tell this story to their children to stress the importance of patience, a hard work ethic, good manners, politeness and above all, obedience to one's elders, because *eliso lyomukuku awaddugala wewalaba* (There is wisdom in old people's eyes).

The Price of Disobedience

Once upon a time there was a very poor family with four children. Both the father and the mother worked very hard, but they still were very poor. Now, one would have thought that if one works hard, that person would get rich; but that was not the case with this family. Having run out of options to get rich, they decided to get advice from a diviner. "My dear wife, we have been hard working people for a long time, and now we have four children, but no money. If we cannot make money by working hard, maybe, just maybe we can make some through magic," suggested the husband. The following day, they visited a diviner. The diviner assured them that they would make money by following his advice. He gave them two small clay pots he had smeared with medicine and instructed them to put those pots out in the sun every day and to keep them in the house every night. He also warned them to never leave those pots outside whenever it was raining because the rain would wash the medicine off. These pots were irreplaceable once the medicine was off; their magic would be gone, and the diviner never gave more than two such pots to each family. "Is that all we have to do?" inquired the husband doubtingly. "That is all you have to do. Continue working as hard as you have been doing, though; but in addition, remember to put the pots out every morning and to take them in every evening. Also remember to never leave them in the rain. Before long, you will start getting rich. But if you fail to follow my instructions at any time, even your accumulated riches will disappear," stressed the diviner. The couple returned home in jubilation.

Once home, the couple followed the instructions to the letter, and within a few months, they started accumulating wealth. They soon started buying necessities and nice extras they never had before. When they had gathered enough wealth, they also built a better and larger house, and they started living the good life. The parents clearly explained the situation to their children and instructed them to be active participants in taking great care of the pots, especially putting them into the house whenever there was rain. All was going well so long as the family followed the diviner's instructions. One afternoon, the man decided to go for a drink with his friends as he was used to doing; but before leaving, he reminded the wife that the pots were outside in the sun, where they were supposed to be, except at night and when it was raining. After finishing her chores, the wife too decided to pay a visit to her neighborhood friend; but before leaving, she too reminded the children to take care of the pots.

Once both parents were out of the home, the children started playing all over the place, and they had a lot of fun that day. When they were still playing, signs of impending rain appeared, but all four children ignored these signs, and it soon started dripping. The children started telling each other to go out and bring the pots in, but each refused and assigned the responsibility to another. Before they could decide on who was to go bring the pots in, torrential rainfall poured. As soon as it stopped raining, the children rushed outside to check on the pots, but the pots were nowhere to be seen; they had totally disintegrated during the rain. The children, who knew exactly what the loss of those pots meant, waited fearfully for their parents to return home. A short time after it had stopped raining, the mother returned, and as expected, she asked the children if they had taken the pots inside the house during the rain. But we know the children's answer to that. The wife was so scared of the husband. Knowing how furious he was going to be, she decided to pack her stuff and clear the compound before he got home. The children begged her to stay, but she explained that she could not. Deep inside she very well knew that their father would kill her over the loss of those pots, so she left them despite their heart wrenching pleas. As their mother disappeared in the distance, the children started singing a very sad song:

Zamunkoola baganda bange enkoola. Zibadde nsumbi zatikidde ebweeru.
Tunakola tutya maama atwabulira. Tunakola tutya maama zitusanze.
(They were pots from a marsh. They were clay pots that broke outside
    in the rain. What can we do now that our mother is leaving us?
    What can we do now mother except to suffer?)

They sang even louder after their mother had disappeared. When their father got home later that night, he found the children sitting up waiting and crying, and they explained the situation to him. It would be an understatement to say that he was furious; he was so furious that the children had to run out of the house and seek shelter with the neighbors that night. For over a month, the father continued to work as hard as he had been doing with his wife, but he got no results. Money was not coming in; he eventually started bartering their stuff for food, and when there was nothing left to barter, he too decided to abandon the children. Once again the children sang their song as their father disappeared in the distance just as their mother had done:

Zamunkoola baganda bange enkoola. Zibadde nsumbi zatikidde ebweeru.
Tunakola tutya taata atwabulira. Tunakola tutya taata zitusanze.
(They were pots from a marsh. They were clay pots that broke outside
    in the rain. What can we do now that our father is leaving us?
    What can we do now father except to suffer?)

The children stayed alone in utter poverty! A very good story to remind children not to disobey their parents.

The Disappearance of Berry Babies

Once upon a time there was a husband and wife who could not have children. They tried to have children many times, but their efforts were not paying off. One day they decided to visit a diviner for advice. After hearing their story, the diviner sympathized with them and he decided to help them. He gave them four small berry seeds and told the wife to swallow them all on getting home. After nine months, the wife would give birth to four beautiful babies. He then instructed them to never reveal to anyone, and definitely not to those kids, that they were berries. "Is that all we have to do, sir?" inquired the husband hesitatingly. "Basically, that is all," responded the diviner encouragingly.

The couple got home and the wife immediately swallowed the seeds; they then settled down and waited enthusiastically for the arrival of their babies. The pregnancy was trouble free, and after nine months the wife gave birth to four very beautiful girls. You can imagine the excitement! They took their babies home, and they brought them up in total joy. The girls grew up fast and they proved to be a handful in all ways; but no matter how mad the husband and wife got, they heeded the diviner's words not to tell these kids that they were berries. Even when they were old enough to do chores, the parents resisted asking them to help just in case something went wrong and they snapped and told the children that they were berries.

One good sunny day the children, who were now ten years old, decided to fetch water for their mother. They had seen all the village kids fetching water and they could not think of any reason why they were never allowed to go to the springs. Their playmates would get together and go to the springs to fetch water for their parents, and they would have a lot of fun; but whenever these four asked their parents to join the group, the parents would either refuse or tell them to join their friends, but not to get water. The containers for drawing water were clay pots, and these parents treasured theirs very much. That was one of the reasons they did not allow their children to take them to the springs. Anyway, on this day, the four children decided that they were going to take their mother's clay pots and bring her water, just like all the other kids did. When their friends beckoned, the four children picked up four beautiful clay pots and headed to the springs. They played all the way there, and on arrival to the springs, they all filled their pots with water. But when one of the four girls was trying to balance her pot on her head, it slipped and fell and of course shattered into pieces!! "Oh, Oh! For sure mom is going to be very mad, but I will explain how slippery it was at the springs, and she will understand," said the girl whose pot had broken, and they headed home. When they arrived home, the girl explained the situation to the mother and begged her for forgiveness, but the mother would not hear of it. She scolded the girl loudly and the girl started to cry. On seeing their sister crying, one other girl also threw down her clay pot and broke it. The mother was furious, which made the third girl also throw hers down, and so did the fourth. Now the mother was really fuming; her beautiful clay pots were gone, and she did not have any means of replacing them. Before she knew it, she had told the children how useless they were, and how stupid. "I am not surprised, though, that you are this stupid, intentionally breaking my precious pots; after all, you were berries and not children."

The children got every word their mother said, and when she caught her breath and started apologizing to them, the children held each other's hands and started walking away from the home singing:

Maama agambye nti sitwali baana twali ntula
(Mother has said that we were not children, but berries).
Agambye atya? (What did she say?)
Nti sitwali baana twali ntula (That we were not children but berries).

The more the mother apologized, the louder the children sang as they picked up speed. Although she followed them for a while, they at last simply disappeared in the ground just as she was about to catch up with them, and she returned home, once again childless.

Parents are cautioned to weigh what they say to their children, no matter how angry one becomes with one's children! Children are precious and fragile gifts, so they should be handled accordingly.

Friendship Tales

Friends!! We all love to have some, but they have to be handled with care if we want them to be around us for a while. Friendships also require self-sacrifice, and one gets as much out of them as one is willing to put into them. It is also important to keep in mind that if a friendship goes sour, it can produce disastrous consequences.

How Frog Became Man's Best Friend

Once upon a time there was a man by the name of Kitezi who married a wife, and they had one boy. They lived a happy life, but their land was not so productive, so they ate mostly meat for their meals. Since their

121

home was in the vicinity of a thick forest, and the man was a reasonably good hunter, most of the time he would bring home good meat. But one time, there was a drought and most animals left the area; meat became scarce as a result. One day, after having had no meat for several weeks, and no other ample food, either, because the land was scorched, Kitezi asked his son to gather their hunting gear and their hunting dogs and go with him to the scanty bush to hunt.

On getting to the bush, they set their traps as usual and waited, not really expecting anything spectacular, maybe some birds! And if they were really lucky, they might catch a rabbit, but that would be wishful thinking. Anyway, they sat and waited and waited. Suddenly one of the dogs started howling, and the pair rushed to see what was happening. To their delight, they spotted a huge deer trapped in one of their nets. They quickly speared the deer, dragged it to a nice shade and started skinning it and cutting it up for easy carrying back home. As they were skinning the animal, the boy felt really, really hungry and begged the father to roast some of the meat for him before leaving the bush. "And where are we going to get the fire from my dear?" asked Kitezi. "I will go around and look for twigs and I might find fire too, you never know!!" replied the boy. When the boy was some distance off, he spotted a hut and rejoiced, knowing that he was going to find fire in that hut; and for sure he did. But as he was leaving the hut with a fire log, its rightful owner, a huge lion, blocked his exit. "Why are you stealing my fire?" asked the lion. "Sir, I am not 'stealing' your fire; my father and I have just caught a huge deer and we are very hungry so we needed fire to roast some meat to eat before we head home. I was going to bring your log back after making our own fire," explained the frightened little boy. "Did you say you are hungry? Well, now, that makes two of us. Today is definitely my lucky day, because most animals left this area due to the drought, and I haven't had a decent meal in months; little boy, you are going to be my lunch," bubbled the excited lion.

Now the boy was not breathing; he was totally gripped in fear. Suddenly an idea hit him, and what a great idea — surely providence was on his side. "Sir, since I am famished myself, you will not benefit as much if you eat me now. Why don't you come with me to the place where my father is with the meat. On getting there, we will roast the meat, and I will eat my fill, and then you can also eat some meat and me as well; then you will really be full." The lion could not believe its luck. "What a brilliant plan, my dear boy. Well, what are we waiting for? Let's get going." And they headed towards Kitezi with the fire log in the lion's hand. Kitezi spotted the pair from afar, and he immediately knew that he and his son were in trouble, very big trouble. The dogs, too, sniffed danger and they took off. The lion was so happy to see Kitezi and the meat; this definitely was its lucky day. The father begged the lion to spare their lives, but the mighty lion would not hear of it. "Sir, we are very, very poor people. We were very hungry so I told my wife that we will find some meat and take it to her for our dinner; please, do spare us. We will give you half of this deer meat or even all of it if that happens to be your wish," pleaded the helpless, very frightened father. But all fell on deaf ears. "Mr. Kitezi, I want you to roast enough meat to satisfy the three of us now. We will eat the meat, then you will eat your son, and I will eat you, so hurry and start the fire," demanded the excited lion. Kitezi started the fire and when it was ready, he cut up some of the meat and started roasting it, wondering what he was going to do to save first his son and, if possible, himself too.

Before the meat was quite ready, a big frog approached the group, all excited because of the aroma. But more important, he needed company. With the place so dry, he could not find any creatures to spend time with on land. And if he stayed in the now almost dry forest all by himself and his family, they would eventually die. What he needed most now was someone to save his life by giving him water for his family whenever they ran short of it. But on seeing the lion so happy and the two people so miserable, the frog tempered its excitement and demanded to know what was going on. "Mr. Frog, Mr. Lion here is going to eat some roast meat with us, then he wants me to eat my son, after which he will eat me," explained the frightened Kitezi. The frog pushed the trembling Kitezi aside, pumped itself up and started spitting in the lion's face, after which the frog made a modest proposal to the lion. "My friend, I like your plan, but listen, it even gets better. The four of us can eat the meat as soon as it is ready, then Kitezi will eat his son, then you will eat Kitezi, and I will swallow you," suggested the frog. Now you would think that the lion would laugh at the frog for being so ridiculous, but not at this particular menacing looking frog. It was spitting and gaining size all the time. It even jumped on the lion's ears, scratched its head and claimed that after swallowing the lion, it would be ready for its midday nap. The lion, having experienced some of the frog's bites and saliva in its face, decided to abandon the venture. But the frog would not hear of it. It chased the lion, swelling, spitting, and climbing on and off its tail until they were far out of sight. Kitezi and his son hurriedly gathered some pieces of meat and ran home as fast as they could.

On getting back to the spot, the frog looked around for his friends, but they were not anywhere near, so he journeyed to the village to look for them. Eventually he found them, and Kitezi threw the biggest party of the season for his new friend the frog and offered him accommodation on land. "I cannot accept your offer my friend. I have children and even eggs to hatch in the swamp, but even if I had no family back there, I would not have taken residence on land because I cannot survive on dry land for long. Let me go back home, but I will be visiting you whenever I run out of water so that you can replenish my swamp," explained Mr. Frog. Kitezi and all the guests thanked Mr. Frog profusely, agreed to help him as needed, and gave him a hero's send-off. Mr. Frog promised to be back soon, and he kept his promise. You can occasionally see Mr. Frog on land looking for his friend Kitezi whenever he needs him, and the Baganda people do not kill or eat frogs; now you know why!

Mrs. Dog and Mrs. Leopard

Once upon a time, Mrs. Dog and Mrs. Leopard were great, great friends; they did everything together. They also had a lot in common, like absentee husbands, so they shared a residence. One time, they both got pregnant and carried their pregnancies to term. Mrs. Dog was the first one to give birth, and she had twins!! There was great joy in all corners. Two weeks later, Mrs. Leopard also gave birth to twins, and it was double joy. Mrs. Dog's husband and relatives were able to come see the twins, but Mrs. Leopard's in-laws lived far away and they did not get the news. And as for the father — what father? Weeks passed, then a month. At the end of that first month, Mrs. Leopard told Mrs. Dog that she wanted to take the children to be given names and to also see their relatives since they hadn't come to see them. [Among the Baganda, parents must take their newborn babies to the babies' paternal grandfathers, who give them clan names.] Mrs. Dog applauded the idea. "Since you haven't seen these relatives in a while, and your mother-in-law and father-in-law are quite old, you better buy some meat and we'll cook a big meal for them, and we'll take it to them, together, of course, with the kids," suggested Mrs. Dog. "Great idea," assented Mrs. Leopard. "But since I do not have money now, let me work and get some, and we will go when I can afford it," she added. "Just let me know when you are ready," said Mrs. Dog.

A week or so later, Mrs. Leopard told Mrs. Dog that she had gotten the money to buy the meat, and they should go the next day before that money evaporated. Actually, what Mrs. Leopard had gotten was not money but a brilliant idea, or so she thought at the time. The next day, Mrs. Leopard assigned Mrs. Dog the task of fetching water to be used for the cooking, and she said that she would go to get the meat and also gather the food items to be cooked. As soon as Mrs. Dog left for the springs, which was quite a distance off, Mrs. Leopard went into the house, got Mrs. Dog's twins and put them in the pot all ready to be cooked. She covered the pot with banana leaves as is usually done. When Mrs. Dog returned with the water, Mrs. Leopard told her to add water to the already covered pot and start the fire while she went to get the drinks. When Mrs. Leopard was some distance off, Mrs. Dog, who was feeling uneasy but did not know why (call it a mother's instinct), went to check on her babies before adding water to the pot and starting the fire, and sure enough, they were not there!!! She ran back to the kitchen, uncovered the pot and found her twins in there, fortunately still breathing!! She rescued her babies and took them to her relatives with instructions to keep them until she returned. On getting back home, she put Mrs. Leopard's babies in the pot, covered it exactly as Mrs. Leopard had left it, added water and started the fire. She then went into the house and put stones in Mrs. Leopard's babies' crib, and covered them exactly as Mrs. Leopard had left them.

By the time Mrs. Leopard returned with the drinks, the "food" was ready. "Let's go immediately before the food gets cold," suggested Mrs. Dog. And she also added, "Let's not uncover this pot because that will definitely make the food cold, and we might even be tempted to eat some of it." "I totally agree," said Mrs. Leopard, and they got dressed for the journey. Mrs. Dog suggested that it would not be a good idea to wake up Mrs. Leopard's babies when they had a long journey in front of them. "Just lift them up and carry them the way they are! Babies are always cute no matter what they are wearing." "Great thinking, my friend," responded Mrs. Leopard. "Screaming babies can make even a short journey quite long," she added. And Mrs. Leopard, too, had a suggestion: "Since I am carrying the babies and you are carrying the pot of food, we better leave your babies behind; there is no way you can carry them and the pot that far." "I totally agree. Besides, we will be back before the sun sets, and I asked my relatives to check on the babies anyway," added Mrs. Dog.

When the pair was ready, Mrs. Leopard put the secured "babies" on her back and balanced the container of drinks on her head. Mrs. Dog put the very heavy pot on her head for easy carrying, and the journey got under way. The onlookers commented about the size of the pot Mrs. Dog was carrying. "Where are you two heading with such heavy loads?" they inquired. Mrs. Dog explained that Mrs. Leopard was taking her babies to get names and to meet their relatives. The onlookers wished them a good journey, and the pair journeyed on. About halfway, they met still another group. "Where on earth are you two going with such loads?" they too inquired. This time Mrs. Leopard responded foolishly, if you call it that, "I know where I am going and what I am taking. Poor Mrs. Dog here is the one who has no clue as to what she is carrying." "Of course I do have a clue," responded Mrs. Dog, who, as we know, definitely had more than a clue!! Just before arrival, they ran into Mrs. Leopard's sister-in-law, who welcomed them so warmly and asked why they had made such a long journey with heavy loads. Obviously the lousy Mr. Leopard had not even told his relatives that his wife had given birth to twins, and in his defense we can say that he, too, did not know since he hadn't seen his babies either!! "I am bringing the twins I had over a month ago to be given names and to meet you all," explained Mrs. Leopard to her sister-in-law, who got so excited she ran all the way home to alert her parents that "important" visitors were on the way.

By the time the pair arrived at the in-laws' place, the in-laws had already invited their own guests to join them in the celebration; the whole place was full. There was joy everywhere. They helped Mrs. Dog with the pot and also took down the container of drinks from Mrs. Leopard's head, but they did not wake up the "babies" on Mrs. Leopard's back. The hosts greeted their visitors and invited them into the house, but Mrs. Dog, who knew that things would get out of hand sooner rather than later, opted to sit outside on the verandah because supposedly she was so hot from the journey. The real reason was that she needed a quick exit at the first sign of trouble. After all the greetings had been exchanged, Mrs. Leopard suggested that it would be better to eat before waking up and showing off her babies because, for one, the food would get really cold by the time they got through all the twins' rituals that they had to perform to welcome them to the family [the Baganda celebrate the birth of twins pompously and extravagantly]. She also added that Mrs. Dog, who had carried the heavy pot all the way, was really hungry! The hosts agreed and went in the kitchen to unpack the meal brought by the guests.

You can imagine the horror when they saw the twins in the pot!!! The father-in-law ran back into the house, lost for words, but he eventually gasped, "What DID you do?" addressing Mrs. Leopard. "Are you a lunatic, or what? How could you?" Since the father-in-law was out of breath, he just violently pulled Mrs. Leopard by the ear and dragged her into the kitchen. Mrs. Dog did not wait long enough to hear more. In no time she was back on the road, and she ran all the way to the nearest medicine man she knew and asked for help. After explaining her situation, Mrs. Dog pleaded with the medicine man to help her immediately; there was no time to waste. "Mrs. Leopard will find me in no time," she pleaded. The medicine man sympathized with Mrs. Dog but told her that he had no medicine for that kind of situation. "But you are in big trouble, my friend. The leopards are vicious, nasty creatures, and if she ever sees you, she definitely will kill you at the spot and then eat you. I have some advice for you, though; but you will have to listen very carefully and follow my instructions to the letter. Go home and pack your stuff, and find a people's home to live in; the humans will welcome you because you are gentler than you know who, and you are also great with human babies. Make sure that you never, ever get out of the house at night. You can spend all your days outside, but soon as night falls, you must go back inside and stay until morning. There are two possible ways to go outside during the night. One would be taking a walk with the humans. And two, if there is a fence around the house you live in, so long as you stay within that fence." Mrs. Dog nodded that she understood all, but before she was able to leave, there was a furious knock at the door, and guess who? The medicine man hid Mrs. Dog in his attic and went and opened the door for his new arrival. The breathless Mrs. Leopard explained her situation to the medicine man, leaving out the part where she had put Mrs. Dog's children in the pot. "My in-laws beat me and threw me out of their house; they swore to kill me next time they see me, so I have to stay in hiding from them, because

I know they meant what they said. They did not give me any chance to explain the whole story. Please help me to find Mrs. Dog. I want to kill her and eat her; she will pay for this," panted Mrs. Leopard. "I sympathize with you, my friend," responded the medicine man, "but I have no medicine for that kind of adventure. I can give you some practical advice, though, if you want to hear it." Mrs. Leopard made herself comfortable. And the medicine man started giving her advice in a clear loud voice intended to alert Mrs. Dog in the attic to the advice coming up: "I want to give you and your descendants this advice, and I want all those ABOVE as well as those below to listen carefully. Are you ready?" "Totally ready, my friend," responded Mrs. Leopard.

"You know how meek and fearful Mrs. Dog can be, don't you?" continued the medicine man. "I know that," responded Mrs. Leopard. "Because of her nature, Mrs. Dog is going to seek shelter in people's homes. If you want to catch her, never go there during the day because she definitely will be in hiding, and the people might kill you. Wait until night and go around people's houses; you definitely will catch her then patrolling those people's homes." Mrs. Leopard thanked the medicine man and left immediately. But since it was still daytime, she went into hiding. A little while later, Mrs. Dog exited the attic after thanking the medicine man profusely, and since it was still daylight, she went and retrieved her babies and headed to the nearest village, where she found refuge with a very good family.

For years, Mrs. Dog lived happily in the village, spending her days outside with her children, hunting, feasting and truly enjoying life. She would sleep every night either in her own house or in the people's house; she never ventured outside after dark. Mrs. Leopard, on the other hand, spent sleepless nights patrolling the villages, looking for Mrs. Dog but with no success. One day during the rainy season special ants, which Mrs. Dog loved so much but had not had in ages, appeared at night in the neighborhood, and they were everywhere. People opened their doors and windows to see the sight, so many "delicious" ants. Mrs. Dog salivated all over the house and all over her children as humans watched delightfully both the ants and Mrs. Dog's show. She tried so hard to contain her greed, but it got the best of her and she slowly ventured out in the night. Before she had eaten even a handful of ants, guess who saw her. And the chase was on. But since Mrs. Dog could not outrun Mrs. Leopard, she (Mrs.

Leopard) soon caught up with her, trampled her to death and ate her for dinner that night. Mrs. Dog's children watched the whole scene, and they swore revenge for the death of their mother. Mrs. Leopard's descendants also swore to continue the fight on her behalf. Since then, whenever one sees the other, there sure has to be trouble, often ending in the death of one of the two or both; they truly hate each other.

If a Muganda person describes a relationship between two people or parties as *bali kabwa nango* (they are like dog and leopard), you automatically know that there is no love lost between those two; you also understand that actually they are a danger to each other!

The Adventures of Eagle and Chicken

Once upon a time, Eagle and Chicken were great friends. They did a lot together whenever they met, which was frequent, but of the two Chicken was the brainy one; Eagle, though physically stronger than Chicken, was more spacey, and at times he could be downright stupid! This situation worked out very well for both, though, and it was one reason why they were such great friends. Chicken was Eagle's brain, and Eagle protected Chicken whenever such protection was needed. Now, in their village there happened to be only one market, so both of them used to shop there, but for different items because they had radically different food tastes.

One day, Chicken checked his pantry and discovered that he had no salt to make his midday meal, so he went shopping in the heat. He bought one pound of salt and headed back, but the journey was a bit long, and the sun was so hot, so he decided to seek shelter in the shade and rest while it cooled down. When he sat down, he folded one of his legs in his wings, and only one leg remained out. While Chicken was resting in this position, Eagle also decided to go to the market for sugar, and he found his friend in the shade resting. After examining his friend's posture, Eagle asked Chicken in an alarmed voice, "Where is your other leg, my friend?" Chicken immediately thought of playing a trick on Eagle and responded jovially, "I gave it to the shopkeeper in the market because he loves chicken, and he gave me this salt in return; in other words, I paid for the salt with my leg, and I will grow one to replace it in no time. You too can get that good deal."

Eagle, who was running low on cash, was happy to hear that he could get stuff from the shop using his leg as payment. And he was even happier thinking that he, like his resting friend, would not be affected that much because he would grow a replacement leg in no time. So he hurried to his destination. Once in the shop, he explained to the shopkeeper that he wanted to buy five pounds of sugar and that he was going to pay for them with his leg. "Just chop off one of them," said Eagle confidently. The shopkeeper was startled. *What a stupid proposition*, he thought to himself, *but maybe Eagle is not serious*. "Are you sure, Mr. Eagle, that you want me to chop off your leg in exchange for five pounds of sugar?" asked the shopkeeper. "Very sure, my friend," replied Eagle. So the shopkeeper chopped off Eagle's leg and helped to bandage him. Eagle started hopping back home with his five pounds of sugar, but he was feeling so much pain. "Oh, well, I will ask Chicken to tell me the secret of not feeling pain once I get home," he assured himself. The more he hopped, the greater the pain grew, so he tried to hurry.

As he was nearing Chicken's home in great pain, Eagle spotted Chicken walking on his two legs. "What is going on here? Hello, you had only one leg when I last saw you and you advised me to exchange mine for goods from the market, just as you had done. And you said it was painless. Now I am dying of pain and you are walking on both your legs. Am I missing something?" Chicken, clever as he was, had no immediate response for his suffering friend. He had not prepared any, and this situation took him by total surprise. "Any fool would have known I was kidding, even Eagle," mumbled Chicken to himself. Since Eagle was by now in very bad shape, hurting so badly and groaning loudly, the confused and very scared Chicken simply took off as fast as he could, leaving Eagle furious and in great pain.

Eagle lived with pain for quite a while, but he eventually got better. As soon as Eagle started feeling better, he made a very elaborate plan which he hoped would put an end to Chicken and his antics. "He will have to pay dearly for his mischief," grunted the still very furious Eagle. Eagle made looking for Chicken his mission, and he was determined not to rest until he had accomplished that mission. Every day he would start early in hopes of catching the culprit. But on spotting Eagle, Chicken would take off running, and the two would keep at it with Eagle circling Chicken until Eagle would give up, totally exhausted. Being a good runner, Chicken was able to elude his captor for a while; but one day, Chicken's luck ran out. This time Eagle spotted Chicken resting in a shade of a huge tree, and he approached his victim slowly and quietly. By the time Chicken realized he was in trouble, it was too late; Eagle grabbed Chicken from the side and squeezed him. After chiding his former friend and forcing him to apologize, Eagle ate Chicken and declared that he had solved the problem once and for all. But Eagle eating Chicken that time did not settle the score. Up to this day, there is no friendship between the offspring of those two. Whenever any of Eagle's descendants sees any of Chicken's, he circles him until Chicken gets away or is caught and eaten.

Squirrel and Snake

Once upon a time, Snake and Squirrel were great friends; they did almost everything together. One day, Snake informed Squirrel that he had been invited to visit his in-laws, and that he needed his best friend, Squirrel, to accompany him. Squirrel was quite excited about this visit; he had heard that Snake's relatives were generous hosts and great cooks too. Early on the promised day, Squirrel put on his best garments and waited for his friend to come knocking. Snake arrived shortly, and the journey got under way. On arriving at Snake's in-laws' residence, the pair was given a very, very warm welcome. Squirrel felt sure that all he had heard about Snake's in-laws was true: they were generous hosts and great cooks. It was soon lunchtime. Since Squirrel had not eaten any breakfast, due to excitement, he was quite happy to hear such news. As soon as several very delicious dishes were put in front of the guests, Snake informed Squirrel that he had to "sit" properly while eating so as not to insult their hosts. "Sure, my friend, I had no intention of sitting badly," responded the hungry, eager-to-eat Squirrel, not knowing that sitting properly for Snake and his relatives meant lying flat on one's stomach. In no time Snake was sitting properly (lying flat on his stomach), and he instructed Squirrel to do the same, but Squirrel had never performed this task before, and the more he tried to do it, the harder it became for him. Snake informed Squirrel that he was going to start eating because he was quite hungry, and that Squirrel could join him as soon as he sat properly!!!. Since there was no way Squirrel would ever "sit" properly, he eventually gave up trying and resorted to watching Snake eat all the food.

When the relatives came for the dishes, Snake thanked them profusely for a great feast and made fun of the fact that Squirrel had eaten nothing because he could not sit properly. They all had fun at Squirrel's expense: "How on earth can such a grown-up squirrel fail to sit properly?" they jeered. By evening, the visit was over, and the two "friends" returned to their homes. Squirrel had been a perfect gentleman through it all; he did not show any anger even though he was literally dying of both hunger and anger. He patiently waited for his turn for revenge on Snake; in the meantime, their relationship continued undisturbed.

The Baganda have a proverb that can be translated as "If one is waiting for something one really likes, days fly." It was soon Squirrel's turn to take revenge on Snake. "My dear friend, my in-laws have given me an invitation to their house, and I would love it if you please can accompany me," cordially announced Squirrel to Snake. "Of course I will accompany you, and unlike you, my friend, I will sit properly come mealtime. When do we go?" "On the seventh day of this coming week," responded Squirrel without showing that he was taking more offense with Snake's uncalled-for sitting properly joke. Seven days later, the two friends embarked on their second journey, this time to Squirrel's in-laws. As soon as the guests arrived, the hosts brought out appetizing munchies, but before they could eat, they had to sit properly in an upright position and stay that way throughout mealtime, something impossible for Snake to do. "Come on, my friend, you can sit up. You cannot eat sleeping on your belly or side; it is absolutely bad manners, and it will offend our hosts," instructed Squirrel. The harder Snake tried to sit up, the more difficult the task became; in the meantime, Squirrel kept busy eating. Delicious dishes followed munchies, and once again Snake tried to sit up and eat, but to no avail. Squirrel had his fill, and when the hosts came for the dishes, Squirrel thanked them profusely for such a delicious feast and apologized for his friend who failed to sit up and eat. "How can a grown-up snake fail to sit properly and eat?" jeered Squirrel's relatives while Snake puffed up angrily. Snake did not wait to return home with his now ex-friend.

That basically was the end of the beautiful relationship that had existed between Snake and Squirrel. Whenever Snake sees Squirrel, he reaches to bite him and Squirrel always takes off in time to escape the vicious bite.

Crested Crane and Fox

The Squirrel and Snake tale as told above comes in several versions starring various pairs of physically different creatures performing various activities. But all these stories point out two basic lessons: do unto others as you would like them to do unto you, and always be aware of and respect differences among people, especially those natural differences that no one is responsible for or can change even if one wanted to. Here is a shortened version of another one of these stories.

Once upon a time there was a great friendship between Crested Crane and Fox, but it came to an untimely end. One day Crested Crane invited his friend Fox to accompany him to his birthplace for a big family reunion, and Fox agreed. The two friends embarked on their journey quite early because they had a distance to travel and on foot. By the time the two friends arrived at Crested Crane's home, Crested Crane's relatives had already arrived, and they had been waiting on this pair to arrive so that they could eat. The cooks served the delicious food immediately and they invited all the guests to gather in one room to eat. As soon as all the guests were properly seated, the master of ceremonies gave a brief speech and asked the guests to start eating. They all settled down and were soon eating and conversing merrily with the exception of our dear friend Mr. Fox. Although Fox tried very hard to eat the delicious food in front of him, he could not; it had been served in beakers for the convenience of the crested cranes, of course. Poor Fox, whose mouth was not pointed, could not reach into the beakers, but none of those around him paid any attention to him and his problem. About halfway through the meal, one crested crane, at long last, realized that Fox was not eating and wanted to know why. "My good friends," started Fox, now addressing all of those around him, "my mouth cannot reach into these beakers; therefore, I cannot get any food from them. Can you please put some of this food in a more fox friendly container?" "Is that a joke?" jeered one of the cranes in response. The whole group burst into uncontrollable laughter, including Fox's best friend. Fox kept his cool through it all until the party was over. On the way back to their homes, the two friends conversed as if nothing had happened, and that was because Fox too had a counterplan already in place.

A few months later, Fox returned the favor by inviting Crested Crane to his birthday celebration. Crested Crane groomed himself for the occasion and arrived in time to see the celebrations start. Once all the foxes were in place, the cooks started passing around delicacies, and the guests started enjoying themselves, with the exception of Crested Crane, of course. The foxes had their food served on flat platters, and even though Crested Crane tried so hard to eat from these platters, he could not. Unlike Fox, Crested Crane did not keep his opinion to himself. "Will one of you for heaven's sake bring me something to eat in a beaker?" demanded the now furious Crested Crane. When the response from the serving foxes was "Sorry, but we do not serve our food in beakers," Crested Crane stormed out of the party vowing to never be friends with Fox again: "After all, you are very ugly." Those were Crested Crane's parting words to Fox, who barely heard them because he was having too much fun.

Man and His Best Friend

Once upon a time there was a poor man who lived alone with his dog. The pair looked out for each other and they had a great relationship, but although they had tried hard to get rich, they had not yet succeeded in doing so. One day, when they were really hungry and had absolutely nothing good to eat all around them, the dog came up with a brilliant idea. "Why don't we go to one of the rich folks in the village and offer our services to him? We can, for example, tell him that I will sweep his compound if he gives us something to eat, like a goat," proposed the dog. The man was very excited to hear the dog's proposal; after all, no one had ever heard of a chore-doing dog anywhere in that village!! What a concept!!

The next day, the man and his friend got up hungry as usual, and sat around still hungry as usual. Their plan was to visit a certain rich folk in the afternoon, when villagers are likely to be home after a day's work, and offer their services as agreed on the previous day. Around 2:00 P.M., the pair set out on their journey. When they arrived at their destination, they found the owner of the home seated outside under the shade of a giant tree in his compound. The dog meandered off as dogs are known to do in such circumstances. The owner greeted the human visitor warmly, and they soon started conversing about various subjects, ending with a curious bet from the visitor. The man told the home owner that his dog could help sweep the whole compound since the family seemed so busy. "Are you joking? Who has ever seen a dog doing chores?" chuckled the amused home owner. But the man was serious, and he suggested to the home owner that if his dog swept that compound, the home owner would give the man one of his goats. "Now that will be pure entertainment," replied the home owner, who immediately agreed to the bet. The man called out to his dog, and to the surprise of the family gathered for the entertainment, the dog came singing and dancing:

Mbwa, mbwa (dog, dog). Chorus also sung by the dog: *bayita mbwa mukama wange* (You are calling me, my master). *Mbadde siriwo* (I was not here), chorus. *Ngenze okuyigga* (gone hunting). Chorus. *Nsanze akamyu* (found a rabbit). Chorus. *Kankutte nkalese* (caught it and brought it). Chorus.

The more laughter from the crowd, which by now was quite large, the louder the dog sang and the more the dog danced. "And what a wonder," murmured all those present. "Tell you what," said the home owner to the dog owner, "since your dog has entertained us so much, it does not even need to sweep. I give you one of my goats to thank you for the wonder." The dog owner thanked the home owner, and the pair returned to their home with their prize, the goat.

On getting to the home, the man thanked his dog profusely, and he then called all his friends to join him in celebration. They slaughtered the goat, cleaned the meat, spiced and roasted all of it, and had a great feast. And guess what the dog was given to eat that day: bones, just bones, not even one piece of meat!! The dog ate the bones and life went on as before.

A week later, the man found himself in the same dire situation with nothing good to eat. He approached the dog with a proposal to go to another village and entertain them as they had done a week before. The dog obliged and the journey got under way. On getting to their destination, the dog went its merry way, and the man started conversing with a rich home owner just as he had done a week before in his own village. The home owner talked about his long days in his various fields and how exhausted his family members always were by the time they got home in the evening. The conversation once again ended with the dog owner making a bet with the home owner. "My dog can help your family by sweeping your large compound; that way, your family members can concentrate on their other money generating chores and get their deserved rest at the end of the day." "Either you are joking to make me feel less tired, or this is the most stupid suggestion I have ever heard," replied the home owner. "I am quite serious my friend," responded the dog owner. "And if my dog sweeps your compound, will you give me one of your cows as payment?" added the dog owner. Wanting to get the comedy over, the home owner agreed to the bet. The man called out to his dog the same way he had done a week before, and once again, to the surprise of the homeowner's family gathered for the bet, the dog came singing and dancing:

Mbwa, mbwa (dog, dog). Chorus also sung by the dog: bayita mbwa mukama wange (You are calling me, my master). Mbadde siriwo (I was not here), chorus. Ngenze okuyigga (gone hunting). Chorus. Nsanze akamese (found a mouse). Chorus. Kankutte nkalese (caught it and brought it). Chorus.

And again, the louder and larger the crowd got, the more entertaining the dog became. When it was all over, the amazed homeowner gave the dog owner the cow without asking the dog to do the sweeping, adding that they had had enough entertainment to last them for a while, and a marvelous story to narrate, to whomever wanted to listen, for the rest of their lives. Again the dog owner thanked the home owner, and he headed back home with both the dog and the cow in tow.

As soon as they got home, the man repeated the previous week's activities. He gathered his friends, and as before they slaughtered the cow and cleaned the meat. Since this was a lot of meat, they spiced all of it, but only roasted some for the day, and dried the remaining pieces and kept them for future consumption. And, again, guess what dog got to eat? You got it: bones, just bones, not even one piece of meat. The dog had the pleasure of watching his master and friends partying day after day and only leaving him bones, until the cow meat was all gone. Two or so weeks later, the man approached the dog to do the routine, and once again the dog obliged, and once again the dog was given bare bones. This went on for a while, and the man became rich; he even started having his own goats and cows because he had gathered so many in the process, but whenever he slaughtered one of those animals, he simply feasted with his friends, giving dog only bare bones.

As often happens with people getting unexpected riches, the more animals the man got, the more he needed, and guess who the faithful friend who kept on helping him to acquire all these riches was? But at no time did the man change his behavior towards this friend. One day, the man and his friend set out on their usual mission, but by this time, the dog had had it with his uncaring friend. On reaching their destination, the dog went for a walk, as usual, and the man engaged a group of men in his usual conversation, this time asking each one to donate whatever each had, chickens included. The men agreed, but then they wanted to know what else they could do to the man for wasting their time, besides just withdrawing their offers, if the dog did not perform as promised. By this time, the man had become overly confident about the dog's performance, and a bit arrogant as well, so he bet his own life. "If my dog does not perform as I have promised, you can stone me to death," pledged the over-confident dog owner. The crowd agreed, and the man started calling his dog as usual, but this time the dog did not come immediately! The man called even louder, but there was no sign of the dog. The longer and louder the man called, the more desperate he became, but still there was no sign of his dog. After an hour or so of the man calling, the crowd got restless and stoned the man to death as had been agreed upon. No sooner had the man breathed his last than his dog waltzed in singing and dancing:

> *Mbwa, mbwa* (dog, dog). Chorus also sung by the dog: *bayita mbwa mukama wange* (You are calling me, my master). *Mbadde siriwo* (I was not here), chorus. *Ngenze okuyigga* (gone hunting). Chorus. *Nsanze akanyonyi* (found a bird). Chorus. *Kankutte nkalese* (caught it and brought it). Chorus.

The crowd froze in place speechless, but the dog owner was dead, so they thanked the dog, and since it was a wonder dog, they told it to return to wherever it had come from and begin a new life with whomever was going to be its new owner.

Yes, dog is indeed man's best friend, but only when man reciprocates the love!

Tales of Husbands and Wives

Relationships come in many forms, each with its own unique characteristics; but probably it will not be far-fetched to say that the husband-wife relationship is the most amazing of them all. Think about it: two people meet and get to know each other. Somewhere along the way they decide to get married, and when they do, they become one person — one person in two, that is. These are two unique individuals not in any way biologically related to each other, from different backgrounds, with different upbringings, different lifestyles, different genders, different habits, and the list goes on. These two people promise to become one. In some ways, they are expected to be a salad, complementing each other for that special flavor but retaining some of their individual attributes. After all, differences supposedly attract, and it may have been their individual attributes that attracted them to each other in the first place. On the other hand, they are expected to be a very smooth pudding, totally synchronous, especially in decision making for the good of their families. Little wonder then that this relationship yields many stories in all cultures, some amusing, some tragic. But most of these stories are great learning experiences, often highlighting crucial differences between the two genders. Baganda women, much like women in most African societies, are known for their ingenuity, especially in hard situations. Here are a few Baganda stories that, in most cases, attest to the women's ability to solve their families' problems.

A Dangerous Host

Once upon a time there was a very happy couple blessed with two pairs of twins. They owned several acres of land, and they lived their own version of a good life until hunger spread in the region due to a drought. Most people who had relatives in faraway places left the area, but our happy family had nowhere to go. Every day they would search for food from all around them, and they would find wild fruits like berries and hunger-calming roots to chew on, but they soon exhausted all those. After going hungry for a while, the wife decided that they too should leave; maybe, just maybe, they might find a place that might have some more of those fruits and roots. One day, they gathered what they were able to carry and headed eastward, having heard that there might be some food in that direction!

After traveling for about a month, living on whatever fruits and roots they were able to find, their sights revealed to them what they had only been dreaming about: a very beautiful village with numerous very well kept banana plantations, each plantation full of both ripe and green bananas! They screamed, sang, danced, called each other's names, and simply shouted to make sure that they were not dreaming!! How could this be? How come there were not numerous people here? What was going on here? How come they had made so much noise and no one had come to see who they were? They called in all directions but got no answer. Might this place be the answer to their prayers? Having agreed among themselves that their ancestors might have smiled on them, they gathered plenty of ripe bananas and eventually sat down in one of the peaceful banana plantations to enjoy their meal. They ate as much as they wanted and decided to nap before continuing to thoroughly explore this very generous gift from their ancestors! But as they were going around the village, they found many empty houses, all looking abandoned and in a hurry. The more of these houses they saw, the less jubilant they became, and instead of proceeding noisily and joyously as they had started to do, their mood became somber, and they put on their thinking caps and proceeded quietly and apprehensively.

By the time it started getting dark, they had almost completed their exploration; and because they had filled up on ripe bananas, what they needed now was not food but a place to spend the night. And once again, their ancestors came through, or so they thought. At the edge of the village they found a very neat well kept house that automatically claimed their attention. They approached the house cautiously and called all around for the owner, but they got no response. After thoroughly examining the house and concluding that it too, like all the others they had seen, had no owner on the premises, they decided to make themselves at home, at least for the night. Because they were thoroughly exhausted, they all fell soundly asleep as soon as the wife finalized sleeping arrangements.

Now we all know that if something sounds too good to be true, chances are it is not true, and this situation was no exception to that rule. Around midnight, the owner of the house returned home. Since the village had been empty for over a year, he was able to ascertain from a distance that he had company, and he too, like his guests, proceeded cautiously. On entering the house quietly, he noticed not one but six people sleeping on the floor in the front room!! Were his eyes playing him a trick? Were these really people? Now guess who thought that his ancestors had at long last remembered him! For over a year now, this gorilla had not had any decent meat to eat. Obviously, the bananas were in plenty, and he had kept the village in a very good shape, so he definitely was not hungry. But he needed real meat, and it seemed like he was about to have some, plenty actually for one gorilla. He coughed gently to wake up his guests.

The husband was the first to wake up, and what a sight he saw, a very big gorilla smiling down at them. Just as the man was about to scream, the wife too woke up. On seeing the happy gorilla, she immediately grabbed the frozen-with-fright husband and put her hand over his mouth; she did not want the children to get up and be equally frightened! The gracious host welcomed his guests and narrated the village's story to them. Incidentally he had eaten most of the villagers, except a few who had escaped just in time, and that was over a year ago. Oh, how happy he was to see some more people he was going to eat! But since they looked exhausted, he was going to be hospitable and allow them to have a very good night's sleep; people taste better when they are rested anyway, and he too was too tired to wrestle with them. Having spent over a year without decent meat, he wanted his meal to be enjoyable, so he advised them to continue sleeping. He promised not to disturb them during the night, but to make sure that they were going to be around come morning, he was going to secure and guard the door all night. That night, three individuals did not sleep. The gorilla was too excited to sleep, and in any case, he did not want his guests to escape; the wife kept calm, thinking of plans to escape; the husband was too frightened to be of any help, but he too could not sleep, for obvious reasons.

When morning finally came, and before the children woke up, the gorilla explained his plan to the husband and wife, who were totally awake. Since he had not had any meat in such a long time, the gorilla wanted to make sure that he got ultimate satisfaction; so instead of eating them all at once, he politely requested the husband to kill one member of his family every day for the next five days, beginning with the youngest twin. He assigned the wife the task of cooking whoever was killed every day for him to eat that day. The gorilla then told the husband that he was to kill and cook himself on the sixth day — do not ask me how!! The frightened husband started wetting himself, but the wife soothed him, and she told the gorilla that all would be done according to his wishes. After hearing the good news, the gorilla told them that he was going to run an errand somewhere in the village, and that on coming back, he needed to have his dinner ready. He instructed them to cook and eat so that they would be good tasty meat by the time he finished eating all of them; as of now, they looked haggard and quite unappetizing, even for a gorilla that hadn't had any meat in over a year!! After gathering his stuff, the gorilla secured the high fence around his compound and went merrily on his way. "What are we going to do?" wailed the husband. "This is the end of us; we were surviving with hunger, only to end up in a gorilla's stomach. What are we going to do?" The wife had figured out something. There was a huge heavy tree in the middle of the gorilla's compound; she was going to send her kids up that tree one a day, but she did not explain it to the husband because he was too frightened to pay attention. Instead she went and searched the area around the fence for squirrels, wild rabbits, and any birds. To her delight, she found many of those creatures and she returned home ready to implement her plan. By the time the children woke up, the plan was in place, but then guess who was sleeping — the husband!!

On that first day, the wife secured about five small birds, cleaned them, marinated the meat and cooked a delicious meat dish for the gorilla; she fed the youngest twin, called *Kato*, and hoisted him up the tree with instructions not to move or make any noise when Gorilla was home. [Among the Baganda, a mother of twins is called *Nnalongo* and a father *Ssalongo*. If the firstborn twin is a girl, she is named *Babirye*, and if she is followed with a boy, he is named *Kato*. If a boy comes out first, he is named *Wasswa*, and if followed with a girl she is named *Nakato*. The family in this story had *Ssalongo*, *Nnalongo*, *Wasswa*, *Nakato*, *Babirye* and *Kato*, so *Kato* was sent up the tree first.] When Gorilla got home that evening, *Kato* was nowhere to be seen but there was a delicious meat dish so it ate to its satisfaction. "You've done very well, *Nnalongo*," grunted Gorilla. "*Kato* was so delicious — but small. I am looking forward to feasting on *Babirye* tomorrow; she is a plump girl, so she should be more meat and she might have some more fat, too." The gorilla wished them a good night, and once again it slept by the door, just in case the guests got any ideas!! Since *Ssalongo* had been restless through all the first night, he had slept a good part of the day and by the time he woke up, the sun was about to set, and *Nnalongo* had already prepared the dish and sent *Kato* up the tree just in time for Gorilla's arrival. The couple then could not engage in any lengthy conversation in the presence of Gorilla, but when *Ssalongo* asked *Nnalongo* what had happened to *Kato*, *Nnalongo* assured him that *Kato* was safe, for now, and that was the end of that conversation.

Day two went as smoothly as day one, but it was actually happier than day one because the plan was working very well, and *Kato* was able to come down, play and eat. Unfortunately for *Ssalongo*, as he would find out later, he never took the time to ask *Nnalongo* the details of the plan; he was just happy that a load had been lifted off his shoulders, at least for a while, so he spent his days roaming the village while *Nnalongo* executed the plan. On day two, though, *Nnalongo* cooked more birds and made sure that they were bigger than the ones she had cooked the previous day, to convince Gorilla that it was eating the plump *Babirye*. After feeding both *Kato* and *Babirye*, she sent them up the tree, and once again, she warned the two to be quiet when Gorilla was home. Once again Gorilla ate to its satisfaction, and it once again praised *Nnalongo* for being a great cook. Day three Gorilla went to work; *Ssalongo* went to roam around the village; both kids came down; *Nnalongo* cooked squirrels that were bigger than the birds she had cooked the last two days, fed the children, sent *Kato, Babirye and Nakato* up the tree; *Ssalongo* came home late; Gorilla arrived almost at the same time as *Ssalongo*; Gorilla ate its food and enjoyed it; *Ssalongo* did not ask any questions; and all went to bed happy. Day four went more or less the same as day three, and Nnalongo sent *Kato, Babirye, Nakato* and *Wasswa* up the tree. Day five started out exactly like day four and continued the same way until it was time for *Nnalongo* to cook herself, which she did, of course!! After cooking herself, *Nnalongo* ate with her kids and they went up the tree just in time for Gorilla's arrival home.

When Gorilla got home on day five, it found that *Nnalongo* had cooked herself in the form of a very juicy rabbit; it ate delightedly. Just as Gorilla was finishing his meal, *Ssalongo* returned only to realize that it was only him and Gorilla!! "Well, now, my friend, you've done very well, but all the same I must eat you too, so tomorrow, you must cook yourself for my dinner. I've really enjoyed getting to know your family, and I thank you for having stopped by. So long, my good friend. It will be quite lonely again, but worthy it," and with that said, Gorilla took his usual post by the door, and wished *Ssalongo* a good last night in its house. That night, *Ssalongo* did not sleep, of course. What was he going to do? Remember he had spent his days sightseeing, and he had totally neglected to ask *Nnalongo* the details of the plan!

Very early on day six, Gorilla reminded *Ssalongo* of what he had to do, and it left as was its usual routine. As soon as Gorilla was out of the compound, *Ssalongo* started crying. What was he going to do? He gathered firewood, made a big fire, boiled a huge pot of water and put in his left hand, which, as expected, was scorched in the water. He rapidly withdrew it in great pain. He cried more and then tried cooking the right hand, but he got exactly the same results. His left foot did not fare any better, of course. He also tried cooking the right foot and once again he got exactly the same results. With burned hands and feet all hurting badly, *Ssalongo* decided that it was time to give up trying to cook himself and simply wait for Gorilla to kill him and cook him. But the more he imagined his end at the hands of Gorilla, the more scared he became, so he tried to cook himself again so that he would not suffer that slow agonizing death he imagined would be inflicted on him by Gorilla. As he sat in the shade of the huge tree in the compound in agony, thinking of ways to cook himself, he cried and sang loudly, not expecting anyone to hear him, of course:

> *Maama Nnalongo, wefumba otya, nange nefumbe*
> (Mother *Nnalongo*, tell me how you cooked yourself
>   so that I can cook myself too).

He sang the agonizing song several times, still sitting under the huge tree. Eventually *Nnalongo* and the kids heard him, and *Nnalongo* called to him. At first he thought he was dreaming, but, realizing that he was fully awake and in great pain, he stretched his head and tried to catch *Nnalongo's* voice. Imagine his delight when he realized that he was not dreaming, that *Nnalongo* was for sure calling his name from up that tree. "How did you get up there? Where are the kids?" asked *Ssalongo* now in disbelief. "Please, do help me get up there," pleaded *Ssalongo*. *Nnalongo* and the kids came down from the tree, and *Nnalongo* fully explained the whole plan to *Ssalongo*, who repeatedly interrupted her with thanks and praises. *Nnalongo* asked *Ssalongo* and the boys to go and hunt for two or more huge rabbits while she peeled the bananas. As soon as *Ssalongo* and the boys had the rabbits they needed, they brought them to *Nnalongo* who, as had been her routine, cleaned the meat, marinated it, and prepared a great meat dish for Gorilla — and her family. The family ate as much as they could since they had no idea of how they were going to survive undetected up in the tree. They would have thought of coming down and preparing meals for themselves, but then Gorilla would wonder about the fire, pots, and so on. So after filling themselves with food, they gathered some ripe bananas and went up the tree, but not before they had thought of ways to help *Ssalongo*, who was so heavy, to climb the tree. How were they going to accomplish that feat? Once again *Nnalongo* came to the rescue; she proposed making a very strong rope. Using that rope, the five people were able to pull *Ssalongo* up the tree. Now all six were together, but not comfortable since they knew that their stay up that tree was temporary, and of course dangerous. What next?

Later in the evening of day six, Gorilla returned home as had been its routine, very hungry and ready for its meal. To its delight the meal was in place, and as usual, it ate to its satisfaction. After eating, it slept soundly for the first time in six days since it had spent those nights guarding its meat!! The next day, Gorilla woke up late, all refreshed and quite happy about the week's events. It decided to take the day off work to revel in its comfort, since all would soon sound like it had been a dream! Around midday, Gorilla sat in the shade of the huge tree to feel the breeze, and it soon fell asleep. Since Gorilla's guests had eaten so much, and the kids had already started eating the ripe bananas, they started feeling uncomfortable with stomach pains. Actually, the youngest kid developed diarrhea, and of course wanted to use the bathroom big time. Where was *Kato* going to relieve himself? He soon started crying, silently, of course, but the tears did not solve his problem. Long and hard as they thought, they could not come up with any viable solutions, so *Nnalongo* told *Kato* to simply go ahead and relieve himself, which the boy did immediately.

Remember who was sitting under the tree? As soon as the boy started relieving himself, warm, wet, smelly stuff starting falling on Gorilla's stomach since Gorilla was sleeping on its back. At first Gorilla thought it was the usual birds' droppings, but the more this stuff fell on its stomach the stranger it all seemed; birds cannot let out so much stuff, and definitely not that much warm, wet, smelly stuff! Eventually Gorilla looked up the tree, and imagine its delight on seeing the familiar faces!! At first it was very angry, of course. "Can you explain what you people were feeding me?" boomed the very angry Gorilla up the tree. "Never mind that; it was done and whatever you fed me did not kill me. Now I have a better plan for eating the real you. I am going to cut down this tree and of course you will all die on hitting the ground, and I will have all the meat I was supposed to have had in the first place," said the now excited Gorilla. *Ssalongo* started trembling, but *Nnalongo* held him tight and conversed calmly with Gorilla. "I have a better idea, sir," said *Nnalongo*. "If you cut down this tree and we fall, we will all be in pieces, and then you will not have good meat. So here is my idea. We have a very strong rope we used to get *Ssalongo* up the tree; I am going to throw it down to you, and we will pull you up the tree, as we did *Ssalongo*, so that you can eat us whole, one by one, instead of eating dirty little pieces," suggested *Nnalongo*. Gorilla welcomed the suggestion, and *Nnalongo* threw down the rope. She instructed Gorilla to tie the rope around its waist and signal them to start pulling it up as soon as it was secured with the rope. In no time, Gorilla had firmly tied the rope around its waist, and it was ready to go. When *Nnalongo* got the signal, she asked the family members to start pulling Gorilla up the tree as they had done with *Ssalongo*, but *Ssalongo*, who had momentarily regained his voice, objected furiously. "Woman, are you out of your mind? How can you offer to help Gorilla come up to eat us?" "Well, my dear, do you have a better idea?" responded *Nnalongo*; but of course *Ssalongo* had no suggestions to make. "Please do pull up Gorilla; the sooner we do this the better," instructed *Nnalongo*, and the pulling got under way. When Gorilla was halfway up the tree, *Nnalongo* asked the family to pause pulling because she needed to rest, but she suggested that they rest first while she held onto the rope, and that she would rest after them. The family gladly relinquished the rope to *Nnalongo*, and after making sure that she had the rope to herself, she simply let it go! Gorilla hit the ground with a thud, gave one loud cry, and was no more!!!

The family came down and lived happily thereafter in their dream village delivered to them by their ancestors, thanks to *Nnalongo*'s ingenuity, courage and dignity under pressure.

The Millet-Making Bird

Once upon a time a prolonged drought devastated a village that had been very fertile and prosperous, and hunger spread throughout the area. For months, people struggled to stay alive, but many perished in the process, and those who could move moved to faraway lands in search of food and water. Almost all moved out except one family of six, consisting of two parents and four children, who had to remain in the area because they had absolutely nowhere to go. And so they continued the struggle to stay alive, but with no hope of ever overcoming their enemy, hunger.

Every morning, each family member would set out with a basket to look for traces of food in all directions. At the end of the day, they would return home tired and truly beaten up, but with no food in their baskets! They would then face another long, sleepless, uncomfortable night, not sure that they would all be alive come morning. One day, as the mother was out there searching for things to eat, basket in hand, she saw a very beautiful little bird perched on a tree that had lost all its leaves. The bird surprised the woman when it called her by name to go under the tree and receive a very important message it had brought for her, but since she had nothing to lose by doing as the bird had said, she went to the location. The bird asked her to put her basket on her head and stand still under the tree just below it, and once again, she did as she was told. "Close your eyes, but hold on to your basket," ordered the bird. The bird spread out its wings and millet poured out of those wings into the basket. So much millet was pouring out that in no time, the basket was full. "Go and make a meal for your family," said the bird. "Use as much millet as you want to satisfy your people's hunger, and return tomorrow for more, but do not tell anybody about me, not even your husband. If you ever tell anyone, I will disappear, and that will be the end of your getting millet from me," stressed the bird. "Thank you so much. I will keep all a secret, and I will see you tomorrow," replied the totally amazed but very grateful woman. "I will be here," said the bird and then it disappeared. On arriving at home, the woman hurriedly prepared the meal and waited for her famished family members to return home.

You can imagine how delighted they were to eat a "meal" to their satisfaction. "Where did you get this fine millet flour from?" inquired the husband. "You do not need to know," casually responded the wife, but the man was not satisfied with her response. He, however, stopped asking when he realized that no reply was forthcoming, and he was glad to go to bed on a full stomach for the first time in months. The next day, the woman returned to the promised venue, and once again, the bird gave her millet, and the next day, and the next day, and the next day, for at least one month. But the husband was becoming very uneasy! *Where is she getting all this fine millet from when we are surrounded with emptiness and devastation?* he wondered to himself.

One day, the husband decided to secretly follow his wife to see for himself where she was getting the millet. When the wife picked up the basket and started walking, the husband too started following — from a distance, of course. Incidentally, it was not a long walk, maybe 20 minutes maximum. As usual, the woman found the bird there waiting for her. And as usual, it spread its wings, and millet started flowing into the basket. The man could not believe his eyes; a millet-giving bird — what a treasure!! He slowly moved nearer and nearer until he was within earshot. Then he shouted at the woman: "What a stupid woman you are. Here is such a treasure, and you did not even think of capturing this little bird and bringing it home so that we will eat whenever we feel like?" Not only did the man shout, he also attempted to capture the little bird, which, as expected, had already flown to the next tree, high up in the branches. "My dear lady, you took an oath of secrecy. We made a contract; I was going to give you your daily ration and all you had to do is protect my privacy. Was that too much to ask? Here you are putting my life in danger! Goodbye, my dear lady." And the bird disappeared, never to return. The poor woman did not even get a chance to apologize. The next day, the woman returned to the spot, and the next and the next, but there was no bird to be seen! Hunger continued to ravage the family and they died one at a time until no one was left.

The Pumpkin Patch

(This story is a variation of "The Millet-Making Bird" above.)

Once upon a time there was a family of five living happily in a good arable area. They took advantage of their good fortune and used the land to the best of their ability; they were very productive subsistence farmers growing a variety of food crops for their needs. But one year, they experienced an extensive drought, and they were not able to plant all the crops they used to tend to all year. Slowly their food supplies diminished, and month by month they hoped for rain but got none. They soon exhausted all their food supplies, and they started spending whole days with nothing to eat or drink. Instead of spending long days in the fields, they would roam all over simply looking for something to eat.

One day, as the wife was searching for food, she came across a pumpkin patch surrounded by scrawny trees and dotted with very many ready to harvest pumpkins. She stood there speechless because she had already been to this area a number of times, and she had not seen that pumpkin patch there before. It was a totally uncared for patch, covered with tree branches all over it and thorns as well from the very dry thorny bushes surrounding it. Was it for real? Could she take some of the pumpkins for her starving family? What if they were poisonous pumpkins? Were they witches' pumpkins? Where had this pumpkin patch come from? All kinds of questions went through the wife's mind as she stood there transfixed and staring blankly at the patch. She was trying to leave, but her feet were not moving!

After an hour or so of inactivity on the spot, the wife heard a gentle voice inviting her to take as many pumpkins as she needed to feed her family. The voice informed her that the pumpkin patch was a gift to her for her and her family's long years of dedication to the land, and that so long as she did not try to clear the area, the pumpkin patch would remain healthy, producing as many pumpkins as she needed to feed her family until the drought was over. And one more thing, she was not supposed to tell anyone about this patch. Having agreed to the conditions, the woman collected as many pumpkins as she could carry and headed home to make the meal. The family was delighted, more so the husband, who had exhausted almost all his options for keeping his family alive through this cruel drought, but he really wanted to know where the wife had gotten the pumpkins. "That is going to be my secret," responded the wife, and she thought that she had put a lid on her husband's curiosity.

Every day, the wife would steal herself from her home and go to the pumpkin patch to fetch pumpkins for her family, and each time, the patch looked new, like nobody had picked any pumpkins from it the previous day. The woman was so thankful. Unfortunately, though, each day that went by, the husband became more and more curious. What was really going on? How could anyone give his wife so much food for free every single day? Was his wife really human? The more questions gathered into the husband's head, the more determined he became to find answers. One day, he announced that he was going to the fields as usual, and that he was not likely to return before sunset. This gave the wife more than enough time to go to the pumpkin patch and return unseen by her husband, or so she thought. Instead of going to the fields, however, the husband hid along the route he had seen his wife take whenever she went to get pumpkins, and this time he managed to follow her undetected all the way to the patch.

As usual, the wife collected the pumpkins she needed and headed home. As soon as the wife was out of the way, the husband explored the area and he couldn't believe what his eyes were seeing — an uncared for pumpkin laden patch! "Surely my wife is not serious. How can she not take great care of such a treasure?" murmured the husband to himself. He, however, returned home and said nothing to his wife. A week or so later, the husband gathered his farming tools and headed to the patch, without saying anything to his wife. He cleared the area and he returned home in high spirits, all the time asking himself why women were so careless, especially in an important situation like that one. On getting home, the now exhausted husband asked the wife for something to eat, and after filling up on pumpkins, he asked his wife to sit down for a serious conversation. "Can you explain to me why on earth you did not bother to clean up the life giving pumpkin patch?" demanded the husband. "Please, do not say that you have spent the day cultivating around that place," pleaded the wife. "Of course, I have," responded the husband smugly. "Thank God I discovered that patch when I did, and that I have more sense than you, and definitely better judgment. How can you explain your carelessness?" On hearing what her husband had done, the wife gave out a loud cry and ran to the place to see if the pumpkin patch was still there. Of course, it was not, and neither were there any pumpkins! That was the end of this family's good fortune!

Tales of Beauty

Beauty! Supposedly in the eye of the beholder! Whatever form beauty takes, and however elusive the term is, every person knows what it is when one comes across it. It is universally renowned, loved, and sought after, but it should also be dealt with cautiously, because in addition to being a blessing, it can also be a curse or outright treacherous, as we often find out.

Beauty and the Hunchback

Once upon a time, a man married a beautiful wife and they had three beautiful girls. The girls grew up to be the envy of all parents, both for their behavior and for their beauty; but the middle one was the most beautiful, and they all knew it. When it was time for potential husbands to start calling, the first and last girls accepted their marriage proposals with no hassles, and the parents married them off in style. But things were not so easy for the middle beauty. Since she was so beautiful and very well brought up, both her and her parents expected her to get married to an exceptional person! No, it was not just looks they were looking for; many very handsome young men put in their bids and they were turned down. Were the parents looking for a man from near their home? Probably not, because potential husbands came from near and far, and somehow they all fell short of expectations. Was it riches? That too was not a satisfactory answer. What about fame? Not really. And if we put together riches and fame, will that be a winning combination? Probably not, because princes called from all over, and they were turned down.

So, how was Beauty supposed to pick a suitable husband? Well, we throw in some magic and entertainment. The parents went to a diviner and got seeds for an extraordinary, small, gourd-bearing tree, which they planted promptly in their front yard. In less than a year, the tree was covered with small gourds all over its branches. But they were quite hard to pick, which was no problem because the parents had a plan for this tree and its gorgeous gourds. The suitable candidate for Beauty would have to pick all the small gourds from the tree in no more than twelve hours!! Sounds quite simple, right? In no time, potential husbands started coming in big numbers. And whenever one turned up, Beauty, whose name was Namirembe, would sit on a very beautiful goatskin mat in the shade of the tree and watch her suitor sweat it out while singing a song devised by her parents:

Namirembe noge kano? (Namirembe, do I pick this one?), and she
would respond, singing sweetly: *noga kali akali ewala* (Pick the
one farther away from that).

The singing was supposed to energize them since Namirembe's voice was so soothing; but to most suitors, it seemed like the gourds they would painstakingly pick would return to the tree. They would work for hours on end with no success until time was up. Rich suitors hired the most powerful men they could find to do the picking for them, but they all failed. Princes sent their guards for the task but to no avail.

One day, a hunchback approached the family and asked for a chance to compete for Beauty. He was readily granted permission, with much laughing and jeering, of course, from all present. Able-bodied individuals had failed to accomplish the task; was there a possibility of a hunchback doing what all now thought undoable? The hunchback requested to start picking the gourds early in the morning, so Namirembe, her parents, her two sisters and their husbands, and all the other onlookers woke up quite early and positioned themselves for a day of fun!! The hunchback was hard at work by 7:00 A.M. He, of course, knew the song, as did all by now, but his voice was scratchy and horrible as he proceeded:

> *Namirembe noge kano?* Beauty replied sweetly as usual: *noga kali akali ewala.*

Energized by Namirembe's sweet singing, the hunchback picked up speed and worked tirelessly. To the surprise of all present, the hunchback's gourds did not seem as if they were returning to the tree. By midday, all watchers were starting to get worried. Beauty, of course, was the most horrified. The hunchback's singing became sweeter as he made progress while Namirembe's voice cracked and she eventually broke into tears. The more progress the hunchback made, the more tearful Namirembe became. By 5:00 P.M., the now very happy hunchback had finished picking all the gourds!! And guess who was jeering and having fun now! The parents handed Beauty to the hunchback, and the couple set out to start their married life.

Now, one would like to think that the Baganda no longer make fun of those different from themselves or underestimate people because of differences, but unfortunately they still do, just like all of us! But every now and then, a Muganda person remembers "Beauty and the Hunchback," and tones down the jeering and underestimating of those different in appearance!!

Lukulwase

Once upon a time there was a happily married man by the name of Lukulwase; well, at least onlookers thought that he was a happy man! The couple lived in a huge house anchored on fine wooden poles; it was also supported with strengthening poles inside, one in each corner and a couple in the center. But these poles were more than house holding objects; the couple would split one for firewood whenever it was raining outside and the wife couldn't get firewood from the forest. As soon as the rain would clear, Lukulwase would go to the forest and replace the pole they had used as firewood.

One day, Lukulwase went to the forest to replace one of his poles as he customarily did. This time, though, not only did he find one beautiful pole, he also found another very beautiful pole, and a great surprise: a very, very beautiful woman was standing in between the two poles. The man was smitten by the beauty of this creature! He walked cautiously around her, examining her every feature and making unbelieving sounds as he did the examination. Eventually he gathered up courage and greeted the woman, who immediately responded to the greeting with a very warm smile. The man almost fainted. Gathering courage one more time, he proposed to the woman, who explained that she would have liked to become his wife, but she had one great difficulty — she had only one breast. There was no way she was going to get married to him when she had only one breast, so she made a tantalizing suggestion: she would accept Lukulwase's offer if he found a second breast for her. You may not want to believe this, but this hypnotized man ran all the way to his home, called out his wife, chopped off one of her breasts, and ran all the way back to the forest with it to give it to the forest beauty! And what do you think he found at the spot where he had seen the forest beauty? NO ONE!!! The mystery woman had disappeared, of course. The no longer hypnotized but now totally shocked, frozen idiot fell on the ground, bloody breast in hand, and passed out. He was soon discovered by the angry mob wanting revenge! Let me leave you here to conclude the story yourself.

The Baganda have a proverb coined from this story: *Amagezi amatono — gakubuza eka nemukibira,* literally translated as "Little intelligence does make one homeless." That idiot was not able to live at home, assuming he survived the mob, nor would he survive in the forest.

Beauty and the Gorillas

Once upon a time there was a man who married a beautiful woman. They were blessed with three beautiful children, all girls. When it was soon time for the oldest girl to get married, suitors flocked in from all corners.

152

But the girl found fault with each and every one: too short, too tall, a bit heavy, so tiny, bad teeth, and on and on. The parents, too, knowing that they had the most beautiful girl in the region, set their own standards based on riches. The potential suitor had to be so rich and must give them plenty of gifts! The girl, too, consented! "I am so beautiful," she used to say. "My husband will have to be very rich in addition to good looks." So many potential suitors were exasperated by these people and their demands. Most just gave up trying!

But one day, three very handsome looking gentlemen came knocking. Not only were these men handsome, they were also rich, from the look of their attire and the princely looking carriages they had come in: three people, three carriages, each one loaded with pricy gifts just as the girl's parents had wanted. You can imagine the excitement! The guests introduced themselves as brothers, and said that, as they were looking for a bride for their youngest one, they got news of the most beautiful girl in the region ready for suitors. They also knew that the chosen suitor had to be exceptionally handsome and very rich. They had scrutinized their own attributes, and they were sure that they had a chance. "Of course you have a chance," interrupted the girl's father just as the oldest brother was preparing to conclude the introduction. "We accept," continued the father. The guests thanked the parents, and for over an hour they kept busy unloading gifts from their carriages. When the carriages were empty, the guests handed the father a huge bundle of cowries as well. A quick but elaborate meal was prepared for the guests, who thanked their hosts profusely for it because they had a very long journey in front of them, so they said. After the meal, the guests prepared to leave, and when they were asked to set the wedding date, they explained that since they had come from very far, it would be more convenient to take their bride with them. [Traditionally, the acceptance of the suitor's gifts by the girl's parents signified those parents' approval of the marriage, and marked the beginning of the marriage rituals, culminating in a wedding. But the suitor also had the option to take his bride with him if the parents consented.] The parents consented, and the girl was dressed in the most expensive *busuuti* that she had been given by her aunt to wear as she welcomed potential suitors. The guests adorned her with expensive jewelry and sandals, and it was soon time to say good-bye. The parents bid their daughter farewell and wished her a long, prosperous life; they also cautioned the brothers to handle her carefully because she was precious, and the wedding party got on the road.

Soon after getting out of sight, the brothers picked up speed and moved their carriages frantically, telling their bride that they had a very, very long journey in front of them. She sat contentedly in her now husband's carriage, and they kept moving. By nightfall they were still going, just stopping briefly here and there to catch their breaths and to make nature calls. "I have plenty of time to get to know my husband, so I better sleep," thought the girl, and she soon fell asleep. When morning came, they were still on the road. The second day went just like the first, and on day three, the girl started worrying! "When will we get home?" she sheepishly asked her husband. "Soon, my dear," was his reply, and he moved on. Nighttime of day four, they veered off the clear path and started going along on a very dusty one, not a good sign. *Wealthy people should have great well kept paths leading to their homes, but oh, well, I will soon see the castle*, thought the girl. Before she knew it, they were now traveling through a thick forest, no path was visible, just roughing it in the wilderness! *What a way to get to a castle*, she thought to herself. When they arrived at a clearing in the middle of the forest and the carriages stopped, the carriage drivers — Remember them? The most handsome trio ever known? — they immediately turned into gorillas!!! And they were joined by other more menacing gorillas, all excited to have fresh meat! The excited creatures dragged the very much fear stricken girl out of the carriage, making fun of her: "Here we are, your majesty, one who refused to get married to poor, ugly men because you are so beautiful! You wanted riches and status in exchange for your beauty, didn't you? Well, now, the only way people get riches is if they work for them, and so you are about to start working; we've already paid for you." The gorillas taunted the girl for a while, and after having their fun, they ate her!!! Of course these gorillas were not about to report this poor girl's demise to her parents.

Back at the girl's home, no sooner had the wedding party departed than the now very rich parents started making preparations for their daughter's visit the following week. [According to Baganda custom, the bride spends her first week being pampered by her in-laws; she is fed and even bathed; all she has to do that week is get to know her new home, a home she did not get to see until the wedding day! After one week, the bride is given her own cooking utensils by her mother-in-law, and she is shown her own kitchen. Now she is ready to cook her husband's first meal, so she returns to her parents and gets all the foodstuff, such as bananas, potatoes, and yams, and meats, chicken, fish, vegetables and seasonings, she will need to prepare her husband's first meal.] You can imagine how busy the now rich parents got buying all that stuff for their daughter! They made sure that they bought the best, freshest food items to be spiced just right so as to implant in their new son-in-law, hopefully, a permanent impression of their daughter as the best cook the man had ever known!

Now that their daughter had been married for a week, the parents had everything ready for the joyous reunion! They looked forward to hearing all about their prosperous in-laws and their daughter's impressions of them and of her new home. [The guests normally arrive in the morning so as to make it back in time for the bride to prepare her meal; she can take one or two of her sisters to help her with this very important task.] And so the parents waited, and they waited, and they waited!!! Noon came, then afternoon, then evening, and eventually nighttime!!! "Where is our precious daughter? What happened? Oh, where are they?" The parents did not sleep that night; they stayed up waiting, just in case!! By morning, they were falling to pieces: "What happened, oh, what happened?" Day two came and went; day three came and went; a week came and went; a month came and went. At first hope replaced joy; then apprehension replaced hope; fear replaced apprehension; panic replaced fear. And poor parents — since they had no clue where their daughter had been taken, they simply searched all over the region, blindly, of course, and with no success. Nobody anywhere the search party went had ever heard of, let alone ever seen those three very handsome looking brothers; nobody had any idea of who they were or where they had come from. The search went on for days, weeks, months, up to a year!! Eventually the grieved parents accepted their reality; their daughter was never going to come home, so they held a funeral service, without her body!!!

The Baganda people claim that this girl's disappearance prompted them to add a procedure to the courting rituals. The groom-to-be cannot take his bride home on his first visit. The prospective husband must first introduce himself on the first visit, and then if he is accepted, he returns for a second visit. He can make anywhere up to five visits before he sets a wedding date. During the meantime, the girl's relatives make a thorough background check on their prospective son-in-law, and if they get satisfied that he is indeed who he claims to be, then he can set the wedding date. He must also provide transport for his in-laws and their guests to accompany the bride to her new home on the wedding day!

Tales of Poverty

Poverty is scary, and because of that most will spare no effort when it comes to fighting it. However, people are always cautioned to fight poverty cautiously because, as one of the proverbs states, riches are like dew: they come and they go. Selling one's soul to simply get rich may end up devastating that individual. Here are some tales to ponder along those lines.

The Woman Who Wanted to Get Rich

Once upon a time there was a rich man who married two wives. Both wives gave birth, but only to baby girls; every time each wife had a baby, it was a girl. The man loved the children, but he needed a son to take over his estate. [The Baganda people are patrilineal; the family lines run through men.] One day, he called his wives for a consultation concerning the inheritance issue, but all three could not think of any viable solutions. The man then made a proposal to his wives. "I will give my fattest cow and some other riches to whoever of you will have a baby boy to take over my estate." The wives continued having baby girls, though. But one time, one of the wives got pregnant with twins. Of course, nobody could tell that she was expecting twins, not even her, but all knew she was pregnant. One time when the pregnant woman had gone to fetch firewood from the valley not far from her home, she went into labor and had no choice but to deliver her own baby: actually, it was not one baby; there were two babies, a boy and a girl. The woman was overwhelmed with joy, not because she had given birth to two very beautiful babies, but because she had produced a baby boy, which meant that she was going to get rich as promised by her husband. Since her mind was so focused on getting rich, she did not stop to think that there might be a possibility that her husband would be overjoyed with both babies. So she cleaned the baby girl and hid her in a thicket in the valley so as to return home with just the baby boy.

When she got home with her baby boy, her husband was not around but the co-wife and the children were outside doing various chores, and they congratulated her heartily. Later on the husband too returned home, and on getting the news, he threw a huge party with relatives and friends, and rewarded the mother of the boy as he had promised to do. The now very rich woman lived happily, with no worries whatsoever, not even thinking about her baby girl in the thicket. In her own mind, leaving that girl behind was worth it! Fortunately for the baby, there were cattle herders who used to tend their animals in the valley where the woman had left her. Soon after the poor baby had been left in the thicket, one of the cattle herders found her and took her to his home. Cattle herders are nomadic people, mostly living in valleys and ever moving with their cattle in search of fresh pastures and water, so they are not often part of whatever village they happen to be near at any one time. This time, though, since a huge party had been thrown in honor of a mother of a baby boy in the nearby village, and all the people around had heard the story of how the man had promised riches to whichever wife would give him a baby boy, the cattle herder was able to connect the dots. Despite his suspicions, though, he did not approach the father of the baby girl; instead, he took great care of her, feeding her milk, which he had in plenty, and the baby eventually gained strength.

The girl grew up with the cattle herder, moving from valley to valley but in the same area, and she became a real beauty. One time, when the cattle herder and his family were again in the valley where the girl was born, that girl's brother came to get milk from the cattle herder and he saw a very beautiful age mate. He immediately fell in love with the girl, and on getting home, he informed his parents that he had seen the girl of his dreams. The parents of course brushed him off since he was at that age when every girl such a boy sees seems to be the one. But the boy insisted on hanging around the cattle herder's daughter. When the cattle herder saw that this relationship was getting serious, he sat down his daughter and told her the whole story, so the girl started withdrawing from the boy. When the boy saw that the girl was avoiding him, he thought that she needed a proposal from him, so one day he gathered courage and asked her to marry him. Instead of responding to the proposal, the girl started singing to the boy in a very sweet voice:

Oh Wasswa ngolimba Wasswa (Oh, *Wasswa* you are kidding).
Baatuzaala babiri ng'abalongo Wasswa (We were born like twins).
Maama nandeeka mukisalu Wasswa (Mother left me in the thicket).
Ngagoberera ente ya ssebo Wasswa (Going after my father's cow).

The girl repeated this song a number of times while the boy listened intently. When she finished singing, she simply ran back into the cattle herder's compound. The boy ran home and told his father the whole story. The story sounded credible so the father paid the cow herder a visit, and he was informed accordingly. The cow herder, though, apologized that since he did not have any hard evidence, he had decided to keep his suspicions to himself so as not to shatter a family simply based on suspicions. But now, he did not want these young people to get married to each other just in case they turned out to be brother and sister. The man thanked the cow herder profusely and went to investigate, starting with quizzing his rich wife, of course. The wife verified the story, upon which the man withdrew all his riches from her and threw her out of his home. Another huge party was thrown to reunite the twins.

Sure, riches are desirable, but one should not have to go to such extremes to get them!

Lukomera

Once upon a time, a man by the name of Lukomera married a very beautiful woman by the name of Lulina Amattire, and their marriage was blessed with a very beautiful daughter. It was a peaceful, very happy family — oh well, as happy as any family with no resources can be. Lukomera and Lulina Amattire were both very hard working people, but they were very, very poor. They were so poor that they could not even afford decent clothes to wear and go out of their house as a family; they had only one decent cow-skin wrapper which they used to wrap around themselves in turns when going out. Otherwise they dressed in rags at home. Every morning Lukomera would wrap the cow skin around himself and go out to work in the fields. On getting tired he would return home and his wife would wear the cow skin and take her turn working in the fields, after which she would gather the food for both lunch and supper from the fields and return home around lunchtime. Then it would be their daughter's turn to venture outside. Sometimes she would visit her friends and they would do chores together like fetching water from the well and gathering firewood, after which they would play, plait their hair, share stories and so on. Then she would return home before sunset so that her father could go out in the evenings and spend time with his friends as is the custom. Whenever a family member was out, the other two had to stay in dressed in their respective rags! Poor as this family was, they lived decently with their neighbors, without envying anyone or doing harm to the rich folks around them.

The daughter grew up fast and she was even more beautiful than her mother had been as a young adult. One day, a rich, handsome young man who had seen her several times in the afternoons called and asked for her hand in marriage. After consulting with their daughter and checking the young man out thoroughly, the parents consented to the marriage. Imagine what an experience it was for the girl to arrive in a family where each member had individual clothing. She was given her own wardrobe; her husband adored her, and since the in-laws also loved her a lot, she was quite happy in her marriage. She soon got pregnant and, like her mother, had a very beautiful baby girl. But the grandparents could not come to see the baby, at least not together, and we know why, so the daughter decided to take the baby to them. Since the daughter's in-laws were very rich and they loved her very much, they put together an elaborate package of gifts for the parents, including clothes! The baby was dressed lavishly and adorned with cowries. During those days, cowries were in great demand because they were the currency for buying stuff and paying for services. You can imagine the daughter's parents had never had any spare cowries around the house, definitely not those they could use as adornments. When the daughter and her baby arrived at the home, the parents were indeed very happy to see them, and what a beautiful grandchild!

That evening, an idea hit Lukomera — as the Baganda people say, in order to achieve in life you have to use the head God gave you! And what an idea — it was simple — why not take the granddaughter's cowries to a diviner and get advice on how to become rich? The daughter consented, and in no time Lukomera had arrived at the diviner's house. "And what brings you to my house this evening?" asked the diviner. "You know what I am looking for my friend," replied Lukomera. The diviner posed some questions to determine the identity and intellectual capacity of his guest, whether indeed Lukomera was capable of implementing the suggestions he was about to make to him.

QUESTION ONE: "Lukomera, there was chaos in your house not so long ago; what was it all about?"

RESPONSE: "Beans were accidentally poured all over the floor of the living room, and we had to tiptoe until they had all been cleared out of the room."

QUESTION TWO: "Who is the *dead person* you keep in one of the corners of your bedroom?"

RESPONSE: "That is a leftover part of a banana tree that my wife intends to use someday."

QUESTION THREE: "Why did you and your wife make that terrible noise last week and run out of your house?"

RESPONSE: "Fire ants had invaded our house."

The diviner, having ascertained the identity and capability of his guest, understood the reason for his visit and proceeded to give him the information that was meant to solve his problem. The diviner handed Lukomera a spear and shield and said, "Take this spear and shield with you home; do not talk to anybody on the way, and when you get home, do not talk to anyone. Go to bed immediately in the nude. When the first cock crows, get out of bed and do not dress; grab the spear and shield and run out of the house without talking to anybody, not even to your wife and daughter. Just keep running, no looking back, until you run out of breath. If you follow my instructions to the letter, you will run out of breath in the doorway of a house full of respectable people you have never seen; if you have been a good, decent person, you will know what to do from there on!"

Lukomera returned home that evening with the spear and shield, and did exactly as he had been told to do by the diviner. His wife and daughter tried to make conversation with him, but with no success — mum was the word. Lukomera slept very uneasily until he heard the first cock crowing. He grabbed the spear and shield and he was soon on his way, naked. He kept running until he felt that he could run no more; he then stopped and to his surprise there was a house just in front of him, door wide open. Lukomera approached the house and peeped inside. It was full of respectable looking gentlemen who became very nervous on seeing the naked Lukomera standing in the doorway, because they had just carried out a successful heist and they were busy dividing their loot among themselves. They begged Lukomera not to report them, and they requested him to take as many animals as he wanted to from their herds: cows, sheep, chickens, pigs, and so on. Lukomera was spellbound, totally speechless. When he did not respond immediately, the men got even more nervous, thinking that he had rejected their offer, so they sweetened it with slaves, clothes, cowries, any riches you can think of! Still Lukomera was overwhelmed, but remember he was naked and it was about to be daybreak, so he took some of the clothes and put them on. Then the men gave him slaves to help him carry his riches and they begged him to leave immediately; time was of the essence. Before he could say anything, the house and men disappeared — just disappeared, and Lukomera remained standing in the middle of nowhere with slaves, animals, and much more.

Lukomera returned to his home a very rich man and lived happily thereafter!

Now, this is a good, clean way to get rich. There are also some morals to be learned from this story, including the value of patience; Lukomera was patient, and eventually he got his day in the sun. And Lukomera had lived a decent life, always happy and willing to help his neighbors, no crimes against others, no grudge against rich people, and so on. The Baganda people believe that if you live as decently as Lukomera did despite his poverty, you get your just reward sooner or later! Lukomera got what he deserved!! There is also another proverb demonstrated in this story: "*Lubaale mbeera — nganembiro kwotadde*" ("God helps those who are willing to help themselves," like Lukomera making the first move by seeking out the diviner and following instructions to the letter).

Hare Tales

Probably it is fair to say that very few collections of folktales would be complete without hare tales, that survivor, ever ingenious, at times annoying, but an often lovable small creature.

Hare and Fish

Once upon a time Hare and Fish were great friends. Fish lived in the nearby lake and Hare lived in the village near that lake. Every day, both would meet at the shore and they would spend ample time swapping stories.

One day, Fish's mother fell sick and she was terribly ill for days, so eventually they took her to their doctor, who examined her and told them that she needed another heart to live. They all started thinking of ways to get hold of that heart immediately; the doctor made their task slightly easier by suggesting to them that any heart from any living creature would do. Immediately Fish thought of his friend Hare, who, according to the stupid Fish, had at one time told him that he could live without a heart. "I have the candidate. Give me just several hours," declared Fish, who immediately readied himself and headed to the shore. As soon as Hare appeared, Fish gave him an invitation to visit his family in the water. "My friend, you know very well that I cannot swim, so there is no way I am going to accept your invitation," explained Hare. "Oh, I have a plan for that," replied Fish. "I will carry you on my back all the way there and back. Please do come," insisted Fish. Hare was apprehensive, but after numerous pleas from his friend, he agreed to go on Fish's back.

In no time, the journey was under way, and the two friends kept chatting away, especially through heavy waves so as to keep Hare calm. When they were halfway through the journey, at a spot that Hare could not escape from, Fish explained his mission. "My friend, we really need your help. My mother is on her deathbed; unless she gets a new heart immediately, she will soon die. I thought about you as a very good candidate because you once told me that you can live without a heart; and so soon as we arrive, we are going to take you to the doctor, who will harvest your heart and put it in my mother." You can imagine the expression on Hare's face, but they were in the middle of a gigantic lake, so Hare could not run away; but he also knew that there was no way he was going to survive without a heart. Hare's quick and critical thinking came in handy. "I am so sorry, my friend, about your mother. Of course I am willing to help; but, you see, I keep my heart in my house in the village; I never move with such a precious item. If you had told me before when we were still on the shore, I would have gone to the house and brought it with me. But no need to waste time discussing that; simply swim back quickly and I will go and get the heart for you." Fish was so happy that he had such a great friend, and in no time they were at the shore. Once Hare had cleared the shore and was safely in the village, he called out to Fish. "What a stupid creature you are. Have you ever seen a living creature with no heart? Can anyone keep one's heart in a house? God has saved my life, and now let's part to never see each other, because the next time I or my descendants see you or your descendants, we will kill you."

That was the end of the beautiful relationship that had been developed between Fish and Hare. The Baganda people use this tale to caution against taking advantage of friends. But more importantly, they stress the value of quick, critical thinking; it saved Hare from imminent death.

Hare Saves the People

Once upon a time, Leopard and Hare were great friends. They had made a great home for themselves in a little village of subsistence farmers. Most of the time the pair lived in harmony with their neighbors, as each group took care of its own business without intruding on the other. That is, until edible ants appeared in the village during rainy seasons! In preparation for the edible ants season, the people would clear their respective anthills, all located in the valley below the village, dig trenches around them to trap the ants, and light and hold fires above the trenches to direct the edible ants into the trenches. Preparing for the edible ants season was always a lot of work for all who enjoyed eating them, except for Leopard. Leopard's strategy was simple; all he had to do was turn up in the area at the right time and wait for the edible ants to appear. As soon as the ants would start coming out of the anthills, Leopard would leap from anthill to anthill and eat his fill. This, as expected, did not sit very well with the owners of those anthills, who were always unable to compete with Leopard in collecting these ants.

One day, the people convened a meeting and decided that they had had enough of Leopard leaping where he did not sow when it came to collecting edible ants. They agreed to approach Leopard's friend, Hare, and ask for advice and help the next season. Hare was very delighted and honored to be approached by the people asking for his advice and help. After listening to the people's story, Hare agreed to help them as long as they promised to give him two large baskets of those ants for his work. The people eagerly accepted Hare's proposal and they went about preparing for the edible ants season in their usual way. Hare, too, now had work to do, but being Hare, it would not take him long to find a solution.

On the first day of the edible ants season, it rained in the morning as was expected, and dried out in the afternoon under a moderate sunshine as was expected. The people were joyful; this was the ideal weather condition for the edible ants to appear in plenty soon after sunset. Of course Leopard, too, was jubilant, waiting as usual to eat more ants than any of his neighbors. Hare, on the other hand, was pensive, thinking of ways to save the people from Leopard so as to get his share of the ants as promised. "I've got it," jumped Hare in excitement as evening approached. "Got what?" inquired Leopard casually. "I will explain later; there is no time to waste. I have a very good plan for getting very many ants this season. Just wait; you will see," explained Hare as he dashed out of the house. Hare went and gathered clothing and various musical instruments, including a flute, a drum and a pair of shakers. He dressed up handsomely, making sure that he disguised himself completely. With his music instruments in hand, Hare waited along the path from the village to the valley of the anthills. It was soon dark, and as soon as the people started heading into the valley, Hare put on a musical show and dance like no other in the middle of the path. He sang, danced and invited people to join him in the concert, which some of them, especially children, did. People watched in amazement. "Who is this great entertainer?" "We love him!" "Oh, how funny!" They all marveled. Eventually Leopard, too, emerged from his house, heading to the valley to do the usual; but as soon as Hare saw Leopard, he drummed, sang and danced even more furiously, singing Leopard's praises as the most powerful creature in the area, feared by all. Hare kindly and persuasively invited Leopard to be the guest of honor at the concert and to join him as he drummed, sang and danced. Leopard, who loves power more than anything else, was greatly fascinated by the drumming, singing, dancing stranger, and he agreed to join him as requested. The two drummed, sang and danced for hours while the villagers peacefully collected their ants in the valley below. When Hare started seeing groups of villagers returning from the valley with baskets on their heads, he signed off and thanked Leopard profusely for having honored him by joining him in the concert. Hare then disappeared in the dark, and that was the end of the entertainment session. Before retiring for the night, the grateful villagers put together two very full baskets of edible ants and sent two envoys to deliver the baskets to Hare and Leopard's house, where they found Hare relaxing by the fire. They thanked him profusely, gave him the baskets and left him in total bliss.

Now Leopard, on remembering why he had gotten out of his house that evening, hurriedly made it into the valley, but by that time there were very few people left. And although Leopard worked very hard running from anthill to anthill until late in the night, he did not get enough ants to eat. But the people had successfully collected as many sacks of ants as they had wanted to have. Leopard returned to the house all tired and cold, and of course hungry, only to find Hare sleeping in his warm bed, very much contented, with two large baskets full of edible ants beside his bed. Leopard woke up Hare and narrated his ordeal. "On my way to the valley I ran into a very cheerful entertaining person singing my praises who invited me to join him; we had a dandy time, I tell you. But then, by the time the entertainment was over, there were very few edible ants left in the trenches. I spent a lot of time looking into various trenches, but found very few ants. Eventually I decided to return home because it was getting very late into the night, and I was tired, hungry and beginning to feel cold. But now, here you are, all comfortable in your bed, and you have these two large full baskets of edible ants. Please, do share, how did you get these ants, Hare?" "My good friend, I will tell you the whole story tomorrow; let's get some sleep; it is late," was Hare's response.

The village was all abuzz the next morning, with very happy people all over the place cleaning and roasting their edible ants, some for immediate consumption and the rest for safekeeping. Hare, too, woke up equally excited and ready to clean and roast his ants. Leopard had not had that much sleep because he had gone to bed hungry, so he, too, was up quite early. When Leopard saw Hare preparing his ants, he begged him for some. "My good friend Hare, please do give me some of your ants to eat; I am really hungry." Hare promised to share the ants after roasting them. But Leopard could not wait that long, so he joined Hare at the fireplace and begged to be given some of the roasting ants. At first, Hare obliged Leopard and gave him a mouthful of hot ants, but Leopard wanted more and more. A bright idea came to Hare. "Okay, my friend, close your eyes and I will pour some hot ants into your mouth where they will be cooled by your saliva; that way, you will not burn your hands," suggested Hare. Leopard welcomed the idea, closed his eyes and opened his mouth wide. Hare poured a whole shovel of embers down leopard's throat, which scorched him to no end. After a few days, Leopard passed away, and the villagers have been collecting their edible ants in peace since then.

As any Muganda person will tell you, it is not a very good idea to reap where you did not sow, let alone demanding stuff and even to be fed when you have done absolutely nothing to earn your share.

Hare Saves His Life

There was a time when Leopard and Hare were great friends, but that came to pass because of Hare's antics that always ended up annoying Leopard, not to mention putting Leopard's life in danger. One time, after having spent several weeks without finding meat to eat, Hare came up with a proposal which he explained in detail to Leopard. The humans in the nearby village where both Hare and Leopard were staying had some goats these two could have. They had to be careful, though, not to get caught, so Hare decided that they had to carry out their mission around noon, on a very hot day when the goats were out grazing in the pasture and the humans were resting, exhausted from both their morning chores and the heat. One hot day, Hare and Leopard approached the pasture where the goats were grazing and Hare suggested that since Leopard was strong, he would do a better job of catching and carrying off one of these goats, a mission which Leopard accomplished with no difficulty. When they got to Leopard's abode, the two slaughtered the goat, cleaned the meat and started roasting it. When the meat was about ready, Hare told Leopard that he had an errand to do, but that he would be back in time for the feast. Leopard urged Hare to be quick, and Hare set off. But of course Hare did not go that far. He gathered some noise making items that would sound like human footsteps and hid very near Leopard's abode. He then started rustling, shaking dry banana leaves and stamping. On hearing these noises, Leopard thought that the humans had come to kill him because he had stolen their goat, so he fled the place and went into hiding until late in the night. As soon as Leopard fled the place, Hare went into Leopard's kitchen and ate all the meat, leaving only bones and a few unchewable pieces. After filling up on the meat, Hare slept. Late in the night, Leopard tiptoed back only to find all the meat gone and Hare comfortably sleeping in his kitchen. Leopard woke up Hare and told him his sad story. Hare felt very sorry for Leopard, and told him that by the time he too came back, the meat was gone; maybe the humans had taken it. Hare returned to his house and slept comfortably, having had a very good meal.

The following week, Hare made the same proposal to Leopard, and, as previously, Leopard agreed to steal the goat. They brought the goat to Leopard's kitchen, slaughtered it, cleaned the meat, and once again Leopard started roasting the meat. Just before the meat was ready, Hare again excused himself from Leopard's kitchen, stating that he was going to bring a drink from the village; since he knew exactly where the drink was, he would be back in no time. While Hare was away, Leopard heard exactly the same noises as he had heard the previous week, and once again, he fled to safety. As soon as Leopard was out of the way, Hare entered the kitchen and again ate all the meat. When Leopard returned in the night, he again told his story to Hare, and Hare again sympathized and ended up pinning the crime of stealing their meat on the humans. The third time, the same thing happened. Now Leopard started suspecting Hare, and when Hare made the same proposal a fourth time, Leopard agreed, but this time, he too had his own plan. When Hare told Leopard that he had an errand to make just as the meat was getting done, and Hare left, Leopard too left quietly and hid very near his kitchen. Shortly thereafter he saw Hare coming with dry banana leaves, rustling and stamping!! After doing this for a while, Hare entered Leopard's kitchen with his usual confidence, and started enjoying the meat. Just as Hare was halfway through the meat Leopard pounced on him, but Hare escaped and the chase was on for several hours. Eventually Hare spotted a pool of water, and he immediately plunged into it unseen by Leopard. He then tried to hold his breath under the water until Leopard passed by but since Hare is not that good of a swimmer, he almost drowned in the effort, so he surfaced. No sooner had Hare surfaced from under the water than Leopard appeared, totally out of breath. Hare began shivering more out of fear than cold, but not for long.

"My dear wet Hare, have you seen dry Hare pass by?" inquired the breathless Leopard. You can imagine Hare's relief!! and he enthusiastically responded, "He headed that way, sir, not so long ago, and he looked very tired. If you pick up speed, sir, you will soon catch up with him." Leopard thanked "wet" Hare and he continued the chase, this time with renewed energy because of the information he had gotten from "wet" Hare. The relieved hare took his time resting, and after ascertaining that Leopard had by now run a comfortably long distance, he decided to find a place to spend the night. After running a considerable distance without catching up with "dry" Hare, Leopard returned to his home vowing to catch up with his nasty friend the following day.

The following day, Leopard went to Hare's house to settle the score, but of course Hare had left before sunrise. Leopard was not discouraged; he continued the search. Day and night, Leopard stalked Hare to punish him but each time Hare managed to escape. One day, Hare almost became Leopard's meal because Leopard had managed to slip into Hare's house when Hare was not home, and had waited for Hare's return. Fortunately for Hare, he did not get home that night, but the next day he found evidence of Leopard having been in his house all night waiting for him. That same evening, Hare hatched a plot to keep himself alive should Leopard be in the house when he got home. It was a very simple but quite effective plan. On getting home that evening, Hare stopped in the doorway of his house and called out, "My dear house, I am home; should I come in?" Leopard, who was in the home hiding and eagerly waiting for Hare, sniffed at the call: "What a weird creature Hare is, talking to his house." Leopard kept quiet, of course, and Hare called again.

After calling about five times and getting no response, Hare complained loudly enough for whoever was inside his house to hear: "That is strange; there must be someone in my house because it always responds to my call and welcomes me home. Let me try it one more time, and if I get no response, that will be my cue not to enter." And so Hare called his house one more time in a sweet enticing voice: "My dear lovely house, I am home; please do welcome me home." Leopard immediately responded in a tiny squeaky voice: "Please do come in." On hearing this, Hare pulled out a knife from his bundle he always carried around and opened the door with a thud. Leopard rushed to the door to pounce on Hare, but Hare, who had a vantage point, immediately stabbed Leopard, saying, "What a foolish creature you are; have you ever heard of a talking house?" That night Hare slept soundly, and although Leopard's relatives have continued the fight, they have never succeeded in getting their revenge on Hare.

Hare Eats for Free

Hare, Elephant and Buffalo were once great friends living in the same neighborhood. They generally had a good life, especially Elephant and Buffalo, who used to work very hard. Hare, too, was happy in his own way, mostly doing minimum work; but since the area was fertile, they each had more than enough to eat. One season, though, food became very scarce, but both Elephant and Buffalo were not affected that much. Hare, though, was almost dying of hunger because he had had very meager food resources even during times of plenty.

One day Hare decided that he was not going to die of hunger when both his friends had more than enough, so he approached Elephant humbly and requested help. "My friend I do not have anymore food to eat, and I also do not have money to buy some. Please do give me one of your cows for food; it will keep me going for a while. Since I will be strong, I will think of ways to earn money and buy you another one." Elephant was more than glad to help a friend in need, and so he gave one of his cows to Hare. Hare thanked Elephant profusely, took the cow to his house, slaughtered it, cleaned the meat, roasted all of it for safekeeping, and for a month or so, ate like a king. When Hare finished all the meat, he started thinking of ways to raise money to buy a replacement cow for Elephant, but none came readily to mind. *No need to panic*, thought Hare to himself. But that self assurance did not prevent hunger from gnawing away at hare. Fortunately for him, he still had one more very good friend, so he approached Buffalo just as he had Elephant, and once again humbly begged Buffalo to give him one of his cows for food, promising to replace Buffalo's cow in exactly the same way as he had promised to replace Elephant's cow. Buffalo, like Elephant, readily helped out a friend in need. And once again, Hare had enough meat to last him for one more month.

Now Hare had eaten two friends' cows, and it was time to pay back as he had promised, but he had no tangible plan for making money to replace those friends' animals. He, however, had a good head on his shoulders, and accordingly he soon hatched a plan. Hare's abode was conveniently located on a hill and both his friends lived in the valleys on opposite sides of the same hill. Early one morning Hare went down to Elephant's home. He thanked Elephant profusely for his help and patience, and added, "I bought the replacement cow two days ago. It is a very big and very strong cow. I think it is far bigger and stronger than the one you gave me, and definitely prettier. I cannot wait for you to see it; I know you will be very pleased. But before you see it, I need your help. I have been trying to bring it to you with no success because of its size and strength. So this is what we are going to do. I am going to tie a very strong rope around the cow's neck, and I will signal you to start pulling it down the slope. You will have to pull carefully, though, because this is a very huge and very strong cow."

Elephant agreed to the plan, and since he was bigger and stronger than Hare, he couldn't think of any reason why he would not be able to pull the cow down the slope towards his home. Hare promised to alert Elephant as soon as the plan was in place, but that would be the next day because now Hare had to go to the store and purchase the rope. Since Hare's plan had worked out so well with Elephant, as soon as Hare left Elephant's place he headed to Buffalo's home and gave him exactly the same information. Buffalo thought exactly like Elephant and agreed to the plan, but he too had to wait until the next day.

The following day, Hare woke up early and knotted both sides of a very long rope. He stood in the middle of his hill and threw one end of the rope down to Elephant and the other to Buffalo. He then called to Elephant: "The rope is down there, my friend, do you see it?" Elephant saw the rope and responded affirmatively. Then Hare told him to pick up the rope and wait for the signal to start pulling. Next Hare called to Buffalo and told him exactly the same thing. When Hare ascertained that both Elephant and Buffalo were clutching the rope, he signaled each to start pulling while he stood at the top of his hill watching both sweat it out pulling each other. Since both Buffalo and Elephant are big animals, pulling each other definitely exhausted them. Hare had cautioned them, of course, that it was not going to be a very easy job, but they did not expect it to be this hard. Every now and then one would ask to rest, and Hare would willingly oblige and encourage the other to also take a break. By the end of the day, both Buffalo and Elephant were so exhausted that they simply gave up, but Hare pretended not to see that, and he slept soundly. Two days or so later, Hare went down to Buffalo's place and asked him enthusiastically, "So what do you think about the cow, my friend?" Buffalo responded that he would be better off without that troublesome and quite stubborn cow. "I have enough cows in my possession and I do not want to bring in such a troublesome one to disorganize them. Consider that cow a gift from me to you for our friendship. Good luck, my friend; you will need it dealing with that cow." Hare once again thanked Buffalo profusely and headed to Elephant's place, where he asked exactly the same question and he got a similar response. The three friends lived together happily thereafter.

As far as the Baganda are concerned, strength is good, but intelligence will always be better.

Other Sample Tales

Below is a sampling of some other significant Baganda prose narratives that are, like the ones above, valuable windows into the Baganda culture and value systems, but they cannot be comfortably fitted in the categories above.

Kitezi

Once upon a time there was a famous hunter by the name of Kitezi. Kitezi had a wife and several children whom he sustained as a hunter. He would go out into the forest and set several traps each day hoping to get that day's meat; and if he happened to trap a large animal, he would rest for several days before returning to the forest because there would be plenty of meat to keep his family going. One day, he set out on his hunting trip as usual, and he set several traps as usual. Imagine his delight when he found, not one small animal or bird as was often the case, but a big, well nourished deer trapped in one of his nets. But as he was getting ready to spear the deer, he heard it plead with him to spare its life. "Please, do let me go," pleaded the deer. "I would have let you go but I have children to feed, and you are it," replied Kitezi. But the deer kept on pleading. "I too have kids, and like you, I was also looking for something for them to eat; they cannot survive without me." Kitezi, being a kindhearted man and also a struggling parent, understood the deer's plea, and let it off the hook. It thanked him profusely, and they parted ways.

But one day, when the deer was in the forest in the vicinity of Kitezi's village, it heard people talking loudly, some shouting, others sympathizing! "What is going on over there?" the deer wondered, and it continued to listen. Eventually it heard Kitezi's name being mentioned. Incidentally Kitezi had committed a very big crime; the deer did not hear the details, but it heard that he had been sentenced to death. He was being kept in prison, and the villagers expected him to be executed any time now! "Oh my! Kitezi! That is the kind, gentle man who spared my life," mused the deer. "He is a kindhearted father. If he is executed what will become of his family? No, I do not care what crime he committed, I must find a way to save him, but how — what"? The deer scratched its head for a while, and eventually an idea came to it. It hurried back to its place, dressed up in its Sunday best, picked up a broom, and waltzed into town sweeping, singing and dancing as it went along:

Njera, njera, njera, njera (I am sweeping, sweeping, sweeping, sweeping).
Omusajja Kitezi, njera (The man Kitezi).
Wamponnya jjo, njera (You recently spared my life).
Nange njagadde nkuwonye, njera (I also want to spare yours).

The more the deer sang and danced the larger the crowd of onlookers became. "What? Did you say there is a dressed-up, singing and dancing deer cruising our streets?" people asked each other, all in disbelief. Word spread quickly throughout the village, and the people followed the deer, which was now heading towards the prison. So mesmerized was the crowd that those who ran ahead of the deer to report the incident to the prison guards were just babbling, totally incomprehensible when they tried to narrate this deer story. So the prison guards left their stations and waited at the gate for the so called sweeping, singing, dancing deer wanting to save Kitezi. Of course these prison guards were armed and ready to kill the ridiculous animal, but they did not get the chance. Flanked by crowds of speechless staring people, the deer bypassed the prison and continued down the street. On hearing the news, the head prison guard sent one of his men to go and see what was going on. This messenger too got so caught up into the spirit of the sweeping, singing, dancing deer that he forgot to return with the information. A second guard was sent, and he too got stuck in the same way. A third, fourth, and many more guards were sent. But none were coming back, and before long there were no guards left at the prison gate; they were all enjoying the deer's unbelievable show! And you dare not blame them! Since these guards had left in a hurry with the intention of returning immediately, none of them had remembered to lock or even close the prison gates. The prisoners, of course, seized this chance to free themselves, and they were far gone out of the region long before the guards could return; the deer had intentionally held their attention that long.

About four or maybe five hours later, the dancing deer, too, disappeared, maybe somewhere in the forest. No one saw where it went, not even the guards whose original motive had been to shoot the ridiculous animal. But one thing was for sure: Kitezi was safe!!

Armed with stories like this one, the Baganda people have proof that

"Do unto others as you would like them to do unto you" is not just an empty cliché, but practical words of wisdom to cherish and live by.

Kabasa

Once upon a time there was a very poor family of three: a father, a mother and a son named Kabasa. Although the mother used to work hard, the father did absolutely nothing except drink. He would wake up early in the morning and go to look for where he could get a drink; all his neighbors and even little kids in the village knew him as Mr. Drunkard. Despite their poverty though, the mother and her son had a great relationship, keeping each other company and comforting each other while Mr. Drunkard was away. Unfortunately for the son, the mother died when Kabasa was still very young, and he found himself alone with Mr. Drunkard. Mr. Drunkard was very much saddened by the death of his wife, whom he lovely dearly in his own drunken way, and for a while, it seemed as if he was going to give up drinking and take care of Kabasa. But after several months of grieving and taking care of Kabasa, Mr. Drunkard picked up his usual routine. He would wake up early in the morning and traverse the village looking for drinks. Poor little Kabasa would spend days without bathing and he would be given food randomly by kind neighbors. Then there were times when Mr. Drunkard would fail to return home, and Kabasa would sleep in the house all by himself, often leaving the door open for his father to stagger in any time during the night. Eventually, Mr. Drunkard decided to remarry. "You know Kabasa, I cannot take care of myself, let alone take care of a kid like you, so I am going to marry someone who will take care of both of us." That is how Mr. Drunkard explained to Kabasa his decision to marry. And, in a way, he was right because he was not marrying for love; that would simply complicate his life. All he needed was someone to take care of him and Kabasa, or rather someone to give him freedom to go and drink without worrying about Kabasa. Unfortunately the bride-to-be did not get the memo informing her accordingly.

It did not take Mr. Drunkard long to find the lady he was looking for, and he soon got married to a woman who also had a child of more or less the same age as Kabasa. Now there really had been a great misunderstanding between Mr. Drunkard and his bride. The bride-to-be was a very poor single mother looking for someone to take care of her and her son; she wanted a man who would, in addition to fulfilling all her and her son's needs, also be a great role model for her son. You have always heard that looks can be deceiving, and in this case, that statement couldn't be more true. Unless one had heard of Mr. Drunkard before, one could not tell by just looking at him when he was sober that he was a drunkard. The bride-to-be immediately fell for the soft-spoken handsome widower, and the widower also found the smiling beautiful lady, with a boy of about Kabasa's age, totally irresistible. They soon got married, but disappointment was the immediate reaction on the bride's side because of the utter poverty she found all around Mr. Drunkard's place. The house was so small and dirty, with a leaky roof and no real furniture. So long as it was still honeymoon time, Mr. Drunkard resisted drinking and behaved so well towards Kabasa, his stepson and definitely his bride, which gave the lady some comfort. *With some hard work*, thought the lady, *things will get better*, but that was not to be.

As soon as the honeymoon was over, according to Mr. Drunkard, he resumed his schedule. At first the woman thought that if she told him clearly what her expectations were and that she could not stand him being that drunk, he would drop the habit, but that was not the case. The hard work was done, though; instead of going early to drink, Mr. Drunkard would put in a few hours of farm work each day. But then he would disappear, not to return until late in the night, and that is if he returned at all. Day in day out, the couple quarreled but nothing changed. Eventually the woman decided to make herself and her son comfortable because she really did not have any options. But her decision was disastrous for Kabasa. She decided that her son was not going to do any chores. She was going to use Kabasa as their servant, and not only was Kabasa a servant, but a totally abused and rarely fed boy. With his father rarely home and no one to turn to, Kabasa accepted his fate. He had to wake up before sunrise each day and start his chores, which included fetching all the water to be used that day from the well down in a valley, making breakfast, cleaning the dishes, gathering wood from the forest about a mile away for cooking, cleaning the compound, making lunch, washing dishes, preparing dinner, washing clothes as was needed, and doing about everything there was to do around the compound. Despite his hard work, Kabasa was never appreciated, and not only wasn't he appreciated, he also was beaten and kicked, often both by the woman and her son.

When both boys reached school age, Mr. Drunkard enrolled the stepson in school but not Kabasa because he had chores to do around the home, so said the wife. With the stepson gone all day, the woman had all the freedom to abuse Kabasa with no witnesses around. Eventually the villagers had enough of the cruel woman, and they sat Mr. Drunkard down and commanded him to enroll Kabasa in school, which he did despite the woman's objections. School gave Kabasa some breathing space, and now his miserable days were only weekends. One Sunday afternoon, the woman and her son decided to visit their relatives, but of course they expected their dinner to be ready when they got home. Unfortunately for Kabasa, it rained all afternoon and all evening, and since the kitchen roof was leaking, just like the main house roof, he had no way of making a fire to cook the dinner. He tried to start the fire, but rain would extinguish it every time. Because he was wet, cold and quite exhausted, Kabasa fell asleep in the kitchen, with rain falling on him, but not before crying as usual and cursing his mother for having died and left him almost a total orphan; he sang his usual sad song:

> *Maama wankola bubi okufa; singa tewafa, sandibonyebonye bwenti*
> (Mother, it was very bad of you to die; if you hadn't died, I
> wouldn't be suffering like this).

Kabasa sang this song over and over until he fell asleep. During his sleep, he heard a voice, just like his mother's, smoothly responding to his song:

> *Kabasa mwana wange guma; okubonabona si kufa*
> (Kabasa my son be strong; suffering is not death).

Kabasa immediately got up from his uncomfortable sleep, feeling renewed energy but wondering about the voice. Could it have been his mother's voice?

Unfortunately for Kabasa though, by the time his stepmother and stepbrother returned, dinner was not ready. He tried to explain that it had been raining all the time but his explanation fell on deaf ears, and he got his usual dose of beatings and kicks and was told to go to bed with no dinner. "What a stupid useless boy. It always rains but we always eat," grumbled the furious woman. Since Kabasa was only a boy, he did not think that telling his stepmother about his mother's voice would cause him even more problems. On hearing the story, the stepmother beat Kabasa even more and told him that he was simply insane now that he claimed hearing voices of dead people. But a plan hatched in the stepmother's head. Since Kabasa was behaving insanely, why not get medicine from a witch doctor to make him totally insane? That way, he would be dismissed from school, and he might even end up dead somewhere, and the good thing about it all was that no one would accuse her of any wrong doing; they would blame it all on Kabasa's insanity. The following day when Mr. Drunkard was of course away as usual and both Kabasa and his stepbrother were at school, the woman went to see a witch doctor who prescribed some poisonous medicine to be put in Kabasa's food. This medicine was supposed to make Kabasa totally insane. The woman returned home jubilantly and prepared a very good dish for Kabasa, laced with poison. Her plan was to be nice to Kabasa that evening and offer him that food. After preparing the food, the woman went for a walk. While she was away, the children and Mr. Drunkard got home, and as was their usual practice, Mr. Drunkard and his stepson ate the poisoned food ravenously while Kabasa sat under the shade in one of the trees in the compound. According to their usual routine, Kabasa was not supposed to eat anything without his stepmother's permission, but the beloved people could eat whatever they wanted and whenever they wanted, and so they did. By the time the woman got home from her walk, the two people had consumed all the poisoned food and were now resting, but Kabasa was busy washing dishes. "Did you enjoy your food Kabasa?" grinned the wicked woman. "Which food, Mom?" asked Kabasa humbly. "The one I left in those dishes you are washing," responded the satisfied woman. The grin on the woman's face was to soon disappear; she could not believe what Kabasa's response to her question was. Oh no, now her people had consumed poison and they were going to become insane. What was she going to do? That food had been prepared for Kabasa. She said all of this loudly and Kabasa heard the whole of it!!

Instead of going to school the next morning, Kabasa gathered his meager possessions and headed out of the village. He now knew that the woman wanted to kill him, and although she had not succeeded this time, Kabasa was not going to wait around for her to succeed. He walked for days on end, sleeping in corn fields at night and eating wild fruits during the day. He wanted to go as far away as he possibly could although he did not know where he was going. Most nights he would stay up singing his sad song:

Maama wankola bubi okufa; singa tewafa, sandibonyebonye bwenti
(Mother, it was very bad of you to die; if you hadn't died,
I wouldn't be suffering like this).

Kabasa would sing this song over and over until he fell asleep. And as had happened that one Sunday when he was asleep in a wet kitchen, he would again hear his mother's voice smoothly responding to his song:

Kabasa mwana wange guma; okubonabona si kufa
(Kabasa my son be strong; suffering is not death).

After traveling for what might have been a month, Kabasa felt that he had put enough distance between him and his wicked stepmother, so early one morning, he stopped at one of the homes in a village he had arrived in overnight and begged the family living there to take him in. He narrated his whole story to them, and he told them that since he was a great worker, thanks to his wicked stepmother, he would serve them in return for food and shelter. But the family had an even better idea. There was a very wealthy woman in the village who had no living relatives of her own, and she needed someone to take care of her and her property. That was music to Kabasa's ears because he was used to working hard, and with no appreciation, of course. They accompanied him to the old woman's house, who welcomed him like a relative, and soon Kabasa started living the good life. He took very good care of the woman and her property, and the woman became very fond of him. As time went by, Kabasa confirmed his mother's message; since that suffering had not killed him, he now had a chance at a life, a very good life, actually.

One day, the dear old woman fell very ill. When she was on her deathbed, she called in the village chief and a number of other prominent people in the village, and after explaining to them how she had been blessed to spend her last days in the hands of such a wonderful, hard working, very caring, kind young man, she willed her whole estate to Kabasa, and she died shortly thereafter. Kabasa became the envy of the whole village and one of the richest people in the area, but they all loved him because of his good behavior. He soon got married to a very beautiful, well behaved young woman from the village, and he started his own family. He continued working very hard, as he was used to doing, and he was blessed to have found a woman with the same values.

Years later, when Kabasa had two children of his own, he heard that there was a famine in the area he had originated from, and for the first time since his arrival to this village, he wondered what had happened to his father and stepbrother after they had eaten poisoned food meant for him. Well, he was soon to find out. As the famine spread, people started moving searching for food, and a great number had already stopped by Kabasa's home and he had fed them and replenished their supplies. One afternoon when Kabasa's children were playing outside in their gigantic and very well kept compound, they saw a family of three entering their compound. But these people were quite different from the usual families stopping by. For one, the two men were singing, or rather shouting something incomprehensible — definitely deranged people — and they were cripples, dirty, with saliva pouring out of their mouths. They were dressed in rags, and the more the woman with them, who was also dirty and dressed in rags, tried to quiet the pair, the louder they shouted something like: *Ffe tuli birongwa* (We are strange things, not people). As these people neared the playing children, the children fled into the house screaming for their mother. The mother too could not believe what she was seeing, but she could hear the woman begging for food, anything to eat, and water to drink. She decided to call in her husband, who was in the back resting, before offering these strange people anything. "My dear husband," began the wife, "although we have been feeding all kinds of people and allowing them to rest on our property, we should send these ones away immediately because they are deranged and quite uncontrollable, which means that they can be dangerous." Kabasa, who had immediately recognized the family, told the wife to feed them and let them rest, despite her objections. Since she was a good woman, she gave the strange people food and water, and allowed them to rest in one of the side houses used as storage for coffee, cotton, and other farm products. When they finished eating, the very poor, exhausted people fell asleep immediately, and Kabasa told his wife and children to let them be.

The next morning, Kabasa went into the house where the three had slept, and after serving them breakfast, he asked the woman to tell him their story. She told him that the men had been bewitched years ago, and since that time, they had been like that; but she begged him to accommodate them for a few days because they were very poor and tired, and had nowhere to go. Kabasa stared at the woman for a few minutes, and having ascertained that she did not recognize him, he revealed himself to her by saying, "One wet Sunday evening when I was utterly suffering, a wise voice of a dead woman told me that suffering is not death; you will be okay." You can imagine how embarrassed the woman was, and how panicky she became! "Please, sir, do forgive me, please. We have absolutely nothing, but we are not dangerous. I will do whatever you want me to do for you, but please do not send us away yet," begged the woman, now on her knees. Kabasa assured the frantic, totally embarrassed woman that he had forgiven her, and he gave them clothes to wear and allowed them to stay as long as they wished.

Although there are stepparents who mistreat their stepchildren, this story is always a chilling reminder of the consequences of such actions.

Lukwanzi

Once upon a time there was a very good, responsible, caring man who married a wonderful wife. The couple lived happily together for several years, and they were blessed with one son they named Lukwanzi. Lukwanzi blossomed into a very handsome, cheerful, energetic boy, and since the father was a hunter by profession who would spend weeks away from home on hunting trips, Lukwanzi became his mother's best friend and helper. At age 7, Lukwanzi had started calling himself the man of the house whenever the father was away.

Unfortunately, when Lukwanzi was about 10 years old, his mother died, and after one year of mourning, Lukwanzi's father remarried, hoping that the stepmother would be a great mother to Lukwanzi. At first, all seemed to be going well; the stepmother embraced Lukwanzi and the boy returned the favor. When he ascertained that all was in order, Lukwanzi's father resumed his hunting business.

Shortly thereafter, the new wife became pregnant and gave birth to a baby girl. Although this baby was pretty ugly, people did not seem to notice that at first; after all, she was just a baby, and babies are often adorable regardless of physical beauty. But the older she grew, the more ugly this girl became, and her ugliness was soon noticed by all around her, of course, including her mother. Conversely, the older Lukwanzi grew, the more handsome he became, a detail that escaped no one, including the stepmother, of course. The stepmother started neglecting Lukwanzi's appearance. She rarely helped the boy to bathe, and she did not give this

179

boy any lotions, hair combs, and such beauty enhancing items, especially when the father was away, but this negligence did not take away from Lukwanzi's beauty. On the contrary, Lukwanze grew even more handsome, and the people around paid him compliments day in and day out. Having neglected Lukwanzi, the stepmother put all her energy into grooming her daughter. But the more effort she put into her daughter's grooming, the uglier her daughter became, and the more noticeable her ugliness became to all those around, including the mother, of course.

When Lukwanzi's sister was old enough to do chores, she started going to the village springs with her brother to get water for the family. Fetching water from the springs is always a pleasant activity for village children, who call on each other on their way and go in big groups, playing and having fun, but this activity was not that much fun for Lukwanzi's sister. As she grew older, she started noticing her ugliness, and so did the other children, who would not let her forget it. They jeered at her, mocked her, pulled at her hair, and at times even threw dirt in her face while commenting on her ugliness: "But why are you so ugly?" "Has any of us ever seen such an ugly girl?" "Maybe, just maybe, this girl is not fully human." The girl used to cry all the time. She became very sad, then depressed, and eventually she stopped going to the springs with the village children. But that did not solve her problem, because these children would stop by to call on Lukwanzi and inquire loudly as to the whereabouts of his ugly sister. Even the adults started making comments, comparing Lukwanzi's sister to Lukwanzi. "How come that girl is so ugly while the brother is more that handsome?" they would ask each other, even in the presence of the girl's mother. The mother tried to comfort her daughter, but the more she tried, the louder the people's voices became: "That girl is really, really ugly."

Having exhausted all beauty tips, the mother decided that there was only one way of solving this problem: kill Lukwanzi so that the villagers do not have anyone to compare her daughter to day in and day out. "Who knows, my girl might look better if left by herself with no handsome prince beside her to accentuate her ugliness," mused the mother, and then the daughter might even get a suitor. Convinced of her wisdom, the mother patiently waited for Lukwanzi's father to head out on a long hunting trip. As soon as the father started on his journey, Lukwanzi's stepmother headed to a witch doctor, who, after listening to her story, sympathized with her and agreed to help. Her husband had some cows that Lukwanzi took care of, taking them to pasture every morning and returning them into their shed every evening. The witch doctor gave some herbs to Lukwanzi's stepmother, and instructed her to spread them at the gate of the cowshed, claiming that as soon as Lukwanzi stepped across that gate, he would fall and die. The excited mother returned home and found her daughter miserable as usual, but this time she did not waste any time comforting her. Instead she took advantage of Lukwanzi's absence since he was out with the cows, and headed to the cowshed and spread the herbs liberally all around the gate.

After washing her hands thoroughly, the mother went to comfort her daughter as was the norm, but this time the mother was in a great mood and quite chatty as she warned her daughter not to go anywhere near that gate that day.

What the stepmother did not know was that Lukwanzi's dearly departed mother's ghost hung around him to protect him, and so, being a ghost, it had heard the conversation between the witch doctor and Lukwanzi's stepmother. This ghost appeared to Lukwanzi when he was still out with the cows and warned him not to step across the cowshed gate on getting home because of what it had heard transpiring between the witch doctor and Lukwanzi's stepmother. The ghost also cautioned Lukwanzi not to show any sign of anger to his stepmother because for sure the woman was dangerous to Lukwanzi. It was soon evening, and Lukwanzi's stepmother was getting more and more anxious with every passing minute. On getting home with the cows, Lukwanzi greeted his stepmother joyfully as he always did, and directed the cows into the shed without getting near the gate, and as such he escaped the medicine trap.

The next day, Lukwanzi got out of bed as usual, greeted his stepmother and sister joyfully as he always did, completed all his chores around the compound, herded the cows out of the gate without going near it, and headed out with the cows. The stepmother was in disbelief. When Lukwanzi left the compound with the cows, his stepmother headed back to the witch doctor and narrated the previous evening's events to him. The witch doctor was astonished at the boy's "luck," and this time gave the stepmother more potent herbs and instructed her to put them in the boy's dinner. He then told the woman to eat an early dinner with her daughter to enable her to serve the medicated dinner to Lukwanzi when he got home. This for sure was going to work because there was no way the boy was going to go to bed hungry after a day's work under the sun with the cows. Once again the ghost of Lukwanzi's mother was privy to the conversation, and as soon as the stepmother left the witch doctor's place with the medicine, the ghost warned Lukwanzi not to eat dinner on getting home that day. He was to thank his stepmother politely for the dinner, but inform her that he had some stomach pains and was, therefore, unable to eat his dinner. Lukwanzi ate fruits and roots around the pasture all day, and when he got home that evening and found that his stepmother and sister had already eaten, he declined the dinner as he had been instructed to do by his mother's ghost.

Now the stepmother was really getting desperate, and she headed back to the witch doctor very early the next morning. Even Lukwanzi was surprised that his stepmother, who loved her morning sleep, had gotten up that early! The witch doctor too was getting desperate. "Okay, now, we have to come up with a plan that does not involve herbs," suggested the bewildered witch doctor, and his plan was simple. The stepmother, who had neglected taking care of Lukwanzi all these years and had concentrated on beautifying her daughter, was going to act concerned that the once very handsome Lukwanzi was starting to look haggard, maybe exhausted from taking care of those cows all day. The solution was going to be a very good massage by the stepmother, of course, to restore his youthful hue; at least that was what the stepmother was going to tell Lukwanzi. The practical intention of the massage, though, was to make Lukwanzi sleep soundly, after a hot day out with the cows, to enable the stepmother to stab him in his sleep that night. A very good easy plan, mused the witch doctor, but of course this witch doctor, experienced as he was, was not counting on the ghost of Lukwanzi's mother to be part of that plan or any other plan, for that matter.

The stepmother returned home and prepared to execute the plan. She gathered all the items she needed, and when her curious daughter asked what was going on, the stepmother informed her that she was going to give Lukwanzi a massage that evening because he had been neglected long enough. As evening approached, the stepmother began warming the water for Lukwanzi's bath, to be followed with a massage. Of course, by the time Lukwanzi got home he knew the plan, and he had devised his own counterplan, as usual. The stepmother welcomed Lukwanzi home eagerly, gave him warm water for his bath and did the massage to the best of her ability. When it was time to sleep, the stepmother tucked both her daughter and Lukwanzi into their respective sleeping areas, and wished both a great night. After the stepmother had left the room, Lukwanzi convinced his half sister to change places with him just for the fun of it. "We have always slept in the same places; we have never spent any night out of our respective areas. Let's pretend that we are visiting some other place by changing our sleeping spots, suggested Lukwanzi playfully, and the half sister readily accepted the plan.

About 2:00 A.M. the stepmother tiptoed into the children's room with a knife in hand; she immediately headed to Lukwanzi's side and stabbed the sleeping child!!! She then covered the body and tiptoed out of the room as quietly as she had entered. Lukwanzi heard it all, but of course he made no noise. Just as it was about to be daybreak Lukwanzi, who had stayed up all night waiting for this moment, found the stabbing knife near his half sister's body. After wrapping it up in a piece of cloth as evidence, he tiptoed to the door, which he opened quietly, and he got out of the house. He then headed out, running away from the village towards the place where his father had gone hunting. The stepmother woke up at her usual time, ready to declare that thieves had broken into the house and killed Lukwanzi, only to find her daughter dead, and no sign of Lukwanzi. She shrieked, all shaken up that she had killed her own daughter, but of course she was not willing to admit it to the throng of people now gathered in the compound. She pulled out a sharp knife and took off chasing after Lukwanzi, loudly announcing that Lukwanzi had stabbed his half sister. Lukwanzi, who had been hiding in a nearby shrub, heard the shrieking stepmother and took off. Unfortunately the now mad woman spotted him and chased him even faster. The two of them must have run through several villages before Lukwanzi ran into a group of men returning from their hunting trip. As luck would have it, that was his father's group, and the father was among them. The father immediately stopped Lukwanzi, who was holding the bloody knife, and Lukwanzi had enough time to tell his side of the story before the stepmother appeared on the horizon. Whether the ghost of Lukwanzi's mother played a role in convincing the father we will never know, but the father immediately believed Lukwanzi's story because he too had sensed the grudge that his wife had been harboring towards the handsome boy. In no time the mother ran into the group, and on seeing Lukwanzi in his father's arms holding the knife she had used to stab her daughter, she fell down and stabbed herself to death!

This is a good story to remind us that our actions have consequences, and that we should be prepared to handle those consequences, both the intended and the unintended, as is the case in this story. It also strengthens the Baganda's belief, which they share with most Africans, that their dearly departed are never far from them.

Kaleeba

Once upon a time there was a man who married a beautiful wife and they had a beautiful daughter. When their daughter was old enough to get married, the parents devised a plan to find the most suitable man for her to get married to. Their plan was simple; they wanted a strong, reliable man who wouldn't be distracted by trivial things like — for example a singing bird! Yes, a singing bird. Potential suitors would be required to go to the neighborhood springs with a round clay pot, fill it with water, and bring it back balanced on their heads! Simple enough, right? Not really. The parents "contracted" with a bird to distract the suitors; whoever brought the pot back intact with its water would marry their daughter.

It did not take long before the first suitor came along. The parents told him that they did not need any material things from him. All he had to do to win their daughter was take their beautiful clay pot to the well, fill it and bring it back on his head hands off, with water in it of course. The man could not believe his luck. "I am for sure going to wed this beautiful girl. Please, do give me that pot." They readily gave him the pot and pointed him towards the springs. On getting to the springs, the man hurriedly filled his pot and put it on his head for the journey back. As soon as he took his first step, a very beautiful bird began singing from behind him:

> *Semusajja agenda, Kaleeba* (You gentleman heading out)
> *Ndabira abali eka eyo, Kaleeba* (Give my greetings to the people at home).
> *Kanyonyi akali kuluzzi, Kaleeba* (A bird at the water borehole)
> *Kambadde ensimbi, Kaleeba* (Is wearing trinkets),
> *Ensimbi nobutiti, Kaleeba* (trinkets and beads).
> *Kyo kyoki, Kaleeba* [just a chorus, no literal meaning]
> *Kyuka nondeeba, Kaleeba* (Turn and see me).

You can imagine the shock to the man, who hurriedly turned to see the singing bird supposedly wearing colorful, noisy trinkets and beads. In the process, the clay pot fell off his head and it was in pieces in no time!! "Too bad," said the parents to the pleading suitor, "you've lost the girl," and they bade him goodbye! More suitors came and they all met the same fate. You would think that those who came knowing all about this bird would not fall victim to its antics, but they all did. There must have been something magical about that bird, or it had been endowed with supernatural powers!! Word spread far and beyond the region. Still more suitors tried their luck, but they all ended up breaking the pots because of the singing bird.

One day, *akakokolo* (deformed person) came to visit the family and he declared his intention of wanting to marry the girl. He told them that he had heard all about the bird, but that he would not fail like all those others. The parents and their daughter laughed so hard that their tummies hurt from all that laughing, but the *akakokolo* stood his ground. In his husky voice he pleaded to be given the chance: "Let me try it. Do you promise to give me the girl if I succeed in bringing that pot back with water?" "Of course we will keep our part of the bargain, but you know there is no way someone looking like you can do this. Worthy men have failed, as you already know. We do not want to waste our time, but just for the sake of amusing ourselves, we will give you the pot." As soon as the *akakokolo* got the pot, he set out for the springs. On getting there, he filled the pot hurriedly and put it on his head. No sooner had he started moving than the bird started its routine:

> *Semusajja agenda, Kaleeba*
> *Ndabira abali eka eyo, Kaleeba.*
> *Kanyonyi akali kuluzzi, Kaleeba*
> *Kambadde ensimbi, Kaleeba,*
> *Ensimbi nobutiti, Kaleeba.*
> *Kyo kyoki, Kaleeba.*
> *Kyuka nondeeba, Kaleeba.*

The *akakokolo* did not turn to see the bird. "What! This man can resist me?" wondered the bird. "Well, let me put in more effort." The bird sang louder, but still the *akakokolo* did not turn to see it. It started dancing, but the *akakokolo* simply increased his speed. It flew directly over him, but to no avail. It even tried landing on the pot, and still the *akakokolo* did not turn to look at it. The parents and their daughter were still busy laughing when they spotted the *akakokolo* returning with the pot on his head! They squinted to see more clearly, and for sure it was him with the pot secure on his head. Laughter froze on their faces as the *akakokolo* moved closer to them with the singing and dancing bird in tow, but he did not at any one time turn to see it. Soon after putting down the pot, the *akakokolo* requested the parents to hand the girl over. How the girl cried and cried and cried!!! But, oh, well, a promise is a promise, so the parents had no choice but to give her to the *akakokolo* to be his wife.

The Baganda stress the importance of not judging a book by its cover. They also caution against arrogance by despising and underrating people who may be "different" in appearance. Children are often reminded that such behavior made beauty *akakokolo*'s wife.

It Is Everybody's Business

Once upon a time there was a very wealthy farmer who had all kinds of domestic animals on his farm, including chicken, goats, cows, sheep, and pigs. These animals were very well looked after, compared to the other animals in their neighborhood. In addition to rearing animals, the farmer also grew peanuts, plenty of them, but he was having a very hard time keeping the mice out of his nuts. The mice would start eating the nuts long before he could harvest them, so he used to harvest them prematurely so as to get at least some. But once he took his nuts home, the mice would invade the store in which he used to keep them and still eat them.

One day, he came up with a good, practical solution; he set several traps for the mice all over the garden and the store. The mice saw some of the traps, but since they still wanted to eat the nuts, they thought that they would get help from the strong farm animals. "Did you know that your master has set mice traps everywhere to stop us from eating his nuts? Please, do come and help us to remove them because we will die of hunger if we do not get any nuts to eat," pleaded the now desperate mice with the farm animals. But the farm animals collectively refused to help the mice. "Since you are the ones who eat our master's nuts, the traps are a well deserved gift to you. Those traps are definitely not of any business to us," they told the mice, and the mice continued to live in fear.

One night, a large snake got caught in one of the traps, and the farmer thought that he had trapped some of the mice. So he woke up in the dark and went to remove the supposedly dead mice and reset the trap. Unfortunately the snake was not dead yet, so it bit the farmer fatally and by morning, he was dead. Early the next day, when the villagers heard the news, they gathered and collected all the cocks and killed them [traditionally cocks cannot crow in the compound when the man of the house is dead, so they have to be killed or taken off the premises until the burial and mourning period are over]. Also, when the man of the house dies, his goats cannot stay in his compound, so the man's relatives take care of all the goats. When time came for the last rites ceremony, the cows too were slaughtered to feed the guests. Whenever a group of those animals was going to be killed, the mice would make fun of them, saying, "Now, you see how important helping us was? I guess you now understand that getting rid of those traps was indeed your business." The mice lived happily thereafter, and they still feast on farmers' nuts.

The Baganda people use this tale to stress the importance of group responsibility and neighborly duties; whatever happens in one's neighborhood to one's neighbors is always everyone's business!!

African narratives are basically very fluid morality and character building tales, meaning that you can hear the same tale in various versions, each version intended to address a specific audience at a specific time in a specific context. The names of the characters and places can be changed, and specific details can be omitted or added, but the moral lessons of a tale are rarely, if ever, compromised in that process. African storytellers are praised for their creativity and ability to please the audience, but not for their invention of "new" moral lessons. This aspect puts the African storytellers in line with the Moderns in Literature, both groups sharing a motto which, simply put, is not to make new things but to make things new and relevant.

5

Conclusion

No translation can do justice to the rich African oral tradition. As Okot P'Bitek, a famous African oral poetry translator, points out, in translation a piece loses some of its sharpness, vividness, melody and much more. And then, of course, there is the process of transcribing material from an oral text into a written one; once again there is no way one can do justice to such a piece. The creativity of the storyteller, gestures, facial expressions, tonal nuances, poses, the audience's responses, reactions, contributions, the actual environment — the list goes on — are partially lost in the process. But the scholars of the African oral tradition have come a long way in their effort to accurately capture and reproduce African oral pieces, these scholars being aided by technological advances. There was a time when all such scholars had to work with were pens and paper; this was always an awkward situation, often with a scholar unfamiliar with the language listening to a narration and trying to put it all down on paper through a translator. Then there came tape recorders, followed by videos, and now there are all kinds of digital devices, all of which have strengthened the integrity of the process, greatly improved the accuracy of the materials collected and rendered them with more authenticity while at the same time improving the quality of, and validating, the overall resulting scholarship being done in the field. In collecting, transcribing and translating the materials for this volume, the author reproduced, as accurately as possible, the semantics, and also retained most of the aesthetic and poetic characteristics that could be reproduced.

What the reader is given in this study is a glimpse into the thought process, creative capacity, value system, culture, history, and overall essence of everyday life of the Baganda people of Uganda as captured in their songs, legends, myths, epigrams and prose narratives. The author analyzed the major issues and subgenres in the study of the African oral tradition; introduced the Kingdom of Buganda, its history and people; and examined the nature, functions and subgenres of their oral literature; reproduced and elaborated on a famous Baganda people's legend and a myth; cited sample Baganda epigrams in Luganda and translated and explained each one; and also reproduced and investigated sample Baganda prose narratives and songs in translation. Each section opens with a short introduction and concludes with a brief commentary; explanations are given where needed, and cultural and historical information is provided as well. Hopefully the author has whetted the reader's appetite enough to prompt them to pursue further studies not only in the Baganda oral literature but also in as many of the oral literatures of the various ethnic groups on the continent as one can, as well as in the overall African oral tradition.

Based on what has been covered in this study, let us peek into the future of the scholarship on the African oral tradition. This study of the Baganda oral literature is a valuable addition to the growing body of tangible evidence for the defense in the debate of whether Africa had a vibrant past characterized by dignity and wisdom as well as aesthetic and poetic creations long before its encounter with the West. Although theoretically a good number of Africanists would like to claim that this debate is now almost, if not totally, behind us, in reality it is still ongoing; and it is likely to continue as long as Africa is still regarded as a mere curiosity and its people often characterized as "other." The entertainment industry constantly reminds its audience that Africa is still a curiosity. Achebe gives several examples to illustrate that this debate is alive and well. One of the significant topics in that debate is Africa's history, and as Achebe pointed out in his 1975 Chancellor's Lecture at the University of Massachusetts, renowned historians like Hugh Trevor Roper are still of the mind-set that African history did not exist prior to colonialism. Another topic being debated is the lack of African aesthetic and poetic creations. Once again Achebe finds the issue alive and well as he takes a walk around his place and an elderly person wanting to know what he teaches is surprised to hear that there is such a thing as African literature! Instead of claiming or wanting to claim that that debate is closed, we should focus on ways to continue debunking those myths. Such ways include sustaining our efforts to recognize the African oral tradition as a knowledge system, and strengthening the fight to keep alive as many African languages as we possibly can. The International Society for the Oral Literature of Africa (ISOLA) is a step in the right direction, and it should be sustained and supported by all Africanists interested in this valuable, rewarding, and ever intriguing scholarship.

On the surface, Africans seem to have lost almost everything of value to them during colonialism, but they retained their oral tradition, which in turn helped them to sustain the essence of their cultural space and vestiges of their identity during that period. The African oral tradition also played a vital role in the wake of colonialism by empowering Africans, especially writers, to reclaim their cultural space, dignity, wisdom and aesthetic and poetic attributes. The oral tradition can still be put to great use in the 21st century and beyond. Let us take advantage of the global growing interest in the African oral tradition and ensuing scholarship to highlight it as a viable knowledge system capable of debunking the myth of Africa as a mere curiosity. Reexamining our approach to the study of renowned African writers such as Chinua Achebe, Wole Soyinka, Ngugi wa Thiong'o, Flora Nwapa, D.T. Niane and Jomo Kenyatta is a great start.

Writers in marginalized societies have several duties, including correcting their people's distorted records, recording their people's histories, and preserving their people's collective memory, which is essential for these people's cultural survival. The African writers referenced above have met those challenges by successfully reconstructing the languages of the colonizers and making them their own. Then, using those reconstructed languages, they have been able to reclaim the copyrights to their people's own stories they had lost during colonialism. Much authentic African people's literature, as Nadine Gordimer characterizes it, and many authentic African languages expressions are now in print; the more of that we put in print, the less credible the debates on the lack of, for example, African history, and aesthetic and poetic creations will become.

And now we turn to the language issue. As Ngugi points out, "Language, any language, has a dual character: it is both a means of communication and a carrier of culture.... [It] is the collective memory bank of a people's experience in history" (*Decolonising*, 13, 15). If you destroy a people's language, you can successfully marginalize them and even deny their existence if the need to do so arises. One of the colonial success stories was the near destruction of native languages. For example, students were punished for speaking their native languages at school, and most of them grew up believing that their languages were inadequate to express complex ideas. The oral tradition, though, stands as evidence of how unfounded and misguided such beliefs were. African languages, as can be seen in the people's oral tradition, are as complex, if not even more so, as any other language. Since we cannot have authentic oral tradition without authentic languages that anchor it, preserving African languages should be a priority for the African oral tradition scholar.

There is something of value for every Africanist and casual reader in this study of the Baganda oral literature. Anyone interested in the study of any aspect of Africa, in any discipline, whether as a beginner or a seasoned researcher, will find this study valuable. For the casual reader, the legends, myths, epigrams and prose narratives are aesthetically pleasing and semantically worth reading. The tourist may also want to check out *Ddindo* and *Ttanda*. The African oral tradition is not just a glimpse into the African past but also a window into the African present and future because it is a living, dynamic, fluid tradition which has survived many challenges in the past and will continue to flourish by adapting to whatever context comes along, including globalization and urbanization. It has the capacity and resilience to remain relevant, practical and functional by responding to and addressing contemporary issues, sometimes serving as a guide into the future, as well as accurately portraying and reporting current social phenomena. Although it is a great aesthetic tradition, the African oral tradition is definitely more than art for art's sake. In times of trouble and uncertainty, it might be what African societies need to strengthen their people, entertain, heal, and console as well as provide hope, encouragement and even solutions as needed. In particular, it is my hope that this study of the Baganda oral literature will widen the scope of the study of not only African literature but also of comparative literatures globally, as well as of the overall African oral tradition, that it will enrich these disciplines, enliven the literary discourse around them, and leave the readers with an added perspective, greater insight and a deeper understanding of the essence of the African oral tradition so crucial to the study, teaching, and global dissemination of knowledge about Africa.

Glossary of Luganda Words and Phrases

Abalongo   twins

Abalongo ba Kabaka   king's twins

Abalongo twabazaala Babiri   "we got the twins as a couple"; also a song title

Abatabazi Abedda   the soldiers of long ago; also a song title

Akagoma ka Lubendera   a small drum played to soothe crying babies

Akakokolo   a severely disfigured person, frightful to look at

Akatandalo   a wooden rack built above a fireplace, used as a kitchen shelf; a rack often built near a kitchen for drying plates, pans, cups, and other like items

Amasiga   three clay blocks or large stones arranged in a triangle to hoist the pots above the fire in a kitchen; also another name for a fireplace used for cooking

Amazzi genyanja   lake and ocean water; also a song title

Babirye   When one has twins and a baby girl comes out first, she is named *Babirye*

Baganda (pl.); **muganda** (sing.)   people belonging to an ethnic group of Bantu people found in South-Central Uganda

Balwaana   They fought; also a title for a song about war

Basajja Bannange Twabonabona   "My fellow men, we suffered"; also a title for a song about war

Bemba   Legend has it that *Bemba* was a very cruel leader of the Baganda who was overthrown by *Kintu.*

Bikajjo   sugar cane

Binyeebwa   ground nuts; peanuts

Buganda   a kingdom of the Baganda people in South-Central Uganda

Busuuti   a traditional seven-yard Baganda women's dress

Butungulu   onions

Bwangu Bwangu   quick, quick; also a title of a song to *lubaale*

Chwa Nnabakka   the 2nd king of Buganda (circa 1230–1275)

Ddindo   the physical location of *Kintu*'s royal court in Buganda

Ddungu   a non-clan affiliated boy's name; also a *lubaale* name; the deity of hunters

Ddungu Lubolooga   Ddungu the great, the strong; also a song title

Ddungu Omulungi   Ddungu the beautiful, the wonderful; also a song title

Ebika (pl.); **ekika** (sing.)   clans; social groupings of Baganda people by family origins, each group headed by a hereditary clan chief and identified by a set of its own specific last names

Ebikokkyo (pl.); *ekikokkyo* (sing.)   Baganda riddles

Ebitontome   oral poetry

Ekibanja   a tract of land owned by a family, traditionally used for subsistence farming; a hereditary traditional family farm

Ekibbo (sing.), **ebibbo** (pl.)   a dish-like container made with reeds and banana stalks which is used for various activities around a home

Ekkomagiro   a shed used to make traditional materials out of the barks of fig trees

Ekyalo   village; the smallest sociopolitical unit of anywhere between ten and one hundred families, headed by a democratically chosen chief

Ekyayi (sing.); **ebyayi** (pl.)   a dried bark of a banana tree — can be used as a rope

Ekyogero (sing); ebyogero (pl.)   a baby basin; a combination of herbs used to clean an infant at birth and for a month thereafter to bathe the baby

Ekyoto   a fireplace used specifically for cooking

Emizingonyo (pl.); **omuzingonyo** (sing.)   a stalk-like middle part of a banana leaf

Endagala (pl.); **Olulagala** (sing.)   banana leaves

Enfumo (pl.); **Olufumo** (sing.)   prose narratives; folktales

Engero ensonge   proverbs

Engule   monarchy's crown

Ennume tetinta nga ndaawo   A he-goat does not behave like a she-goat.

Eryato   a wooden boat; a wooden boat-shaped container for fermenting traditional Baganda people's beer

Ggulu   This word has several meanings, including the Supreme, heaven, and a very pleasant place.

Gwenjagalira bbawe ekyoka kimunyoola   "The one whose husband I love is having a heart burn"; also a song title

Jjajja   grandparent

Jjajja Tabaala   granny rejoice; also a title for a song to a deity

Jjunju   the 26th king of Buganda (circa 1780–1797)

Kabaka   king; king of Buganda

Kabikkuse   It has been opened; also a song title

Kadongo kamu   traditional Baganda storytelling musical lyrics, played using only one musical instrument

Kato   When one has twins and a baby boy comes out second, he is named *Kato*.

Katonda   creator

Kayikuzi   digger; can also mean a troublemaker. In Baganda mythology, it is the name of *Walumbe*'s brother, who came down on earth to return his brother to *Ggulu* but failed because of human inability to follow directions.

Kiganda   an adjective describing Baganda traditions and activities such as dance, dress, value system and music

Kintu   In Baganda mythology, he was the first human on earth, and is, therefore, the father of the Baganda; 1st king of Buganda (circa 1200–1230); also a popular non-clan affiliated boy's last name

Kirabo   gift; also a non-clan affiliated name, given to a particularly precious baby, one who was particularly hard to get, or who was born in strange, unusual circumstances. A very helpful person can also be called *kirabo*; also an endearing adjective

Kisanyi   a type of spider that supposedly twists (dances) as it moves

Kisawe   a public tract of land, often used as a playground. Every village used to have one.

Kkoyi kkoyi   a unique call, sort of an invitation issued by a caller to those the caller wants to challenge in riddling

lubaale   deities that speak through humans. Traditionally a *lubaale* figure has to be invited by a diviner when needed to intervene, give advice, or settle disputes. It takes over a human form from those present, and it then addresses the issues for which it was invited.

Lubiri   royal court

Luganda   the native language of the Baganda people

Lya or ddya   the expected audience's response to *kkoyi kkoyi*, an indication that the audience has accepted to be challenged by the caller

Maama Abaawo   "if my mother was here"; also a song title

Maama siife nze   Mother, I will not die.

Matooke, amatooke   a type of banana

Mbogo   buffalo

miyembe   mangoes

Muliraanwa Bwayisa   "when a neighbor brews beer"; also a song title

Mutebi   the 36th king of Buganda (circa 1993–)

Muteesa 1   the 30th king of Buganda (circa 1856–1884)

195

Muteesa ll   the 35th king of Buganda (circa 1939–1969)

muwogo   cassava

Mwanga ll   the 31st king of Buganda (circa 1884–1899)

Nabutono   small person; petty name for small people; also a song title

Nakato   When one has twins and a baby girl comes out second, she is named *Nakato*.

Nalubaale   a lake in South-Central Uganda globally known as Lake Victoria, and the source of the river Nile

Namajjuzi   a river in Buganda. According to mythology, this river was born from a woman's tears.

Nambi   in Baganda mythology, she was the first woman on earth; also a popular non-clan affiliated girl's name

Namirembe; mirembe   peace; also a popular non-clan affiliated girl's name

nanansi   pineapple

ndaggu   yam

Ndawula   non-clan affiliated boy's name; the 19th King of Buganda (circa 1700–1710); a song title to a deity of the same name

Nfudu   tortoise; in Baganda mythology a faithful servant who killed *Bemba*

niina   tomatoes

Nkuluze   a Luganda dictionary

Nnaggalabi   *Bemba's* royal court

Nnalongo   mother of twins

Nnalongo Weeryowe   "mother of twins prepare"; also a song title

Nnyanga   bottomless pit

ntula   berries

okukomaga   the art of turning a fig tree bark into a soft usable bark cloth by hitting it repeatedly with a grooved wooden hammer specifically made for that purpose

Okutinta; tintatinta   to play a brainteaser game of the same name

Olubugo (sing.), **embugo** (pl.)   a soft bark cloth made from the bark of a fig tree; a traditional Baganda material used as a dress, sheet, burial cloth

Olukiiko   Buganda parliament

Olumbe   a traditional last rites ceremony during which an heir is installed in the place of the dead person; sickness

Omutuba   fig tree

Omwenge   traditional Baganda people's beer made from bananas

Omweso   chess; a Baganda people's board game which was popularized by *Kintu*

Ssalongo   father of twins

Ssemakookiro   the 27th king of Buganda (circa 1797–1814)

Ssere   an annoying, prickly, sticky weed that hangs on the clothes of those who get near it; can also mean a nagging, unwanted, disturbing person

Taata   father

Ttanda   a final resting place, grave; the physical location of the mythological battle between *Walumbe* and his brother *Kayikuzi*, in Buganda

Tulime   Let's cultivate; also title of a song

Walulumba   title of a song

Walumbe   literally death, or any life threatening circumstance or person

Wasswa   When one has twins and a baby boy comes out first, he is named *Wasswa*.

Appendix: Sample Luganda Songs

WAR SONG: "Balwaana Balwaana" (They Fought, They Fought)
[Defending the Kingdom of Buganda from attacks by neighboring kingdoms such as Bunyoro was one of the most important tasks the king of Buganda had to perform. Most of the time he was expected to lead his troops in such a war. This is one song congratulating the 26th and 27th kings for their bravery and success in some of those attacks.]

CHORUS:

> Ssemakokiro ne Jjunju Obuganda bwonna babuwanguzanga mpiima
> (Ssemakokiro and Jjunju conquered Buganda with heavy spear
> shaped weapons.)

SOLO (Each of the following lines is followed by a chorus):

> *Obuganda nebufuna eddembe* (*Buganda* got peace)
> *Ssabasajja atembenkere baaba* (The first among men deserves to rest)
> *Ne Nabagereka mu Lubiri e Mengo* (with the queen in his royal court
> at Mengo).
> *Bannange nakwata effumu* (My friends, the king took a spear)
> *Amazima nakkirira ettale* (and he went into the wilderness).
> *Nabuuka neyeejaga abange* (He jumped and rejoiced).
> *Nabwaama Nabwaama* (He crouched) [x2];
> *Nabwaama ngayagala amutte* (he crouched wanting to kill him).
> *Ate nasooba bakama bange* (He then moved slowly).
> *Amuva emabega nalimukuba effumu* (and speared whoever was coming
> from behind him).

RELATIONSHIP SONG: "Nabutono" [nickname for a very small person]
[This song alludes to an incident, narrated in Buganda oral literature, of a king who was dethroned when he slipped out of his royal court to have an affair with a very small beautiful woman.]

CHORUS:

> Nabutono amaanyi gandi muggwe (Nabutono, all my strength
> is in you) [x2].

SOLO (Each of the following lines is followed by a chorus):

> *Kabaka wa Buganda agenze luddawa?* (Where has the king of
> Buganda gone?)
> *Basirikaale enfaafa baamukuuma* (So many soldiers guard him).
> *Kabaka wa Buganda bamuwambye* (The king of Buganda has
> been captured).
> *Basirikaale enfaafa baamukuuma* (So many soldiers guard him).

TWINS SONG: "Nnaalongo Weeryowe" (Mother of Twins Dress Up)

[Twins are prized among the Baganda; many special ceremonies are put on for
them and their families, and they get special treatment and special names as well.
This song is sung when the twins and their parents are being introduced to their
community.]

> *Nnaalongo weeryowe tuleeta* (Mother of twins, dress up we are bringing),
> *Ssaalongo weeryowe tuleeta* (Father of twins, dress up we are bringing)
> *Tuleeta Abalongo bo* (We are bringing you your twins) [x2]
> *Nnyabo Nnaalongo weeyagale* (Dear Mother of twins, rejoice).
> *Tuleeta Nnaalongo weeyagale* (We are bringing, rejoice),
> *Tuleeta Abalongo bo* (We are bringing you your twins) [x2].
> *Nnyabo Nnaalongo gwenjagala* (Dear Mother of twins whom I love),
> *Leero Nnaalongo weeryowe* (Today, Mother, of twins dress up).
> *Tuleeta Abalongo bo* (We are bringing you your twins) [x2].
> *Ssebo Ssaalongo gwensuuta* (Dear Father of twins whom I prize),
> *Era Ssaalongo weeryowe* (Father of twins, dress up).
> *Tuleeta Abalongo bo* (We are bringing you your twins) [x2].

LAST RITES SONG: "Mbogo Mbogo" (Buffalo, Buffalo)

[When an adult dies, the Baganda hold a very elaborate last rites ceremony known
as *okwaabya olumbe*, about a month or so after one dies. During this ceremony,
an heir for the deceased is installed and given all the responsibilities the deceased
had. It is an overnight ceremony of singing, dancing, and feeding the guests. This
is one of the songs that might be sung during this ceremony, if the deceased was
a parent, to empower the heir who is assuming those parental responsibilities.]

CHORUS:

> *Kyewaggula erizaala enkambwe* (A rebellious buffalo will beget a
> dangerous buffalo).

SOLO (Each of the following lines is followed by a chorus):

> *Mbogo mbogo eno* (This very buffalo),
> *Mbadde ngiyigga* (I was hunting for it);
> *Mbadde nginoonya* (I was looking for it),
> *Mbogo omulungi* (Beautiful buffalo).
> *Nnyabo lubaale gwempita* (The deity I am calling upon),
> *Lubaale owange* (My deity),
> *Omulungi gwempita* (The beautiful one I am calling),
> *Embogo yange eno* (My very buffalo),
> *Mbogo liggo* (Strong buffalo),
> *Mbogo mbogo eyo* (That buffalo).

LUBAALE SONG: "Ndawula" (a specific deity's name)

[This is a song that might be sung when a group is calling on this specific deity for help.]

CHORUS:

> Ndawula Ndawula ono (This Ndawula),
> *Ndawula talinnya miti* (*Ndawula* does not climb trees);
> *Ndawula akwata baana be* (*Ndawula* only serves his children).

SOLO (Each of the following lines is followed by a chorus):

> *Ndawula Ow'omukwano* (*Ndawula* my friend)
> *Naleeta obulungi* (brings beauty),
> *Nanoonya obugagga* (looks for riches),
> *Nabajemu abaleeta* (catches rebels),
> *Naleeta abalungi* (brings beautiful people).
> *Ndawula Kyalubimba* (*Ndawula*, overboiling pot),
> *Naleeta oluzalo* (brings fertility),
> *Ne lubaale amuleeta* (even brings other deities),
> *Nemirimu agireeta* (brings jobs),
> *Nabaana abaleese* (brings children),
> *Ndawula Kyalubimba* (*Ndawula* overboiling pot).

NEIGHBORLY SONG: "Muliraanwa Bwayisa" (When My Neighbor Brews Beer)

[Traditionally the Baganda used to help their neighbors to make the local brew, and after it was ready, all the neighbors had to do was turn up and drink until it was gone. Then it would be someone else's turn to make the brew and host the group. Most of the time people would sing and dance as they drank, and below is one of the songs they might sing praising their host.]

> *Muliraanwa bwayiisa* (When my neighbor brews beer)
> *Nange nensanyuka* (I too get very happy).

Omwenge gwa munnange (It is my friend's beer).
Nange nsanyukamu (I get very happy).
Muliraanwa bwayiisa (When my neighbor brews beer)
Nange ne ngiisa (I too brew beer).
Omwenge negutugatta (Beer brings us together)
Netwesanyukira (And we make merry).
Omwenge bwegulimbula (When I can no longer find any beer)
Ndyedaagira ennaku (I will feel very sad).
Omwenge gwa munnange (It is my friend's beer).
Nagenda n'ekiro (I can even go to have some even at night).

LULLABY: "Sirika Sirika" (Stop Crying, Stop Crying)

[Among the Baganda, older sisters and brothers are the primary babysitters of their siblings, and they generally enjoy singing to them, especially if they want them to stop crying or to entice them to sleep. This is one of the lullabies one might hear being sung.]

Sirika sirika nkwokere ekkovu (Stop crying so that I can roast a crab for you).
Maama bw'anadda nti omuwadde ki? (When mother comes back she will ask: what did you give the baby?)
Muwadde ekkovu eryokunnyanja (I have given baby a crab from the sea) [x2].

Bibliography

Abalogu, Uchegbulam N., Garba Ashiwaju, and Regina Amadi-Tshiwala. *Oral Poetry in Nigeria*. Lagos: Nigeria Magazine, 1981.

Abrahams, Roger D. *African Folktales: Traditional Stories of the Black World*. New York: Pantheon, 1983.

Achebe, Chinua. *Anthills of the Savannah*. Oxford: Heinemann, 1987.

_____. "An Image of Africa." *Joseph Conrad: Third World Perspectives*. Edited by Robert Hamner. Washington, D.C.: Three Continents, 1990.

_____. *Things Fall Apart*. London: Heinemann, 1996.

Addo, Peter E. Adotey. *Talking Drums*. Pittsburgh: Dorrance, 1999.

Andrzejewski, B.W., and I.M. Lewis. *Somali Poetry: An Introduction*. Oxford: Clarendon, 1964.

Angano ... Angano: Tales from Madagascar. Directed by Cesar Paes. Videocassette. California Newsreel, 1989.

Baker, Rob, and Ellen Draper. "If One Thing Stands, Another Will Stand Beside It: An Interview with Chinua Achebe." *Parabola* 17, no. 3 (Fall 1992): 19–27.

Bascom, William R. *African Folktales in the New World*. Bloomington: Indiana University Press, 1992.

Beier, Ulli, ed. *Yoruba Poetry. An Anthology of Traditional Poems*. Cambridge: Cambridge University Press, 1970.

Berry, Jack, and Richard A. Spears. *West African Folktales*. Evanston, IL: Northwestern University Press, 1991.

Bryan, Ashley. *The Ox of the Wonderful Horns and Other African Folktales*. New York: Atheneum/Macmillan, 1993.

"Buganda." Home page. http://www.Buganda.com (accessed 28 July 2009).

Bukenya, Austin, and Wanjiku Mukabi Kabira, eds. *Understanding Oral Literature*. Oxford: African Book Collective, 1994.

Chiwome, Emmanuel Mudhiwa. "The Interface of Orality and Literacy in the Zimbabwean Novel." *Research in African Literatures* 29, no. 2 (Summer 1998): 1–22.

Cloete, M.J., and R.N. Madadzhe. "Bury My Bones but Keep My Words: The Interface Between Oral Tradition and Contemporary African Writing." *Liberator* 25, no. 2 (August 2004): 27.

Connor, Steve. "Alarm Raised on World's Disappearing Languages." *Common Dreams NewsCenter*. http://www.commondreams.org/headlines03/0515–05.htm (accessed 13 June 2008).

Dadi, Bernard B. *The Black Cloth: A Collection of African Folktales*. New York: Atheneum, 1987.

Damane, M., and P.B. Sanders, eds. *Lithoko: Sotho Praise-Poems*. Oxford: Oxford University Press, 1974.

Damme, Wilfried. "African Verbal Arts and the Study of African Visual Aesthetics." *Research in African Literatures* 31, no. 4 (Winter 2000): 8.

Deng, Francis Mading. *The Dinka and Their Songs*. Oxford: Clarendon, 1973.

_____. *Dinka Folktales: African Stories from the Sudan*. New York: Africana, 1974.

Dickinson, Emily. "Tell All the Truth but Tell It Slant." *Literature: An Introduction to Fiction, Poetry, and Drama*. Edited by X.J. Kennedy and Diana Gioia. New York: Longman, 2003, 747.

Egejuru, Phanuel Akubueze. *Towards African Literary Independence: A Dialogue with Contemporary African Writers*. Westport, CT: Greenwood, 1980.

Egudu, R.N. "Achebe and the Igbo Narrative Tradition." *Research in African Literatures* 12, no. 1 (1981): 43–54.

El-Shamy, Hasan M. *Folktales of Egypt*. Chicago: University of Chicago Press, 1980.

Finnegan, Ruth. *Limba Stories and Story-Telling*. Oxford: Clarendon, 1967.

_____. *Oral Literature in Africa*. Oxford: Clarendon, 1970.

_____. *The Penguin Book of Oral Poetry*. London: Penguin, 1978.

Foley, John M. *Oral Tradition in Literature*. Columbia: University of Missouri Press, 1986.

Ford, Bernette G. *The Hunter Who Was King and Other African Folktales*. New York: Hyperion, 1994.

Forster, Edward Morgan. *Two Cheers for Democracy*. London: Edward Arnold, 1951.

Fuja, Abayomi. *Fourteen Hundred Cowries and Other African Tales*. New York: Lothrop, 1971.

Furniss, Graham, and Liz Gunner. *Power, Marginality and African Oral Literature*. London: University of London, 1995.

Giray-Saul, Eren. *Nsiirin! Nsiirin!: Jula Folktales from West Africa*. East Lansing: Michigan State University Press, 1996.

Gordimer, Nadine. "People's Literature: A Testament of Faith in the Untapped Creative Resources of South Africa's Excluded Masses." *UNESCO Courier* (February 1992): 34–40.

Gukiina, P.M. *Uganda: A Case Study in African Political Development*. Notre Dame: University of Notre Dame, 1972.

Irele, Abiola F., and Simon Gikandi, eds. *The Cambridge History of African and Caribbean Literature*. 2 vols. Cambridge: Cambridge University Press, 2004.

Iyasere, Solomon O. "Oral Tradition in the Criticism of African Literature." *Journal of Modern African Studies* 13, no. 1 (1975): 107.

Iyewarun, Samuel A. *African Folktales*. Kansas City, MO: Tivoli, 1998.

Jackson, Gale. *Khoisan Tale Beginnings and Ends*. Brooklyn, NY: Storm, 1998.

Jacobs, Harriet. *Incidents in the Life of a Slave Girl*. Oxford: Oxford University Press, 1988.

Johnson, John William, Thomas A. Hale, and Stephen Belcher, eds. *Oral Epics from Africa: Vibrant Voices from a Vast Continent*. Bloomington: Indiana University Press, 1997.

Jones, D.J., E. Palmer, and M. Jones. *Oral and Written Poetry in African Literature Today*. London: Currey, 1989.

Jones, Eldred Durosimi, Eustace Palmer, and Marjorie Jones, eds. *Orature in African Literature Today: A Review*. Trenton, NJ: Africa World, 1992.

Kaschula, Russell H. *African Oral Literature: Functions in Contemporary Contexts*. South Africa: New Africa Education, 2001.

Kenyatta, Jomo. "The Gentlemen of the Jungle." *African Short Stories*. Edited by Chinua Achebe and C.L. Innes. Oxford: Heinemann, 1987.

Kipple, Mary A. *African Folktales with Foreign Analogues*. New York: Garland, 1992.

Kizza, I. *Africa's Indigenous Institutions in Nation Building*. Lewiston, NY: Edwin Mellen, 1999.

Ki-Zerbo, Joseph. "Oral Tradition as a Historical Source." *UNESCO Courier* (April 1990): 43–47.

Korty, Carol. *Plays from African Folktales*. Studio City, CA: Players, 1998.

Leslau, Wolf. *Gurage Folklore: Ethiopian Folktales, Proverbs, Beliefs, and Riddles*. Wiesbaden: F. Steiner, 1992.

Lindfors, Bernth. *Folklore in Nigerian Literature*. New York: Africana, 1973.

_____, ed. *Forms of Folklore in Africa: Narrative, Poetic, Gnomic, Dramatic*. Austin: University of Texas Press, 1977.

Lusweti, B.M. *The Hyena and the Rock: A Handbook of Oral Literature for Schools*. London: Macmillan, 1984.

Matateyou, Emmanuel. *An Anthology of Myths, Legends, and Folklore from Cameroon: Story Telling in Africa*. Lewiston, NY: Edwin Mellen, 1997.

Mazrui, Ali, and Toby Kleban Levine, eds. *The Africans: A Reader*. New York: Praeger, 1986.

Miller, Annetta. *Sharing Boundaries: Learning the Wisdom of Africa*. Nairobi: Paulines, 2003.

Miruka, Okumba. *Encounter with Oral Literature*. Oxford: African Books Collective, 1994.

Muli Wa, Vincent. *East African Folktales: From the Voice of Mukamba*. Little Rock, AR: August House, 1997.

Musere, Jonathan. *African Proverbs and Proverbial Names*. Los Angeles: Ariko, 1999.

Ngugi wa Thiong'o. *Decolonising the Mind: The Politics of Language in African Literature*. Portsmouth, NH: Heinemann, 1986.

_____. *The River Between*. London: Heinemann, 1965.

Niane, D.T. *Sundiata: The Epic of Old Mali*. Essex: Longman, 1996.

Nussbaum, Stan. "Profundity with Panache: The Unappreciated Proverbial Wisdom of Sub-Saharan Africa." In *Understanding Wisdom: Sources, Science and Society*, Warren S. Brown. Philadelphia: Templeton Foundation Press, 2000.

Obiechina, Emmanuel. "Narrative Proverbs in the African Novel." *Research in African Literatures* 24, no. 4 (Winter 1993):123–141.

O'Brien, Dennis. "Linguists Rush to Save Dying Languages." *Chattanooga Times Free Press*, 20 July 2003, A6.

Offodile, Buchi. *The Orphan Girl and Other Stories: West African Folktales*. New York: Interlink, 2001.

Ojaide, Tanure. *Poetry, Performance, and Art: Udje Dance Songs of the Urhobo People*. Durham, NC: Carolina Academic, 2003.

Okot, p'Bitek. *Hare and Hornbill*. London: Heinemann, 1978.

Okpewho, Isidore. *African Oral Literature: Backgrounds, Character, and Continuity*. Bloomington and Indianapolis: Indiana University Press, 1992.

_____. *The Epic in Africa*. New York: Columbia University Press, 1979.

_____. "How Not to Treat African Folklore." *Research in African Literatures* 27, no. 3 (Fall 1996): 119–129.

_____. *Myth in Africa*. Cambridge: Cambridge University Press, 1983.

_____. "The Preservation and Survival of African Oral Literature." Available at http://isola.binghamton.edu/CallForPapers-english.htm (accessed 29 October 2004).

Olatunji, Olatunde, O. *Features of Yoruba Oral Poetry*. Ibadan, Nigeria: University Press, 1984.

Ong, Walter J. *Orality & Literacy: The Technologizing of the Word*. London: Routledge, 1982.

Opland, Jeff. *Xhosa Oral Poetry: Aspects of a Black South African Tradition*. Cambridge: Cambridge University Press, 1983.

Ostler, Rosemarie. "Disappearing Languages: Of the 6,000 Languages still on Earth, 90 percent could be gone by 2100." *Whole Earth* (Spring 2000). http://findarticles.com/p/articles/mi_m0GER/is_2000_Spring/ai_61426207 (accessed 13 June 2008).

Owomoyela, Oyekan. *African Literatures: An Introduction*. Waltham, MA: Crossroads, 1979.

Oyler, Dianne W. "Re-inventing Oral Tradition: The Modern Epic of Souleymane Kante." *Research in African Literatures* 33, no. 1 (Spring 2002): 75–95.

Petersen, Kirsten Holst, and Anna Rutherford, eds. *Chinua Achebe: A Celebration*. Oxford: Dangeroo, 1990.

Pitcher, Diana. *Tokoloshi: African Folktales Retold*. Berkeley: Tricycle, 1993.

Porter, Laurence. "Lost in Translation: From Orature to Literature in the West African Folktale." *Symposium* 49, no. 3 (Fall 1995): 229–240.

Radin, Paul. *African Folktales*. Princeton: Princeton University Press, 1970.

Rowell, Charles H. "An Interview with Chinua Achebe." *Callaloo* 13, no. 1 (1990): 86.

Scheub, Harold. *African Oral Narratives, Proverbs, Riddles, Poetry, and Song*. Boston: G.K. Hall, 1977.

_____. *The Xhosa Ntsomi*. Oxford: Clarendon, 1975.

Schmidt, Nancy. "Nigerian Fiction and the African Oral Tradition." *Journal of the New African Literature and the Arts* 5/6 (1968): 10–19.

Shelton, Austin J. "The 'Palm-oil' of Language: Proverbs in Chinua Achebe's Novels." *Modern Language Quarterly* 30, no. 1 (1969): 89–111.

Somjee, Sultan H. "Oral Traditions and Material Culture: An East Africa Experience." *Research in African Literatures* 31, no. 4 (Winter 2000): 97.

Stuart, James. *Izibongo: Zulu Praise-Poems*. Oxford, Clarendon, 1968.

Washington, Donna L. *A Pride of African Tales*. New York: HarperCollins, 1997.

Umeasiegbu, R.N. *Words Are Sweet: Igbo Oral Literature*. Nairobi: East African, 1980.

Vuiningoma, J. "Literacy and Orality in African Literature: The Case of Ngugi wa Thiong'o." *Commonwealth* (Spring 1987): 9–11.

Wallbank, Thomas Walter, et al. *Civilizations Past and Present*. Volume II, *From 1648*. New York: HarperCollins, 1996.

Index

www.ingramcontent.com/pod-product-compliance
Lightning Source LLC
Chambersburg PA
CBHW031132270326
41929CB00011B/1594